MERCOSUR and the European Union

Mikhail Mukhametdinov

MERCOSUR and the European Union

Variation and Limits of Regional Integration

Mikhail Mukhametdinov
Harvard University
Cambridge, MA, USA

ISBN 978-3-319-76824-3   ISBN 978-3-319-76825-0 (eBook)
https://doi.org/10.1007/978-3-319-76825-0

Library of Congress Control Number: 2018937084

© The Editor(s) (if applicable) and The Author(s) 2019
This work is subject to copyright. All rights are solely and exclusively licensed by the Publisher, whether the whole or part of the material is concerned, specifically the rights of translation, reprinting, reuse of illustrations, recitation, broadcasting, reproduction on microfilms or in any other physical way, and transmission or information storage and retrieval, electronic adaptation, computer software, or by similar or dissimilar methodology now known or hereafter developed.
The use of general descriptive names, registered names, trademarks, service marks, etc. in this publication does not imply, even in the absence of a specific statement, that such names are exempt from the relevant protective laws and regulations and therefore free for general use.
The publisher, the authors and the editors are safe to assume that the advice and information in this book are believed to be true and accurate at the date of publication. Neither the publisher nor the authors or the editors give a warranty, express or implied, with respect to the material contained herein or for any errors or omissions that may have been made. The publisher remains neutral with regard to jurisdictional claims in published maps and institutional affiliations.

Cover image: SinghaphanAIIB / Getty Images
Cover design: Thomas Howey

Printed on acid-free paper

This Palgrave Macmillan imprint is published by the registered company Springer International Publishing AG part of Springer Nature.
The registered company address is: Gewerbestrasse 11, 6330 Cham, Switzerland

CONTENTS

1 Analytical Framework for the Comparison of Regions 1
   1.1 Research Question and Related Propositions 6
   1.2 Book Structure 8
   1.3 Integration Theories 11
   1.4 Themes and Criteria of the Comparison 17
   1.5 Summary of the Analytical Framework 25

2 Economic Integration and Interdependence 33
   2.1 Breaches in the MERCOSUR's Common Market System 35
   2.2 Economic Interdependence and Cohesion of Regional Economic Regimes 41
   2.3 Divergences in Economic Performance 54
   2.4 MERCOSUR's Economic Effects 56
   2.5 Case Study: Monetary Cooperation 65
   2.6 Conclusion 73

3 Structural Factors of Regional Integration 87
   3.1 Number of Member States and Challenges of Enlargement 89
   3.2 Intra-bloc Size, Power and Interest Asymmetries 92
   3.3 Foreign Policy Divergence 100
   3.4 Institutional and Legal Order 104
   3.5 Conclusion 112

4 Cultural Diversity and Community-Building 119
 4.1 Cultural Homogeneity and Heterogeneity 122
 4.2 Historical Perspectives on Regional Unity 127
 4.3 Inter-state Relations in the Southern Cone Prior
  to MERCOSUR 145
 4.4 Case Study: Linguistic Policies 153
 4.5 Cultural Work of Regional Institutions 158
 4.6 Conclusion 162

5 External Factors and Geostrategic Considerations 173
 5.1 The EU and the USA: 'Natural Allies,' Unequal
  Partnership, and Diverging Interests 174
 5.2 MERCOSUR Changes Emphases 179
 5.3 MERCOSUR and the EU: Dualism of the Relationship 194
 5.4 Conclusion 196

6 Conclusion 211

Index 227

LIST OF ABBREVIATIONS

ABC Treaty	the 1915 treaty between Argentina, Brazil, and Chile
ACE 14	Agreement on Economic Cooperation 14 between Argentina and Brazil
APEC	Asia-Pacific Economic Cooperation
ASEAN	Association of Southeast Asian Nations
Benelux	Belgium, the Netherlands, Luxemburg
CACM	Central American Common Market
CAN	Andean Community of Nations
CAP	Common Agricultural Policy
CAUCE	Argentinean-Uruguayan Convention on Economic Cooperation
CET	Common External Tariff
CFSP	European Common Foreign and Security Policy
CIS	Commonwealth of Independent States
CSN	South American Community of Nations
EC	European Community
ECJ	European Court of Justice
ECSC	European Coal and Steal Steel Community
EEC	European Economic Community
EMU	European Monetary Union
EU	European Union
EU-15	European Union with 15 members
EURATOM	European Atomic Energy Community
EUROSUR	a project of a transatlantic free trade area between the EU and MERCOSUR proposed in 1995

FDI	Foreign Direct Investment
FTA	Free Trade Area
FTAA	Free Trade Area of the Americas
G-7	Group of Seven (USA, Canada, Britain, Germany, France, Canada, Italy)
GATS	General Agreement on Trade and Services
GDP	Gross Domestic Product
GRP	Gross Regional Product
GU(U)AM	Georgia, Ukraine, (Uzbekistan), Azerbaijan, Moldova
IMF	International Monetary Fund
LAFTA	Latin American Free Trade Area
LAIA	Latin American Integration Association
MERCOSUR	Common Market of the South
MERCOSUR-4	Argentina, Brazil, Paraguay, Uruguay
MERCOSUR-5	MERCOSUR-4 + Venezuela
MERCOSUR-6	MERCOSUR-4 + Chile and Bolivia
NAFTA	North American Free Trade Agreement
NATO	North Atlantic Treaty Organization
NPT	Treaty on the Non-Proliferation of Nuclear Weapons
NTB	Non-Tariff Barrier
OCA	Optimum Currency Area
OECD	Organization for Economic Co-operation and Development
PARLASUR	Parliament of MERCOSUR
PCA	Permanent Court of Appeal
PEC	Protocol of Commercial Expansion between Brazil and Uruguay
PICE	Programme of Integration and Economic Cooperation
PTA	Preferential Trade Agreement
SAARC	South Asian Association for Regional Co-operation
SACU	Southern African Customs Union
SADC	Southern African Development Community
SADCC	Southern African Development Coordination Conference
SAFTA	proposed South American Free Trade Area
SEA	Single European Act
SM	MERCOSUR Secretariat
UN	United Nations Organization
UNASUR	Union of South American Nations
UNGA	United Nations General Assembly

UNSC	United Nations Security Council
US$	US dollars
US(A)	United States of America
USAID	United States Agency for International Development
USSR	Union of Soviet Socialist Republics
WB	World Bank
WTO	World Trade Organization
WW1/2	World War One/Two

List of Maps

Map 4.1 The world before the Spanish accession to NATO.
Source: Russett, 1975, pp 26–27   130
Map 4.2 The world before the Spanish accession to NATO.
Source: Russett, 1975, pp 72–73   131
Map 4.3 The world after the fall of communism.
Source: Based on Huntington, 1997, pp 26–27   132

LIST OF TABLES

Table 1.1	Main comparisons of the monograph	9
Table 1.2	Analytical framework for the comparison of regions	26
Table 2.1	Extra-regional and intra-regional trade of MERCOSUR, the EU, and selected countries	43
Table 2.2	Relation of MERCOSUR-5 intra-regional trade to total trade and production	44
Table 3.1	Political variables and their effect on regional consolidation	113
Table 4.1	Cultural diversity in MERCOSUR-4 and the Iberian sub-region of the EU	126
Table 4.2	Five ethno-social groups in MERCOSUR-4 and the Iberian Peninsula	127
Table 4.3	Languages used in primary texts of the European Commission, 1986–1999	155
Table 5.1	The evolution of geostrategic perceptions of the EU and MERCOSUR	198
Table 6.1	Relative significance of selected dimensions for integration and relative progress of integration achieved in these dimensions	216

CHAPTER 1

Analytical Framework for the Comparison of Regions

Recent years have brought uncertainty over regional integration efforts and disappointment about asymmetric development results enforced by regional blocs. However, interest in regionalism remains strong. Increasing political and social instability along with coups and revolutions across the world lay new hopes on regions as potential sources of stabilizing influence. In South America, interest in MERCOSUR is sustained by dramatic turmoil in Venezuela after the death of Hugo Chávez in 2013, and controversial presidential impeachments in Paraguay (2012) and Brazil (2016). Through suspension of Paraguayan membership in 2012–2013 and Venezuelan membership since 2016 MERCOSUR has shown itself as an actor capable of influencing domestic politics in its member states. At 26 years of age it has a fairly long history and a number of unique features that tell it apart from other regional organizations. Some observers consider MERCOSUR to be the world's second most integrated multilateral regional group after the EU.[1]

However, in relation to the EU, MERCOSUR's integration achievement differs significantly across various dimensions of social life. Its institutions are less developed and they deal with a narrower scope of issues, particularly in the economic and political dimensions of integration where MERCOSUR lags behind. A peculiar feature of the MERCOSUR process is that over half of its legislation is not enforced. The 'dead letters' of MERCOSUR's intergovernmental agreements at times make it difficult to understand what MERCOSUR really is and what it does, and they certainly account for what may be perceived as a failure of integration. This monograph evaluates the current condition of integration in MERCOSUR, explains why, in comparison with the EU, MERCOSUR has not advanced in its development, and suggests that the future shape of this polity will remain different from the EU. To these ends the monograph proposes a special analytical framework for the comparison of MERCOSUR with the EU, which can be used for the analyses of other contemporary regions.

Both MERCOSUR and the EU are perceived as *regions* in the literature on regional integration, which elaborates on a wide range of cooperation issues within various groups of countries. The majority of scholars adhere to a broad definition of *regional integration* as 'institutionalized cross-border cooperation.' There are no excessive criteria in the definitions of *institutionalized*, *cross-border*, and *regional*.[2] The degree of institutionalization may vary from formal organizations to informal political consultations. Cross-border cooperation may apply both to spontaneous social interactions across borders between territories of contiguous states and to government-promoted inter-state cooperation. Regions can be defined as groups of contiguous territories linked by a degree of interdependence that incorporates interaction and possibility of cooperation.

Some authors insist that integration should be defined in more narrow terms to distinguish it from coordination and other forms of cooperation.[3] Thus *coordination* most commonly implies exchange of information. A deeper form of shared action, *cooperation* means taking joint decisions. *Integration* more accurately refers to policies and decisions stemming from binding agreements and supranational institutions. The following stage of merging national policy emitters into one entity and the single policy coming from such entity is called *unification*. I propose to define regional integration primarily as intentional harmonization of national policies among several countries as pursued by a common regional authority. Such understanding of integration automatically brings forward the necessity to consider the specific areas where integration (or policy harmonization) is taking place, thus highlighting the dimension-specific and issue-specific character of the process across various temporal and spatial examples of regionalism. However, integration in narrow terms is not the exclusive focus of this monograph because other forms of cooperation accompany it and affect regional cohesiveness.

There are several grounds for the comparison of MERCOSUR with the EU. Both are geographically contingent areas. Both have expressed commitments to a common market and have undertaken measures for its full or partial implementation.[4] The two blocs have accepted states' competences in the field of commercial policy and have received powers to represent their members in international commercial agreements as a single entity. Thus they have acquired international juridical personalities and recognition as actors in international law with the ability to be subject to international agreements. On the surface, the two blocs appear to have parallel institutional systems, and every major EU institution has an analogue in MERCOSUR. Also, the two blocs share relative similarity in terms of the economic process. They generally confirm the conventional logic of economic integration sequence from an FTA to a customs union and then to a common market.[5] Common to both blocs is frequent rhetoric about integration and promotion of integration symbols, which, for example, have led to the emergence of courses on regional integration in universities and the appearance of MERCOSUR and EU logos on national passports issued by their member states.

However, MERCOSUR unites former colonies, which were and remain dependent on trade with former colonial powers and on acquisition of capital and technology from rich countries. Regional integration in MERCOSUR is unable either to substitute this historical North–South relationship, nor to significantly reduce the dependence of its members on better-developed partners. The EU, on the contrary, is a group of predominantly rich and self-sufficient countries. MERCOSUR is also a more recent process. It was founded in 1991 while the EEC has operated since 1957.[6] MERCOSUR has fewer member states, five versus 28 in the EU. MERCOSUR's basic indicators differ substantially from those of the EU correlating from 1:1.8 (population) to 2.9:1 (territory), 1:4.4 (GRP), and 1:2.5 (GRP per capita).[7]

The degree of commercial interdependence within the EU is 10 to 15 times that of MERCOSUR (See Table 2.1.B). There are 24 official languages in the EU and only three in MERCOSUR reflecting dramatic differences in the degree of cultural diversity. Further, the EU with its three principal actors Germany, France, and Britain (to be replaced by Italy after Brexit) is unfamiliar with the degree of power asymmetry in MERCOSUR where Brazil stands out as a predominant country. The two blocs have had different geopolitical motivations. These are most prominently characterized by the different nature and impact of the US policy in relation to the two regions, and by consequences of WW2 in Europe and the lack of a security dilemma in the Southern Cone prior to the formation of the blocs.

Unsurprisingly, MERCOSUR and the EU achieve varying results across different regional policy domains. The contrast between their measures in economic and cultural integration is particularly illustrative. Thus the EU is characterized by higher economic density, and it has been successful in the facilitation of intra-regional economic exchange through the euro, a single currency among the majority of its members. Rather than an economic community of the EU type, MERCOSUR represents a cultural community with a more meaningful policy of cultural integration. It has committed Brazil to the teaching of Spanish and the Spanish-speaking countries to the teaching of Portuguese in secondary education. Such an undertaking would be impossible in absence of the regional organization.

Despite parallel institutional structures in MERCOSUR and the EU, there is a striking variation between the forms of regional institutions and the ways they operate: the EU is an organization with various supranational competences compared with the strictly intergovernmental structure of MERCOSUR. The EU exercises supranational authority in many economic, environmental, juridical, and security spheres. Depending on the area, EU institutions can take decisions by consensus, absolute majority, or qualified majority. In MERCOSUR there is no regional bureaucracy, and all officials responsible for the integration agenda are representatives of the member-state governments. The major regional institutions with decision-making powers are collegiate. They do not operate on a permanent basis, but meet periodically and produce decisions through intergovernmental mechanisms that always require unanimity.

In the analysis of quality and outcomes of integration, regional institutions have an important position both as by-products of integration and as agencies that affect the processes through their various functions and roles, which stem out from their specific features. Supranational institutions in the EU are believed to pursue interests of the bloc as a whole, and at times they are able to enforce decisions contrary to the will of individual states.[8] However, the MERCOSUR intergovernmental system is restricted to advancing only those measures of integration that have been agreed upon by all member states. This might reduce the scope, depth, and speed of integration. The strictly intergovernmental character of MERCOSUR has often been blamed for a slow progress of integration after the mid-1990s, including the inability to achieve a common market.[9]

Concurrently, MERCOSUR lags behind the EU not only in institutional development but also in economic integration. Malamud observes that 'despite its name, the bloc has not become a common market. At best, it has established the blueprints for a customs union, but even the free trade agreements are repeatedly infringed.'[10] In the early 1990s MERCOSUR's dynamism was astonishing. Measures for trade liberalization were taken rapidly: between 1991 and 1998 intra-regional trade increased four-fold from US$6 milliard to 24 milliard (Table 2.2), and intra-MERCOSUR exports grew relative to total region's exports from 10% to 24% (Table 2.2). However, after 1998 MERCOSUR's dynamism faded and the bloc 'entered a pattern of cyclical crises and rebounds that have defined it.'[11]

The slow progress of institutional development and policy harmonization in MERCOSUR vis-à-vis the EU might seem surprising as a number of factors could have allowed expectations of a faster progress of MERCOSUR integration, especially given the popularity of integration discourse in the region. For example, MERCOSUR has to reconcile far fewer member states over common policies; and there are fewer cultural barriers to intra-regional integration among its countries. The more rapid transformation of the world economy today than in the years of the EC formation in the 1960s–1980s may have been expected to accelerate the consolidation of the common market in South America. When the EEC was born, few foresaw the freedom of capital movement within its borders; on the other hand, MERCOSUR has evolved in a period when capital transfers are so significant that they cannot be ignored. Also, the historic precedent of European economic integration offers lessons and a model to pursue, and policy-makers in MERCOSUR are well aware of this integration experience.

The literature has recorded several explanations as to why MERCOSUR's economic integration and institutional development have been slow after the initial advances of the early period. There is an argument that the Southern Cone's low susceptibility to democratic ideals and the lack of political will prevent MERCOSUR from forming EU-like supranational institutions.[12] Another view blames the persistence of 'magical realism' and 'cognitive dissonance' in the minds of MERCOSUR policy-makers: suggesting that because of their incompetence they are incapable of generating action, so they only produce integration rhetoric.[13] More recently, there appeared a softened version of this account: *Merco-bureaucrats* 'misunderstand the European experience with integration.'[14] A third view indicates greater difficulties of integration in MERCOSUR among its relatively poor and underdeveloped countries in conditions when they keep being affected by a series of never-ending economic crises: the Mexican in 1994, the Asian in 1997, the Brazilian in 1999, the Argentinean in 2002, and the European and North American since 2007.[15] One study explains the limited success of South American integration due to a 'lack of the necessary economic underpinnings' (small volumes of intra-regional trade) and an unwillingness on the part of Brazil to pay the costs of genuine integration.[16]

This monograph offers a complex explanation of MERCOSUR's modest development relative to the EU. Its narrative is based on important aspects of four salient approaches to regional integration available to date: neofunctionalism, intergovernmentalism, social constructivism, and neorealism. The monograph identifies a number of significant factors shaping the South American bloc through a comparison of MERCOSUR with the EU along such important parameters derived from the four theories as economic interdependence, economic convergence, intra-bloc size and interest asymmetries, cultural heterogeneity, discourses on regional unity, and geostrategic motivations. As the conclusions of the monograph are grounded in theory and are also confirmed empirically, they may have greater relevance for understanding MERCOSUR than some of the studies cited above.

1.1 Research Question and Related Propositions

As indicated, MERCOSUR is different from the EU as a geographic region, as a regional organization, and as a generator of different regional policy both in scope of activities and in depth of policy harmonization. Based on this observation, the monograph examines why the MERCOSUR process has distinct outcomes from those of the EU across various integration dimensions. This question is of particular significance for economic and institutional realms where MERCOSUR lags behind. The monograph addresses the following important questions in relation to MERCOSUR's economic and political process: Why is MERCOSUR's economic integration limited in comparison with the EU? Why is MERCOSUR's common market regime loose and partial? Why are MERCOSUR institutions weaker and less influential? Why is the MERCOSUR process characterized by a serious implementation gap? The monograph also supports three related claims: (1) Integration outcomes are highly contingent on regional endogenous properties; (2) Cultural and geoeconomic factors have played greater role in the consolidation of MERCOSUR in contrast to the EU process, which is better developed in political, security, and common market dimensions; (3) Theories used to explain the EU (neofunctionalism, liberal intergovernmentalism, social constructivism, and neorealism) are suitable for the understanding and explanation of MERCOSUR's underdevelopment in relation to the EU.

(1) Studies of Latin American regional and sub-regional integration often relate difficulties of integration to low interdependence among Latin American countries, which they attribute to low diversification of national production structures, existing intra-regional barriers to trade and capital flows, and insufficient cross-border infrastructure.[17] However, the causes of low interdependence are more endemic and insurmountable: the mere size of the countries in terms of territory, conditions of regional physical and economic geography, and demographic settlement patterns predetermine low levels of economic concentration and cross-border interaction in MERCOSUR. Attempts to overcome low interdependence by introducing economic institutions targeting growth of regional exchange are therefore destined to have limited effect.

(2) In correspondence with different integration inputs, the two regions display variation in terms of integration achievement across various policy domains. Integration develops faster and deeper in the areas where it is warranted and where it does not meet resistance. Because MERCOSUR differs from the EU along all possible characteristics, the results of its integration in each specific integration dimension are correspondingly different. Thus certain policy domains are more susceptible to policy harmonization and integration in MERCOSUR, while others are in the EU. While MERCOSUR is characterized by relatively modest progress of development in economic integration, it is undertaking ambitious measures in cultural integration, like striving for a bilingual community based on its natural advantage of only two regional languages, Spanish and Portuguese.

(3) The explanations of MERCOSUR's limited integration achievement are sought through a comparison of MERCOSUR with the EU along a number of criteria measuring the following parameters of the comparison: economic interdependence, economic convergence, intra-bloc size and interest asymmetries, cultural heterogeneity, discourses on regional unity, and geostrategic motivations. These parameters and their more specific criteria are derived from neofunctionalism, liberal intergovernmentalism, social constructivism, and

neorealism. These theories are 'foreign' to MERCOSUR in the sense that they were developed to explain other regions. Therefore, their application towards MERCOSUR is not guaranteed. However, each of them is capable of giving useful insights about the South American bloc, and it is common for the studies of MERCOSUR to deploy all these theories. This monograph, however, offers a systematic approach to show how integration theories can be used to explain MERCOSUR and its outcomes in relation to the EU. The variation between MERCOSUR and EU development and institutionalization is in line with the predictions of the four theories.

1.2 Book Structure

Comparisons between MERCOSUR and the EU may involve myriads of random facts and analogies. Many of them can be related to the differences between the two cases with various degrees of confidence and tentativeness. In order to avoid conclusions with little or uncertain value, the monograph proposes an analytical framework for the comparison of MERCOSUR with the EU using four salient integration theories. The enquiry using multiple integration theories is based on the approach to inter-theory dialogue known as *analytic eclecticism*.[18] *Eclecticism* prescribes the use of elements of multiple theories in search for explanations to complex phenomena. Through the proposed framework the monograph examines why and how MERCOSUR integration develops unevenly across various dimensions of social life.

The framework rests on the analysis of integration development in MERCOSUR and the EU in four dimensions: economic, politico-institutional, historico-cultural, and geostrategic. Each of the four dimensions uses one integration theory to identify the principal theme or parameter of the comparison in the dimension. The main themes of the comparison are economic interdependence (derived from neofunctionalism), state size and interest asymmetries (from intergovernmentalism), cultural diversity (from constructivism), and geostrategic considerations (from neorealism). The comparison between the two blocs in each integration dimension is done along several specific criteria measuring each parameter. Table 1.1 lists the principle themes of the comparison that lay out the quadridimensional structure of the monograph. Full description and explanation of the analytical framework with additional themes and criteria follows in Section 1.4. Each of the four substantive chapters undertakes a comparison of

Table 1.1 Main comparisons of the monograph

	Integration dimension	Applied theory	Principal theme of the comparison
Chapter 2	Economic	Neofunctionalism	Economic interdependence
Chapter 3	Politico-institutional	Intergovernmentalism	Size and interest asymmetry
Chapter 4	Historico-cultural	Social constructivism	Cultural diversity
Chapter 5	Geostrategic	Neorealism	Geostrategic considerations and incentives

MERCOSUR against corresponding EU indicators in a respective integration dimension by the use of the criteria explained in Subsection 1.4.4.

The structure of the monograph is based on the proposed quadridimensional analytical framework. The analysis of MERCOSUR's development in four dimensions of social life divides the comparison into four main parts. Each of the four substantive chapters is responsible for the comparison of MERCOSUR with the EU in one of the four dimensions using one of the baseline theories. There are additional non-key comparisons as well. The chapters highlight important differences between the two processes in the respective dimensions of integration. They also analyse relevant factors of integration and their implications for MERCOSUR. Introductory Chapter 1 discusses the integration theories that form the bases of the MERCOSUR's comparisons with the EU in the subsequent substantive chapters. It also builds up the analytical framework for the comparison of the regions deriving the specific criteria of comparison from the discussed theories.

Chapter 2 is concerned with the relatively low propensity of MERCOSUR for intra-regional economic cooperation, low economic interdependence, scarce trade and intra-regional investment, and divergence in economic performance (which is greater than in the EU). These difficulties of the bloc arise from natural conditions of economic geography, the size and the number of the countries, demographic dispersion, and low diversification of production patterns. As regional cross-border transactions in MERCOSUR are relatively low, there is little interest in securing them in legal terms. In consequence, economic regimes of the bloc are much looser than those of the EU.

Chapter 3 discusses factors of size and interest asymmetries. No country in the EU represents 70% of the region's population and economy as Brazil does in MERCOSUR. The power asymmetry in favour of one country is a great obstacle to policy harmonization. It reduces the scope of mutual interest and is responsible for greater foreign policy divergence and a lower degree of institutional cohesion. In addition, MERCOSUR is more difficult to sustain as a club of poorer countries as they have often prioritized not regional integration, but their foreign policy in relation to wealthier countries from outside the region. However, MERCOSUR has an important advantage over the EU in the more manageable number of member states.

Chapter 4 illustrates the greater propensity of MERCOSUR for integration in the cultural domain. Relative cultural homogeneity is conducive to MERCOSUR's cultural integration, which is occurring even though it was not desired and envisaged during the bloc's creation. However, alone, without a viable politico-economic agenda, cultural homogeneity is unable to sustain political and economic integration. Therefore, additional historic perspectives emphasize the common cultural base of the Southern Cone countries contrasting it with *Europeanness*, which has more of a political than of cultural definition, at least in comparative terms.

Chapter 5 evaluates the hypothesis about MERCOSUR and EU's transformation from hegemonic to counterhegemonic projects. This analysis reveals that external motivations for integration in MERCOSUR are different from those of the EU, and that the impact of US involvement in the affairs of the two blocs has also been of different character and strength. In the external context, MERCOSUR's integration aims to consolidate the bloc's economic capabilities, while the EU is trying to achieve greater political influence. Relations between MERCOSUR and the EU are also important. The EU takes MERCOSUR as an ally in the attempts to counterbalance the USA. At the same time European interests in relation to MERCOSUR economies are not different from those of the US interests in relation to MERCOSUR and other peripheral economies. Obviously, MERCOSUR and the EU have different positions in the hierarchy of international relations.

Chapters 2 and 4 contain case studies that support their conclusions and illustrate the differences in integration results between MERCOSUR and the EU. These cases are in-depth studies of two broad policy domains, monetary and linguistic. Money and language are chosen as quintessences of everything economic and cultural. The two cases clearly show that the blocs have dissimilar integration potential across the two specific policy domains, and that varying degrees of economic and cultural cohesion produce policies of different scope, depth, and consequences. These integration results are highly conditioned by the pre-existing regional features. The case studies also demonstrate that, contrary to common expectations, there are areas in which MERCOSUR integration proceeds further than integration in the EU (linguistic integration). Both cases confirm one of the key assumptions of the monograph that integration is more warranted and easier to achieve among similar countries that require uniform policy solutions to the problems they are facing.

Together the four main chapters illustrate how the proposed analytical framework may be used for assessing MERCOSUR relatively to the EU and what conclusions can be derived from these comparisons.

1.3   INTEGRATION THEORIES

Among regional integration groups the EU receives most scholarly attention, and no other integration bloc has been studied and theorized to the extent of the EU. As there are no theories of global regionalism, scholars who study regions resort to European integration theories. They refer to regional integration as a multidimensional phenomenon and lament the inability of any of the existing theories to fully explain the formation and development of regions.[19] If no theory can offer an exhaustive explanation of integration in one region like the EU, the comparison of integration outcomes between any regions will surely benefit from an exploration based on multiple theories. The specificity of EU Studies is such that it does not have one dominant approach. Two of the four theories deployed by this monograph, neofunctionalism and liberal intergovernmentalism, contest the dominant position as better-developed theories, because they provide descriptions of the process and explain institutional and regulatory developments. As their combined portrait of integration is incomplete, they are complemented by other theories, including social constructivism and neorealism. The latter came to the field of integration studies from International Relations and were not meant to offer any coherent mechanics of regional integration as defined in narrow terms. Social constructivism draws attention to a number of important factors determining the quality of regional political order such as values, norms, identity, and equality. Neorealism explains how global factors affect the formation and development of regions. This section reviews the four prominent theories, while Section 1.4 selects their core elements for the identification of the various criteria for the comparison of the two regions.

1.3.1 Neofunctionalism

The most influential theory in the field of EU Studies is neofunctionalism. In neofunctionalism, integration is a sporadic and self-sustaining process advanced by pragmatic interests of social groups.[20] The major assumptions of neofunctionalism are essentially transactionalist: the key issues for integration are not of ideological vision and cultural agency, but matters of satisfaction of material needs: 'Converging economic goals embedded in the bureaucratic, pluralistic, and industrial life of modern Europe provided the crucial impetus to integration. The economic technician, the planner, the innovating industrialist, and trade unionist advanced the movement, not the politician, the scholar, the poet, the writer.'[21] The emphasis on actors and their often haphazard interactions is illustrative of the emphasis on integration in terms of process rather than outcomes. Neofunctionalism is mainly concerned with the process and has little to say about its end goals.

However, the neofunctionalist process is not quite automatic. It is guided and manipulated by actors and institutions. Neofunctionalism holds that non-state actors (regional organizations, interest groups and regional social movements) are responsible for integration. Organized interests and interests of supranational bureaucrats exercise pressure on national governments. Governments are forced to accommodate region-wide interests of economic agents by conceding authority to regional organizations. However, states are not unimportant actors in integration. They may accept or ignore the preferences of interest groups and institutions. Governments set the terms of formal agreements even though they do not exclusively determine the direction and extent of subsequent changes. Supranational institutions also have an important role in integration development, as they experience pressures of having to justify their roles. Neofunctionalists explain that supranational authorities in the EU contribute to further European integration while the lack of supranational authorities in other regions restricts integration development. In addition to sets of actions among sub- and supranational groups, neofunctionalism explains integration process through such dynamics as functional spillover, political spillover, and the upgrading of the common interest: the pursuit of integration in one policy area creates pressures in neighbouring policy areas, placing these areas on the political agenda and leading to further integration.

Once initiated in a specific policy domain, integration creates groups that benefit from the development of integration and its spread to other policy domains. The benefiting interest groups push the process further.

Increasing socio-economic interdependence causes citizens to shift some of their expectations to regional institutions. This causes a 'spillover' into political integration: 'Political integration is the process whereby political actors in several distinct national settings are persuaded to shift their loyalties, expectations and political activities toward a new centre, whose national institutions possess or demand jurisdiction over the pre-existing national states.'[22] Thus intensifying social and economic transactions may lead to the formation of a certain regional identity. However, neofunctionalism recognizes that not all sectors contain equal spillover potential. Moreover, spillovers to political domain, and especially culture, are not guaranteed. The assumption that deeper integration requires a supranational regulatory authority, pushing political integration to follow economic integration, has come under sustained scrutiny. It has been argued that incremental political integration, as predicted by neofunctionalism, is not taking place across the globe.[23]

1.3.2 Liberal Intergovernmentalism

The most significant approach after neofunctionalism is liberal intergovernmentalism.[24] With neofunctionalism it shares the emphasis on economic interests as the principal driving force of integration. Like neofunctionalism, it stresses the importance of institutions as a necessary means of facilitating and securing the integration process. However, it focuses on the central role of national governments, on the importance of powerful domestic economic interests, and on bargaining among national governments over distributive and institutional issues. As regional integration reveals itself most in economic activities, liberal intergovernmentalism prioritizes the economic preferences of national governments, which pursue integration to secure the commercial advantage of domestic producer groups.

Thus integration is a series of rational choices by national governments that reflect interests of powerful domestic groups and the relative power of each state. It overlooks on-going economic, legal, and social changes. Like most realist explanations, liberal intergovernmentalism assumes that states are central actors in international politics and that policy-making in the international realm takes place in intergovernmental negotiations. Thus state preferences are central for the outcomes of negotiations. If in realist intergovernmentalism state preferences are derived from the position of the state in the international power structure and the interest in autonomy and security, in liberal intergovernmentalism state preferences are formed by the outcomes of domestic negotiations on interests of domestic groups. Therefore liberal intergovernmentalism emphasizes priorities of domestic oligarchy.

Further, the agreed integration policy is a result of intergovernmental negotiations on specific cooperation issues. This result comes from the aggregate of actions dependent on state preferences and their bargaining capabilities. States calculate the utility of all possible courses of action and choose the action that maximizes their utility under given circumstances. As the outcomes of international negotiations depend on bargaining power, small and weak states are insignificant actors in integration as they are unable to exercise much influence on the process. Better-informed and stronger governments manipulate negotiations. This is why economic integration generates distributional conflicts among the involved states. However, weaker countries that are not interested in specific agreements can threaten non-cooperation and may receive concessions.

Liberal intergovernmentalism recognizes that foreign policy goals vary and depend on governments' response to shifting pressures from domestic social groups. Yet states continue to be unitary actors even though their options are neither fixed nor uniform. This is so because national governments are able to develop consistent preferences at a time when domestic groups do not play significant roles in negotiations beyond the state. Thus national governments call the tune of integration when pursuing interests generated at the domestic level. Also, national governments create institutions to facilitate more efficient management of the regional system. Institutions are governments' tools for the achievement of governmental goals. They do not take power away from the national governments. On the contrary, institutions enforce the power of the governments. Economic interests go a long way in giving a plausible account of state behaviour, but in some cases geopolitical, security, and ideological interests may be decisive. Liberal intergovernmentalism allows for such interests especially in conditions when the domestic constituency behind a policy is weak or diffuse or when the implications of a policy choice are unimportant or uncertain.

1.3.3   Social Constructivism

With important links to politics, geography, culture, and history, regional integration goes far beyond economics. Constructivists in particular stress 'natural' conditions as important though imprecise elements of regionalism.[25] These 'natural' conditions evolve out of geographical, cultural and historical proximity and provide the 'humus' for regional integration. That is, shared values, social interactions, and similar organizational structures facilitate the development of common aspirations and mutual identification. These, in turn, make it more likely that a common political culture and consensus about political and economic objectives evolve.[26] Constructivists are interested in notions like regional awareness, mutual responsiveness, loyalty, durable sense of community, major societal values, shared knowledge, learning, ideas, and normative and institutional structures.

Commercial agreements alone are not sufficient to cement long-lasting alliances as wars may separate countries or bind them together more strongly than any economic rationale. Therefore historic relations account for a wide range of integration factors beyond economic relations. It is impossible to explain integration without allowing for the effects of previous cooperation, conflicts, social and governmental interests, and institutional decisions. Constructivists believe that there is much more *Europeanness* than assumed just by judging the results of the EEC, EC, and EU. Likewise, identification processes in the Southern Cone encompass a longer time period than the history of MERCOSUR.

Key to constructivism is the idea about the mutual constitution of agency and structure. Human agents do not exist independently from their social environment and culture; they reproduce and 'construct' social reality through their daily practices. The social environment defines people as social beings and conditions their actions. In turn, human actions affect and change the environment. Common rules, policies, and law enable us to study how integration shapes social identities and interests of actors. The evolution of national and supranational identities is important as they change over time and encourage new forms of cooperation while cooperation further redefines the identities.

Not only does integration constrain the range of choices available to actors (states, corporate actors, and citizens) by formal and informal rules, but also by the ways in which actors define their interests. So-called *soft institutions* have been addressed by a literature that studies the influence of world-views, principal beliefs, routinized practices, and norms. In integration studies, the constructivist focus on *soft institutions* has offered a new perspective on regional integration as a process that involves the constitutionalization of shared norms, principles, and procedures including law and social sciences.[27] Other important notions in social constructivism are communication and discourse. A focus on discourses allows examining more closely how integration blocs are constructed discursively and how actors understand the meaning of integration. Argumentative rationality means that participants in a discourse are open to the influence and persuasion of better arguments regarding social organization while relations of power and social hierarchies recede to the background. Integration blocs are affected by discursive and behavioural practices and also have their own influence on these practices.

1.3.4 Neorealism

In efforts to explain regional integration scholars often look to neorealist ideas, which locate the source of regionalism at the level of the international system.[28] For these authors regional integration is a response to external challenges. Regional blocs are formed and stimulated to expand their political power, economic competitiveness, and negotiation capacity relative to the rest of the world and against the international hegemony in particular. In the current global order the USA remains 'the global hegemon of the regional hegemons, the boss of all the bosses' whose task is 'to be the motor and monitor for the international order and the model and mentor for the regional spheres of influence.'[29] US hegemony is understood primarily as the capacity of power exercised by the USA (economic, political, military, ideological, technological, and cultural) to influence internal and foreign policies of other countries.[30]

The USA represents about 4.4% of the world population; however, it is in possession of 15.2% of the global wealth.[31] Financial resources, military force, and advanced technological capability secure the USA a privileged position in the international system. The hegemon is willing to impose its political and economic will on other countries. To resist subordination to US interests, countries form alliances at the bilateral, regional, and international levels that enable them to speak to the USA with a stronger voice. Middle powers, such as large developing states, occupy an intermediary position in the power stratification system and have their own power ambitions.

Global and regional hegemonic powers (the USA and middle powers) affect regional organizations in several ways. One of them is pushing countries to integrate against them (GU(U)AM against Russia, SADCC against South Africa, the GCC against Iraq, MERCOSUR against the USA, ASEAN against China). Another way is to restrict the exercise of the hegemonic power (of Germany in the EU, of Brazil in MERCOSUR). When power differences are too large, the third scenario is possible: smaller countries seek accommodation with the hegemon in hope of receiving special rewards (Mexico in NAFTA for the sake of access to the US market). In such cases regionalism adopts the character of subordination to the hegemon.

It is common that regional groups serve the interests of powerful states. One major actor sets the agenda in the organization (the USA in NAFTA, Brazil in MERCOSUR, Russia in the EAEU, India in the SAARC, South Africa in the SACU). In this sense regionalism has always existed when powerful countries and empires dominated in different international systems. Hegemons press for regional integration in order to pursue their interests, to generate support and legitimacy for their policies, but also to share burdens and solve common problems such as the provision of security.

The movement towards regionalism can also be characterized as a response to 'a security dilemma' in which each regional movement attempts to enhance its bargaining position relative to other regions. When the trend to the united and closed market in Western Europe became clear, the USA and Canada started a regional agreement of their own. In response to European and North American regionalism Japan undertook efforts to create a regional economy, and there also appeared APEC, NAFTA, and MERCOSUR.[32] Also, neorealism allows a consideration of collective security problems. From the perspective of security studies, regionalism may be a response to conflicts and threats. However, security threats often disrupt and destroy regional alliances instead of strengthening them.

1.4 THEMES AND CRITERIA OF THE COMPARISON

The analytical framework using the described theories is designed to identify and explain differences in MERCOSUR's integration outcomes relative to those of the EU in four dimensions of social life: economic, politico-institutional, historico-cultural, and geostrategic. Each of the four theories offers one general theme for the comparison: economic interdependence, state size and interest asymmetries, cultural diversity, and geostrategic motivations. According to the respective theories, these themes are the key notions affecting regional integration and cooperation. More narrow criteria are derived from these four themes for the actual comparison. There are additional themes and criteria as well. Below is the explanation of the position of the dimensions of integration, the theories, and the themes and criteria of comparison within the proposed analytical framework.

1.4.1 Why Several Theories?

Diverse manifestations of regionalism constitute a theme that merits 'a comprehensive examination even at the expense of theoretical parsimony.'[33] As a complex process across many dimensions of social life, regional integration requires various explanations depending on an issue area. The four approaches discussed in the previous section are all influential theories of integration. However, each of them offers only a partial and incomplete story of integration. Like the factors they emphasize, the approaches have varying degrees of relevance for different geographic instances of regionalism and for a single region in different periods of its evolution. Together they add to each other in the provision of a more detailed picture of regionalism. Integration theories illustrate the multidimensional character of European integration. Therefore, a complex comparison of MERCOSUR with the EU has to be grounded in accounts of multiple explanatory approaches as well.

In order to provide a complex explanation based on several theories, the monograph relies on the approach towards inter-theory dialogue known as *analytic eclecticism*.[34] This approach is preoccupied with problems of wider scope and complexity that cannot be resolved by an application of a single theory. *Eclectic* work combines various pre-existing well-established research traditions and produces explanations based on these multiple traditions. Due to the nature of research problems and organization of the inquiry, *eclectic* studies do not test theories, fill in gaps within theories, or resolve inter-theory debates. Neither do they attempt a synthesis of the used theories, but they operate with the respective theories selecting their relevant ideas. Conclusions from *analytic eclecticism* aim to provide an explanation of the studied phenomena. Sil and Katzenstein observe that *eclectic* work in its combination of different traditional approaches cannot operate with the full-length accounts of the theories it incorporates, but it usually employs only selected elements of each theory. In any case, it is impossible to apply 'full' versions of the European integration theories towards the study of MERCOSUR, as these theories are 'alien' to the South American group in the sense that they were composed from the studies of a different region: Europe. Besides, one can never be sure what a standard full account of any theory is anyway, because authors offer varying interpretations of each theory.

1.4.2 Why Dimensions?

The monograph aims to evaluate the quality of integration in MERCOSUR across several integration dimensions. Even though regionalism is most tangible in the areas of trade and investment, integration touches upon various aspects of social life, receives strong impulses from non-material factors and extends to the domains of security, politics, and culture. As both MERCOSUR and the EU are multidimensional processes, understanding them overcomes strictly economic and institutional realms of integration. Whereas existing studies of regionalism usually focus on a single issue, the broad focus of this monograph on exploring various dimensions brings into clearer relief the differences, similarities, and interrelations among multiple issue areas. Such multidimensional approach contributes to a fuller understanding of regionalism.

Most of the regional initiatives prioritize trade and investment and are subject to economic analysis. Whether an integration project is stuck at the level of an FTA or proceeds further into social and political spheres, the study of political dimension of integration is unavoidable because political circumstances of decision-making are involved in generating regional policy in any social domain: economic, social, cultural, or pertaining to foreign policy. Culture is marginalized in European integration studies because little integration or convergence is occurring among national cultural policies in the EU, if any. The necessity to include this dimension of integration is prompted by the experience of MERCOSUR that has agreed to pursue such an unprecedented goal as the achievement of a bilingual regional community through the mandatory teaching of Spanish and Portuguese as foreign languages. While the effects of linguistic, historic, and cultural affinities among the populations on the actual political and economic processes are not easy to measure, MERCOSUR's relative cultural homogeneity prompts noteworthy regional policies in the cultural areas. Finally, the external dimension of integration is incorporated to illustrate how the hegemonic structures have affected the two regions in notably different ways.

Clearly, MERCOSUR is different from the EU in each integration dimension. In some domains regional policies are easier to harmonize and homogenize in one region, thus making them subject to regional integration effort; other kinds of policies are easier to pursue in the other region. Therefore, the monograph determines which specific integration dimensions in MERCOSUR have greater or smaller potential for integration in relation to its counterpart region and explains why it is so.

1.4.3 What Is the Relationship Between the Dimensions and the Theories?

The analytical framework of the monograph is grounded in four theories serving to explain integration in four dimensions. Neofunctionalism depicts regional integration as a chain reaction advanced by interests of economic actors. It is effective in the analysis of economic integration through the notion of interdependence promoting integration. Intergovernmentalism attributes the integration process to rational decisions of governments. Most intergovernmentalist analysis is about achieving outcomes in bargaining over economic and political matters. Constructivism explains integration as a consequence of pre-existing social, cultural, and economic conditions. It provides important links to culture, history, identity, and factors constraining and shaping utility maximizing behaviour. Neorealism treats integration as a means to increase individual and collective power of states in the global context. With its notions of power it brings in the interrelationship between inter-state cooperation and the power structure of the international system.

The various aspects of the process each individual theory emphasizes correspond well to the main dimension the respective theory is assigned to in the monograph, as each of the four theories is particularly relevant just for one of the four dimensions. Above all, this is true for neorealism in its application to the study of external factors of integration. The use of neofunctionalism is possible in any integration dimension involving interaction, and its key concepts, like interest groups, interdependence, and spillovers do not have to be exclusively economic. However, the economic process suits neofunctionalism well, and this is the domain where it is most commonly applied. As MERCOSUR's key players are states, intergovernmentalist ideas are useful in the analyses of different approaches towards integration among MERCOSUR member governments. Thus criteria based on intergovernmentalism are applied to the study of inter-state politics of integration. This leaves the domain of history and culture for constructivism, which is more used to dealing with these fields than any other theory. Together, the four dimensions and respective theories make up a framework allowing us to look at the most important implications of the MERCOSUR process.

However, all the four theories were intended to describe the integration process as a whole, and they were not designed specially for the analysis of integration in the dimensions as proposed in this monograph. The application of each theory is not bounded by one dimension only. For example, neofunctionalist interactions can be economic, cultural, political, and so on, and neofunctionalism can be applied to the analysis of integration in various dimensions. If each theory could be used for analysis in each of the four dimensions, the monograph would have four times four, sixteen narratives in total. However, due to the limited scope of the theories, not all the sixteen analyses are possible in principle. For example, application of neofunctionalism to external dimension is impossible because neofunctionalist sources of integration are internal to the region.

Some of the narratives are possible but not feasible because there is no reliable data to do them, or they are unable to generate valuable conclusions. Consider neofunctionalism in application to culture. If Germans and the French increasingly interact with each other, the ultimate neofunctionalist prediction is that at some point they stop being French and German and become Franco-German. This is not happening. Even though the neofunctionalist logic does work in culture, the results of cross-cultural interactions in the two blocs remain difficult to identify. In other instances some of the narratives are merged, as it is impractical to keep them separate. For example, the discussion of external factors of integration under the neorealist framework is dedicated to political cooperation and economic integration anyway; therefore, there is only one narrative instead of three (political, economic, and geostrategic) in the four-by-four matrix. The four specified theories are applied to the four dimensions as follows.

Economic Integration As mentioned, neofunctionalism provides the basis for the discussion of MERCOSUR's economic integration in Chapter 2. However, factors affecting economic integration are not limited to interdependence, and the other three theories can explain various aspects of economic integration as well. The intergovernmentalist discussion of integration politics gives a great deal of attention to problems of economic integration in Chapter 3. Neorealism can explain regional economic mobilization stemming from the fears of losing economic competition to extra-regional players, and this shapes the discussion of external factors of integration in Chapter 5. Finally, regardless of any interdependence levels, economic divergences present difficulties for homogenizing national economic practices and regulations. Therefore, an additional discussion about the difficulties of integrating Brazilian and Argentinean economies is incorporated under the constructivist and intergovernmentalist inference that integration is easier to achieve among similar economies and that economic divergences narrow the scope and depth of economic integration (Chapter 2).

Politics of Integration The studies of MERCOSUR hold states responsible for integration. As states are principal actors, their interests and preferences determine the course of the process. Both constructivism and intergovernmentalism agree that similar interests are conducive to actors' engagement in integration. In constructivism integration is prompted by such evolution of existing social structures that converge actors' interests. In intergovernmentalism homogeneity of interests simplify inter-state bargaining over strategic matters and prompt faster agreements on collective action. Therefore, the analysis of politics of integration in Chapter 3 is based on the comparison of states and their interests in accord with the intergovernmentalist and constructivist reasoning that less similar states are more difficult to integrate. The neofunctionalist approach is less suitable for the analysis of political integration because high levels of functional interdependence do not automatically guarantee political integration. In MERCOSUR interdependence levels are relatively low, and they have not played a decisive role in the formation and the development of the region. As in case of economic integration, mobilization as a result of extra-regional threats and competition is an important factor of integration. This mobilization becomes the subject of discussion of the influence of external factors on MERCOSUR and the EU in Chapter 5.

Cultural Integration The proposed framework applies constructivism to culture in Chapter 4. While neofunctionalist and intergovernmentalist analyses of cultural integration are possible, they are not capable of producing any significant conclusions. There is no evidence of emergence of any supranational *Mercosurian* culture as a consequence of regional interaction facilitated by MERCOSUR as could be predicted by neofunctionalism. Likewise, the intergovernmentalist approach to culture may enjoy limited success because regional cultural integration scores low among governmental priorities. Even though culture is greatly shaped by political factors, there is little evidence that regional institutions like MERCOSUR and the EU cause any significant cultural transformations among populations. EU studies literature overuses the term 'European identity' in places where a talk about solidarity or affinity perceptions among selected population groups is more appropriate. Neither does cultural integration occur as a response to external security threats or because of fears of losing economic competition to extra-regional actors. What happens as a result of these external influences is cooperation or mobilization as discussed in Chapter 5. Therefore, the neorealist argument does not apply to culture either.

External Dimension As mentioned, neorealism does a good job explaining economic integration and political cooperation as a reaction to external challenges faced by the integrating countries (Chapter 5). Neofunctionalism does not apply to the external dimension because its source of regionalism is internal to the region: intra-regional functional interdependence. However, constructivism and intergovernmentalism may give important insights to converging national foreign policies resulting in regionalism. Constructivism discusses culture and identity and explains why countries sharing historic, cultural, or ideational affinities feel the need to stand together against competition and threats from the outside, and what may constitute the division between 'inside' and 'outside' (Chapter 4). Intergovernmentalism explains convergence in national foreign policies in relation to material factors. Therefore, the chapter on politics of integration discusses the varying approaches of Brazil and Argentina to their foreign policies that are conditioned by the inherent differences between the two countries and the ways in which they tend to manage their international relations (Chapter 3).

1.4.4 What Are the Themes and Specific Criteria of the Comparison?

Each of the four dimensions contains one or two themes of comparison derived from relevant theories, and each theme is further broken down into specific criteria for the comparison of MERCOSUR and the EU. This subsection explains what these themes and criteria are.

Economic Dimension
Principal Theme. Economic Interdependence In neofunctionalism high economic interdependence provides conditions for the work of the mechanisms that result in the advancement of integration. Economic interdependence can be easily measured by such criteria as intra-regional trade and investment volumes. A number of factors condition regional interdependence levels such as barriers to exchange among the countries and conditions of regions' physical and economic geography and cross-border infrastructure. Therefore they become important criteria for the comparison of MERCOSUR with the EU in the economic chapter.

Additional Theme. Economic Convergence Interdependence is not the only variable affecting economic integration. In practical terms there are difficulties in the development and application of uniform regional policies among countries with different production structures, low levels of macroeconomic convergence, and different economic ideologies that affect their existing national policies. Macroeconomic divergence, heterogeneity of production patterns, and difference in development history constrain MERCOSUR's integration. Therefore they are included in the analysis of the economic chapter under the constructivist/intergovernmentalist inference that economic integration is easier to achieve in instances where the above indicators are lower.

Politico-Institutional Dimension
Theme. Intra-bloc Size and Interest Asymmetries Intergovernmentalism provides core criteria for the study of the MERCOSUR process in the political dimension of integration. This theory holds that states are key actors in integration; therefore state interest in relation to integration becomes the focal point of the analysis. In intergovernmentalism negotiations over integration measures are easier if state preferences coincide. State interest is highly conditioned by the state size and power. Therefore size and power asymmetries have implications for such important outcomes of integration as quality of the regional institutional system, principles of decision-making, and principles of operation of regional law. These, in turn, exercise further influence on the process. Size and power asymmetries in MERCOSUR condition a significant divergence in national approaches towards foreign policy, which reduces the scope and depth of regional integration.

Historico-Cultural Dimension
Principal Theme. Cultural Heterogeneity While there is limited effect of linguistic, historic, and cultural affinities among regional populations on the actual political process, MERCOSUR's relative cultural homogeneity promises to facilitate integration in cultural areas. Therefore factors such as *race, language,* and *religion* are incorporated in the analysis of integration with a goal not to evaluate their effects on the process at large, but on the extent of policy harmonization in respective cultural areas (particularly languages). The stated notions clearly affect separatist claims at the national level, therefore they are useful for the examination of regional cohesiveness at the supranational level. The analysis is done on the inference from constructivism and intergovernmentalism that cultural homogeneity is conducive to integration in cultural spheres.

Additional Theme. Discourse on Regional Unity In addition to the levels of relative cultural heterogeneity and corresponding results of cultural integration in the two regions, the cultural segment of the study compares discourses on regional unity. Dominant discourse serves the needs of those holding power, therefore it provides the links between cultural themes and power politics. The discourse identifies the particular elements of regional unity that can be contrasted between MERCOSUR and the EU. This comparison illustrates that *Europeanness* is characterized by the prevalence of political meanings over cultural definitions whereas the MERCOSUR countries share stronger historic and cultural affinities.

Geostrategic Dimension
Theme. Geostrategic Considerations and Incentives for Integration This segment of analysis does not produce any easily measurable criteria, but it deals with the qualitative analysis of MERCOSUR's incentives for regional cooperation that have been conditioned by its relationship with the USA. The analysis illustrates that geostrategic factors shape MERCOSUR in a notably different way from the EU. While the EU is being affected more by geopolitical factors, MERCOSUR is affected by geoeconomic factors. The monograph employs 'geopolitical' strategy to denote measures that consolidate regional power and influence on other states, whereas 'geoeconomic' strategy is a combination of measures targeting a catch-up in economic development and an increase in economic leverage of the integrating countries against extra-regional actors.

1.5 Summary of the Analytical Framework

Table 1.2 represents the summary of the proposed analytical framework. It identifies all the items discussed above: the four dimensions of integration, the four theories, the six broad themes of comparison derived from these theories, and the more narrow criteria for the comparison of MERCOSUR with the EU. The four theories and their corresponding four themes—neofunctionalism/economic interdependence, intergovernmentalism/size and interest asymmetries, constructivism/cultural diversity, and neorealism/geostrategic incentives—constitute the basis of the analysis of the subsequent chapters. Two additional themes with their criteria—economic convergence and discourse on regional unity—provide bases for additional comparisons.

Table 1.2 Analytical framework for the comparison of regions

Dimension of integration	Applied theory	Principal theme of the comparison	Criteria of the comparison
Economic	**Neofunctionalism** Neofunctionalism explains integration as a spontaneous process shaped by interests of economic agents. Export-oriented producers maximize their utility through economic liberalization and market expansion. Increasing functional interdependence as a result of their operation causes integration to spread into other social domains	Economic interdependence	• Volumes of intra-regional trade • Volumes of intra-regional investment • Degree of economic openness • Peculiarities of physical and economic geography (cross-border infrastructure and population settlement)
	Constructivism/Intergovernmentalism Both constructivism and intergovernmentalism agree that converging interests make integration more likely and easier to proceed. Therefore, divergences in production patterns, development strategies and macroeconomic performance between Brazil and Argentina are discussed as factors constraining integration in MERCOSUR	Economic convergence	• Degree of divergence in national production patterns • Degree of divergence in national development strategies • Degree of divergence in macroeconomic performance
Politico-institutional	**Intergovernmentalism** In liberal intergovernmentalism, integration is an outcome of rational decisions of national governments. It is an intentional and organized process, in which the preferences of individual governments are strongly affected by interests of powerful domestic groups. The governments agree only on the decisions that provide maximum benefit or least damage to their clients (business groups and population)	Intra-bloc size and interest asymmetries	• The number of participant states • Peculiarities of decision-making • Size asymmetries among the member states • Average size of the member states • Image of the region's core countries • The character of regional leadership • Divergences in foreign policy approaches • The quality of the regional institutional system • Principles of operation of the regional law

Historico-cultural	**Social constructivism** For social constructivism, integration is a process highly conditioned by already existing social relations, practices, norms, and values shared by the integrating societies. Human agents (governments, corporate actors, and citizens) are deeply affected by the environment they act in. Regional integration reinforces the trends that are rooted in the history of the regions	**Cultural heterogeneity** **Discourse on regional unity**	• Linguistic diversity • Religious diversity • Racial diversity • Dominant discourse on regional unity
Geostrategic	**Neorealism** Neorealism explains integration as a measure to increase individual and collective powers of the states vis-à-vis the international hegemony. Regional blocs are formed and stimulated to expand their political power, economic competitiveness and negotiation capacity relatively to the rest of the world through individual countries' foreign policy coordination and the mobilization of available resources	**Geostrategic considerations and incentives**	• Geopolitical considerations, including response to extra-regional security threats • Geoeconomic considerations

Notes

1. Malamud, Andrés and Schmitter, Philippe C. 2011. The experience of European integration and the potential for integration in South America. In *New Regionalism and the European Union: Dialogues, comparisons and new research directions*, edited by Alex Warleigh-Lack, Nick Robinson and Ben Rosamond, pp 135–157. Routledge, London. p 135. Malamud, Andrés and Schmitter, Philippe C. 2006. La experiencia de integración europea y el potencial de integración del Mercosur. *Desarrollo Económico*, 46 (181), pp 3–31. p 3. Campbell, Jorge (editor). 2000. *Mercosul: entre a realidade e a utopia*. Relume Dumará, Rio de Janeiro. Campbell, Jorge (editor). 1999. *Mercosur. Entre la Realidad y la Utopía*. Editorial Nuevohacer/CEI, BsAs. Roett, Riordan (editor). 1999. *MERCOSUR: Regional Integration, World Markets*. Lynne Rienner, Boulder.
2. For definitions of regional integration see: Fawcett, Louise. 1995. Regionalism in Historical Perspective. In *Regionalism in World Politics*, edited by Louise Fawcett and Andrew Hurrell, pp 9–36. Oxford University Press, Oxford. Fawcett, Louise. 2004. Exploring regional domains: a comparative study of regionalism. *International Affairs*, 80:3, pp 429–446. Hurrell, Andrew. 1995. Regionalism in Theoretical Perspective. In *Regionalism in World Politics*, edited by Louise Fawcett and Andrew Hurrell, pp 37–73. Oxford University Press, Oxford. Mansfield, Edward D. and Milner, Helen V. 1997. The Political Economy of Regionalism: An Overview. In *The Political Economy of Regionalism*, edited by Edward D. Mansfield and Helen V. Milner, pp 1–19. Columbia University Press, New York. Choi, Young Jong and Caporaso, James A. 2002. Comparative Regional Integration. In *Handmonograph of International Relations*, edited by Walter Carlsnaes, Thomas Risse and Beth A. Simmons, pp 480–499. Sage Publications, London.
3. Malamud and Schmitter, 2011. p 142.
4. Common market is the free supply of services and unrestricted movement of goods, workers, and capital. Above all, the commitment to the common market is reflected in the name of MERCOSUR: MERCOSUR/L = **Mer**cado **Com**ún del **Sur** = **Mer**cado **Com**um do **Sul** = Common Market of the South.
5. As in Balassa, Bela A. 1961. *The Theory of Economic Integration*. Irwin, Homewood, Illinois.
6. The ECSC was established in 1952, the EEC and EURATOM in 1957, the EC in 1967; PICE started in 1986 and MERCOSUR in 1991. Everywhere in the monograph the comparison of the two blocs is *ahistorical*. Age is not an independent variable. The EEC is 34 years older than MERCOSUR. However, Argentina and Brazil of today are not France and

Germany 34 years ago, and contemporary MERCOSUR does not replicate the EU of 34 years ago. Besides, it is not easy to identify uncontested starting points of the two processes. Both 1952 and 1957 can be considered birth years of the EU. The bilateral process of commercial liberalization between Argentina and Brazil started in 1986, and the Treaty of MERCOSUR incorporated two small countries Uruguay and Paraguay into this process. The EEC and the Treaty of MERCOSUR are arbitrary benchmarks: whereas in Europe integration efforts were preceded by WW2, the process of rapprochement in the Southern Cone began early in the twentieth century.
7. Based on CIA data for 2016.
8. González-Oldekop, Florencia. 1997. *La Integración y Sus Instituciones: Los Casos de la Comunidad Europea y el MERCOSUR*. Ediciones Ciudad Argentina, BsAs.
9. de Almeida Medeiros, Marcelo. 2000. A hegemonia brasileira no Mercosul: O efeito samba e suas conseqüências no processo institucional de integração. In *O Mercosul no limiar do século XXI*, edited by Marcos Costa Lima and Marcelo de Almeida Medeiros, pp 190–205. Cortez Editora, São Paulo.
10. Malamud, Andrés. 2010. Latin American Regionalism and EU Studies. *Journal of European Integration*, 32:6, pp 637–657. p 643.
11. Idem, p 642.
12. Kaltenthaler, Karl and Mora, Frank. 2002. Explaining Latin American economic integration: the case of Mercosur. *Review of International Political Economy*, 9, pp 72–97.
13. Malamud, Andrés. 2005. Mercosur Turns 15: Between Rising Rhetoric and Declining Achievement. *Cambridge Review of International Affairs*, 18:3, pp 421–436.
14. Malamud and Schmitter, 2011. p 135.
15. See, for example, Carranza, Mario E. 2010. *Mercosur, the Global Crisis, and the New Architecture of Regionalism in the Americas*. Working Paper 125. FLACSO, Curridabat, Costa Rica.
16. Burges, Sean. 2005. Bounded by the Reality of Trade: Practical Limits to a South American Region. *Cambridge Review of International Affairs*, 18:3, pp 437–454.
17. Idem.
18. Sil, Rudra and Katzenstein, Peter J. 2010. Beyond Paradigms: Analytic Eclecticism in the Study of World Politics. Palgrave Macmillan, New York.
19. Lindberg, Leon N. 1971. Political Integration as a Multidimensional Phenomenon Requiring Multivariate Measurement. In *Regional Integration: Theory and Research*, edited by Leon N. Lindberg and Stuart A. Scheingold, pp 45–127. Harvard University Press, Cambridge. Wiener,

Antje and Diez, Thomas (editors). 2009. *European Integration Theory*. Oxford University Press, Oxford.
20. On neofunctionalism see: Haas, Ernst Bernard. 1958. *The Uniting of Europe: Political, Social, and Economic Forces, 1950–1957*. Stanford University Press, Stanford. Rosamond, Ben. 2000. *Theories of European Integration*. St. Martin's Press, New York. pp 50–73. Strøby Jensen, Carsten. 2003. Neo-functionalism. In *European Union Politics*, edited by Michelle Cini, pp 80–92. Niemann, Arne and Schmitter, Philippe C. 2009. Neofunctionalism. In *European Integration Theory*, edited by Antje Wiener and Thomas Diez, pp 45–65. Oxford University Press, Oxford.
21. Haas, 1958. p xix.
22. Idem, p 16.
23. Rosamond, 2000. Strøby Jensen, 2003. El-Agraa, Ali M. 2011. The theory of economic integration. In *The European Union: Economics and Policies*, edited by Ali M. El-Agraa, pp 83–101. Cambridge University Press, Cambridge.
24. On liberal intergovernmentalism see: Moravcsik, Andrew. 1998. *The Choice for Europe: Social Purpose and State Power from Messina and Maastricht*. Cornell University Press, Ithaca. Michelmann, Hans and Soldatos, Panayotis (editors). 1994. *European integration: Theories and Approaches*. University Press of America, Lanaham. Moravcsik, Andrew. 1993. Preferences and Power in the European Community: A Liberal Intergovernmental Approach. *Journal of Common Market Studies*, 31:4, pp 473–524. Moravcsik, Andrew and Schimmelfennig, Frank. 2009. Liberal Intergovernmentalism. In *European Integration Theory*, edited by Antje Wiener and Thomas Diez, pp 67–86. Oxford University Press, Oxford.
25. On social constructivism see: Risse, Thomas. 2009. Social Constructivism and European Integration. In *European Integration Theory*, edited by Antje Wiener and Thomas Diez, pp 144–160. Oxford University Press, Oxford. Wallace, William. 1990. *The Transformation of Western Europe*. Pinter Publishers, London. Rosamond, 2000. pp 171–174.
26. Mace, Gordon and Bélanger, Louis. 1999. The Structural Contexts of Hemispheric Regionalism: Power, Trade, Political Culture, and Economic Development. In *The Americas in Transition, The Contours of Regionalism*, edited by Gordon Mace and Louis Bélanger, pp 37–67. Lynne Rienner, Boulder.
27. Wiener, Antje. 2006. Soft Institutions. In *Principles of European Constitutional Law*, edited by Armin von Bogdandy and Jürgen Bast, pp 419–449. Hart Publishing, Oxford.
28. For a discussion of neorealist explanations of regionalism see: Hurrell, 1995. Rosamond, 2000. pp 131–135. Hurrell, Andrew. 2001. The Politics

of Regional Integration in MERCOSUR. In *Regional Integration in Latin America and the Caribbean: The Political Economy of Open Regionalism*, edited by Victor Bulmer-Thomas, pp 194–211. Institute of Latin American Studies, University of London, London. pp 207–209.
29. Kurth, James. 1996. America's Grand Strategy. A pattern of History. *The National Interest*, 43, pp 3–19. p 19.
30. Oliva Campos, Carlos. 2002. The United States, Latin America, and the Caribbean: From Panamericanism to Neopanamericanism. In *Neoliberalism and Neopanamericanism: The View from Latin America*, edited by Gary Prevost and Carlos Oliva Campos, pp 3–27. Palgrave Macmillan, New York. p 11.
31. Based on CIA population data for mid-2017 and GDP data for 2017.
32. Gilpin, Robert. 2001. *Global Political Economy: Understanding the International Economic Order*. Princeton University Press, Princeton. pp 342 and 360.
33. Moravcsik about 'the evolution of the European Union' in Moravcsik, Andrew. 2003. Theory Synthesis in International Relations: Real Not Metaphysical. *International Studies Review*, 5 (1), pp 131–136. p 132.
34. Sil and Katzenstein, 2010.

CHAPTER 2

Economic Integration and Interdependence

Regional integration is most often associated with economic liberalization of trade and investment and the effects of regional economic institutions and exchanges. 'Integration' and 'economic integration' are used interchangeably, which reflects the fact that, among all kinds of international relations, economic activities are most susceptible to joint inter-state management. This is evidenced by the launch of FTAs and customs unions and the conclusion of many bilateral, regional, and global commercial agreements on all the continents except Antarctica, with the expectation that economic integration and expansion of economic activity will enhance the welfare of producers, traders, consumers, and will improve conditions of life in the participating countries. As of 20 June 2017, 445 notifications of regional trade agreements (counting goods, services, and accessions separately) had been received by the WTO, with 279 in force.[1] It is of no surprise that economic integration continues to be the major focus in the studies of regionalism.

This chapter discusses major differences between MERCOSUR and EU regional economic systems and explains the relative underdevelopment of MERCOSUR's market using the neofunctionalist argument. Neofunctionalism emphasizes high interdependence as an essential condition of integration. Increasing economic flows and various functional needs within regions cause domestic actors to press governments for policies to further liberalize and standardize regional rules for intra-regional exchange and to promote deeper integration. Regional institutions emerge

© The Author(s) 2019
M. Mukhametdinov, *MERCOSUR and the European Union*,
https://doi.org/10.1007/978-3-319-76825-0_2

to manage increasing levels of cross-border transactions. Differences in the outcomes of economic integration in MERCOSUR and the EU (the varying degrees of consolidation of their common market regimes and economic institutions) can be attributed to the difference in the intensity of intra-regional economic exchanges, which determine higher or lower interdependence levels.

As regional economic interdependence is a key notion in the study of economic integration, the chapter identifies its varying degrees within the two blocs, explains this variation, and relates it to the differences in the consolidation of the two regional economic systems. Compared to the EU, MERCOSUR has limited incentives for intra-regional economic integration because of much lower levels of economic interdependence among its member states. MERCOSUR's relatively low economic interdependence is conditioned by specific physical, geographic, demographic, and structural characteristics of the region. The lower levels of interdependence explain a later beginning of preoccupations with commercial liberalization in the Southern Cone than in Western Europe, relatively weak consolidation of the MERCOSUR economic system if compared to the single European market, and many differences in MERCOSUR's institutions and rules regulating intra-regional economic activities from their EU counterparts.

Section 2.1 describes MERCOSUR's incomplete common market. Section 2.2 examines why economic interdependence in MERCOSUR is low, and explains how low interdependence levels have affected the goals, speed, and qualitative results of the integration reforms. Section 2.4 reviews the studies of MERCOSUR's quantitative effects. The conclusions of these studies are consistent with the assumptions of lesser relevance of the common market and the greater importance of domestic markets and extra-regional economic relations for the MERCOSUR countries. Section 2.5 is dedicated to the study of prospects for the monetary union in MERCOSUR. It suggests that despite being on regional agenda at various times, a monetary union in the bloc is premature because overall economic cohesion of MERCOSUR is much lower than that of the Eurozone.

Besides low economic interdependence, there is another obstacle for the stetting of the MERCOSUR's regional market. The MERCOSUR countries often display a greater divergence in economic performance than the more numerous EU members. From constructivist and intergovernmentalist perspectives, the imposition of uniform economic rules on different countries is both more difficult and less sensible than policy harmonization among similar countries trying to achieve shared goals. Section 2.3 and Subsection 2.5.3 link difficulties of integrating the MERCOSUR economies to implications of divergences in their economic performance, production structures and economic ideologies.

2.1 Breaches in the MERCOSUR's Common Market System

Despite its name being an abbreviation for the *Common Market of the South*, MERCOSUR is far from being a fully operational common market. Even though the contours of such are clearly seen through the bloc's legislation, the MERCOSUR regional market is incomplete in comparison both with the ideal model and the single European market. An ideal common market presupposes a free intra-regional cross-border supply of services, free movement of goods, workers and capital, and a unified approach towards the products and factors of production from the rest of the world. The present-day MERCOSUR cannot be characterized as a common market because of existing obstacles to free intra-regional cross-border circulation of means and results of production, and divergent national norms in relation to the products and factors of third countries. A 2011 article describing the state of affairs in the bloc at its twentieth anniversary describes it as 'an incomplete free trade area struggling to turn into a customs union.'[2] The deficiencies of the MERCOSUR market system are many, and one of the principal tasks of this study is to explain the causes of relative underdevelopment of MERCOSUR's economic integration in comparison with that of the EU. The following paragraphs describe the state of the MERCOSUR integration in the goods, services, labour, and capital markets in their internal and external dimensions.[3]

2.1.1 Goods Market

Even though MERCOSUR's effects are most tangible in the liberalization of trade in goods and especially in the elimination of tariffs, the circulation of goods within MERCOSUR is not completely free due to existing NTBs and some administrative procedures. MERCOSUR's FTA is shallow for a number of reasons:

1) Some goods remain exceptions to the FTA regime, most notably sugar and automobiles.
2) Intra-regional exchange continues to be hindered by trade defence legislation. For example, MERCOSUR competition rules allow antidumping duties on intra-regional trade. No agreement about elimination of antidumping has been reached yet. On the contrary, in certain cases MERCOSUR antidumping norms are less stringent than those of the WTO as they allow violations of WTO rules in intra-MERCOSUR disputes.
3) Even though the elimination of NTBs (particularly of licenses and phytosanitary provisions) has become a recurrent theme, it has not been accompanied by a credible programme of action. MERCOSUR's organs have produced a great volume of legislation harmonizing technical norms including sanitary and phytosanitary standards. However, this impressive body of legislation has had little effect because much of it has not entered in force due to pending 'internalization,' the set of procedures by which MERCOSUR law becomes operational only after it is incorporated into national legislatures of the member states. On the other hand, plenty of legislation aiming to harmonize standards fails to do so because it simply collects and replicates existing divergent national norms. National legislation is divergent not only because it differs among member states, but also because each member state may apply different criteria and standards to each of the other four. This is notably the case in phytosanitary standards for specific agricultural products: for example, Argentina's standards applied to products originating in Uruguay are different from those applied to products from Paraguay, Brazil, and Venezuela.
4) MERCOSUR has not started the process of tax harmonization necessary to achieve indirect tax 'neutrality' in intra-regional trade. In the EEC the harmonization of the value added tax occurred in the 1960s and 1970s. Even if tax rates continue to differ among the countries, indirect tax harmonization could provide greater tax neutrality by ensuring that: (a) export tax rebates are the exact equivalent of the indirect taxes paid in the exporting countries, and (b) imports are taxed in importing countries in a non-discriminatory way as compared to internal products. In MERCOSUR, due to asymmetries in domestic tax legislations and the different indirect tax regimes, export tax rebates do not match the amount of internal

taxes paid in the exporting country. Instead, the rebate is calculated as a percentage of export values. Different rates apply depending on the type of product. This practice opens the door to the use of export tax rebates as a hidden export subsidy on intra-regional trade.
5) Argentina is reported to implement intra- and extra-zonal export duties.[4]

In extra-regional trade MERCOSUR does implement a CET. However, the CET has numerous national exceptions. Besides, MERCOSUR law does not set the principle of free circulation for goods from third countries. Imported goods pay duties when they enter MERCOSUR and, if they travel further, when they cross national borders within the bloc. Member states collect import duties and keep them. In contrast to the EU, not only does MERCOSUR fail to effectively enforce the CET, but it implements neither a common customs code (initially approved in 1994 but never put in force)[5] nor other common procedures applied on imports from non-members (such as trade defence). Thus despite the CET, the four customs territories remain separate; and the term 'incomplete customs union' about MERCOSUR in the academic and technical literature is misleading. The word *incomplete* refers to national exceptions to the common external trade policy. However, not only does a customs union require a CET, but also the merging of national customs territories into a single one, in which MERCOSUR has made little progress. Rather than an FTA or incomplete customs union, MERCOSUR continues to be defined as 'an incomplete free trade area with some degree of harmonization of member states' extra-zonal commercial policies.'[6]

The customs union needs a common customs code and elimination of double taxation. The question of redistribution of import duties arises as ports of entry to MERCOSUR are limited, and Paraguay is very disadvantaged given its landlocked position. In the EU import duties are collected by states and sent to Brussels to become part of the union's budget. Given the size of the Brazilian market and the amount of customs revenues, it is unrealistic to expect that Brazil will accept this model. In the SACU national authorities collect import duties and then redistribute them among member states according to a fixed percentage. This might be a model for MERCOSUR to accept in the future. In 2010 MERCOSUR did approve a new common customs code and agreed to eliminate the double import duty.[7] However, the customs code remains subject to incorporation into domestic law, which is a lengthy and uneasy process.[8]

Neither has complete elimination of double taxation been achieved despite a series of agreements undertaken between 2004 and 2011. The crucial problem of redistribution of income from import duties is left for further intergovernmental negotiations.

The question of completion of the FTA and of the customs union is closely related to the issue of negotiations with third parties. MERCOSUR requires that trade agreements with third countries and blocs be negotiated and completed by the bloc and not by the countries individually.[9] However, due to remaining obstacles to intra-zonal trade, Uruguay and Paraguay still have difficulties accessing Argentinean and Brazilian markets. As a result, tensions appear as the small countries and even Argentina are often more interested in third markets than in the regional market. The third countries themselves may prefer to negotiate with the bloc members separately rather than jointly until the customs union is effectively in place for outsiders to take advantage of the truly integrated regional market.

2.1.2 Services Market

The only existing general set of MERCOSUR rules on services is the Montevideo Protocol with its annexes.[10] It follows the GATS approach, and many commitments undertaken in the Protocol simply replicate those undertaken under GATS. This means that the process of integration in the services area focuses on 'negative' liberalization (removal of barriers), leaving aside 'positive' integration (harmonization of rules and regulatory criteria). The Protocol has been in force in Argentina, Brazil, and Uruguay since 2005 and in Paraguay since 2014.[11] The major problems in service sector liberalization are 'different rules in force in each country that still have to be harmonised, the dispersion of regulatory regimes and their absence in some countries, […] slow incorporation of MERCOSUR services rules into national legislations and weak participation of private interests in negotiations.'[12] Among specific services sectors, only insurance, transport, and telecommunications have been covered by MERCOSUR legislation.

2.1.3 Labour Market

An agreement of 1997, which came into effect in 2005, allowed citizens of the MERCOSUR countries to accumulate social security rights while working away from their homeland.[13] The agreements of 2002 allowed nationals of MERCOSUR, Bolivia, and Chile to travel freely, live, work, and do business within any of the six countries.[14] Article 1 of the Agreement on Residence for Nationals of the MERCOSUR Member States, Bolivia, and Chile promises: 'The nationals of the Member State who wish to reside on the territory of another Member State may obtain legal residence permission in the latter in conformity with the conditions of this Agreement through verification of their nationality and the presentation of the formal documents prescribed by Article 4 of the present Agreement.' Article 4 requires only a set of standard documents such as passport, birth, police and medical certificates, and a payment of a fee. It does not contain any special requirements that would complicate obtaining residence and work permits unless the citizen has criminal convictions. Likewise, Article 18 of the European Constitution grants that 'every citizen of the Union has the right to move ahead and reside freely within the territory of the Member States.'[15] However, the provisions have not come fully in effect even in MERCOSUR-4. Brazil, Uruguay, and Paraguay ratified them between 2005 and 2009 while Argentina is still guided by bilateral agreements on the matter.[16]

As in the EU, MERCOSUR member states retain their own discretion regarding workers and travellers from third countries. Yet the EU went a little further than MERCOSUR: the Schengen Agreement abolished national immigration control within the territory of the union.[17] While Western Europeans obviously have grievances about excessive immigration from poorer Southern and Eastern parts of Europe; intra-regional migration has become a sensitive topic for MERCOSUR as well, particularly for Argentina. Argentina has long been receiving significant numbers of impoverished migrants from Paraguay and Bolivia. The increase of poverty and marginalization in Argentina produced social unrest in 2010, which manifested in the occupation of public lands by thousands of migrants, failed forced eviction, and violence. These incidents compelled Argentina to take a leading role in the promotion of regional initiatives in migration and social spheres.[18] Nevertheless, intra-union migration in MERCOSUR may not exceed emigration to North America or Europe or internal migration within Brazil. Parts of Brazil are currently experiencing disturbances provoked by refugees from Venezuela.

2.1.4 Capital Market

On financial markets' regulation the only existing pieces of legislation refer to internationally accepted norms and standards for financial supervision. MERCOSUR has produced two pieces of legislation on capital movement.

One has been repealed and the other, the Protocol of Colonia, has partial coverage that does not purport to produce broad liberalization.[19] The Colonia Protocol on investment overlaps with the Montevideo Protocol on services. Because the Montevideo Protocol follows the GATS system of definitions, it covers the 'commercial presence' of foreign services suppliers. As in practice 'commercial presence' is the FDI from other member states' firms, these transactions are also covered by the Colonia Protocol on investment.[20] The overlap creates a potential for conflict. The Montevideo Protocol restricts 'commercial presence' to the sectors and issues listed in the respective schedules of commitments. It is less liberal than the Colonia Protocol, which liberalizes FDI in all sectors except those listed as exceptions. However, the Colonia Protocol has not been ratified by a single member and is not yet in force. A new Services Protocol was approved in 2017.[21] Given the destiny of the Colonia and Montevideo Protocols, we may expect its entry in effect in about 20 years.

2.1.5 Conclusion

As discussed, MERCOSUR has not made much progress beyond the liberalization of trade in goods and movement of people. Although the Treaty of Asunción proclaims the target of the common market and sets the principle that economic integration should eventually embrace services and factors of production, it does not contain any operational provisions applicable to economic relations other than trade in goods. The measures to promote the free cross-border supply of services and circulation of capital have been scarce or ineffective if not repealed. The extension of economic integration into areas other than trade in goods was seen as a task of 'secondary legislation' from the decisions of the MERCOSUR organs. This type of legislation has not been effective and MERCOSUR's most tangible results have been reached in the areas openly addressed by 'primary law' such as the Treaty of Asunción's Trade Liberalisation Programme, which dealt with the elimination of obstacles to the free circulation of goods.

In contrast to the MERCOSUR Treaty, the EEC Treaty included provisions that extended integration beyond the trade in goods to services, movement of capital and workers, and the right of establishment. Not all these provisions had similar consequences in terms of policy harmonization. The provisions on the liberalization of capital movement, in particular, were shallower than the rest and required much more secondary legislation to become complete. Moreover, the practical effects of many of the liberalization provisions in all areas, including trade in goods, were curtailed by the existence of divergent national legislation raising indirect barriers. Their elimination has been achieved through further gradual harmonization only partially. However, the fact remains that from the very beginning the EEC Treaty included provisions covering services, movement of capital and workers, and the right of establishment, at a minimum enshrining the obligation to grant national treatment to economic agents from other member states.

In addition to greater restrictions to product and factor movement, the MERCOSUR enforcement system lags behind the analogous EU mechanism. Thus the 2002 Protocol of Olivos reaffirmed the intention of the 1992 Protocol of Brasília to use arbitration as the basis for the MERCOSUR dispute resolution system.[22] Certainly, arbitration is a lax measure if compared with the EU practice of resolving commercial disputes in courts of law. As far as regional competition law is concerned, MERCOSUR competition rules are a more coherent system due to their single source (the Protocol of Fortaleza),[23] as EC Competition law comes from various legal documents. However, there is an essential difference in one of the basic principles of the competition rules in the two blocs. In the EU any measure to restrict competition falls within the competence of the European Competition Law because measures affecting national markets are believed to have an impact on the regional market.[24] In contrast, the Protocol of Fortaleza distinguishes the restriction of competition within the national market from the restriction of competition in the regional market and leaves the former to 'the exclusive competence of the member state.'[25] This certainly disunifies the MERCOSUR market. In addition, it gives rise to conflicting interpretations of whether a specific violation of competition rules affects the common market or domestic markets only.

2.2 Economic Interdependence and Cohesion of Regional Economic Regimes

According to neofunctionalist explanations of integration, increased economic and social interaction lead to the adoption of rules facilitating interaction and economic exchanges and cause policy harmonization spillovers into social, political, and cultural domains of international relations. High levels of regional exchanges require appropriate regulatory systems, therefore the region's motivation and propensity for economic integration is dependent on the intensity of intra-regional exchange and significant interdependence levels. There are objective obstacles of physical, geographic, demographic, and structural character for the MERCOSUR countries to achieve high interdependence. These natural limitations affect the region's propensity for integration along with the goals, speed, and results of the corresponding reforms.

2.2.1 Economic Interdependence

The most convenient indicators of regional economic interdependence are intra-regional trade and investment. MERCOSUR differs from the EU substantially in both. Even though MERCOSUR is a destination for a notable share of its members' exports (13%, Table 2.1.B), the overall level of economic interdependence among the MERCOSUR countries is very low because foreign and intra-regional trade do not make up a high share of their domestic production. The shares of Brazilian and Argentinean foreign trade are by far inferior to those of Chile (See Table 2.1.A). This is an expected result of the comparison of large and small countries, because larger countries are more self-sufficient while smaller countries tend to trade more. However, the principal economies of MERCOSUR Brazil and Argentina are relatively inward-looking not only in comparison to small countries, but also to European giants Germany, France, and Britain (See Table 2.1.A). Naturally, all trade in relation to production is much smaller in MERCOSUR than in the EU (11% versus 33%, Table 2.1.B).

Besides, intra-regional trade occupies a greater share of EU total trade, 63%, whereas in MERCOSUR it reaches 13% only (Table 2.1.B). In peak years for intra-MERCOSUR trade, a maximum 2.2% of regional production was exported to MERCOSUR (Table 2.2), whereas in the EU 21% of regional economic output was designated for the single market in 2015 (Table 2.1.B). Commercial interdependence among the MERCOSUR countries is up to 15 times weaker than within the EU (Table 2.1.B). Intra-union exchange is relatively unimportant for the MERCOSUR individual economies, and the MERCOSUR countries are much less dependent on the common market than their EU counterparts. Even for small countries in MERCOSUR, intra-regional exports did not exceed 32% of total exports in Uruguay and 50% for Paraguay in 2012 (Table 2.1.C), which is well below the EU average of 63%. Intra-MERCOSUR exports and imports in Uruguay and Paraguay range from 5.5% to 18.8% of GDP

Table 2.1 Extra-regional and intra-regional trade of MERCOSUR, the EU, and selected countries

A*

	Exports of goods, % of GDP	Year
Brazil	10.3	2016
Argentina	10.6	2016
Uruguay	12.8	2016
Chile	24.3	2016
Venezuela	26.2	2012
Paraguay	31	2016
Britain	16.3	2015
France	19.8	2016
Germany	38.7	2016
the Netherlands	62.9	2015
Belgium	85.2	2016

B**

	Total exports, % of GRP	Intra-regional exports, % of total exports	Intra-regional exports, % of GRP	% of intra-EU exports to GRP / % of intra-Mercosur exports to GRP
MERCOSUR-4 in 2015	10.6	13.4	1.4	14.6
the EU-28 in 2015	32.9	63.2	20.8	
MERCOSUR-5 in 2008	16	13.8	2.2	9.5
the EU-28 in 2008	31	67.7	21	

C***

		Intra-Mercosur exports, % of total exports	Intra-Mercosur exports, % of GDP	Intra-Mercosur imports, % of total imports	Intra-Mercosur imports, % of GDP
Argentina		27.7	4.7	27.9	4
Brazil		11.5	1.2	9.1	0.9
Paraguay		49.6	13.9	42.5	18.8
Uruguay		31.6	5.5	40.8	9.5
Venezuela		2	0.5	11.9	2

*Based on data from the Federal Statistical Office of Germany
**Indicators for MERCOSUR are based on Table 2.2 data; indicators for the EU are based on Eurostat data
***Based on data from IDB for 2012 (IDB. 2013. *Informe Mercosur #18*. BID-INTAL, Buenos Aires)

Table 2.2 Relation of MERCOSUR-5 intra-regional trade to total trade and production

Year	1991	1992	1993	1994	1995	1996	1997	1998	1999	2000
GRP in milliards of US$*	670.152	701.185	758.503	889.363	1135.746	1215.101	1284.044	1268.811	1000.901	1077.308
Total exports in milliards of US$*	60.68772	64.49483	69.25429	80.19205	90.63318	99.2361	107.5796	99.56563	95.75846	119.1851
Intra-MERCOSUR exports in milliards of US$*	6.178927	8.184515	11.07888	14.1927	18.1818	19.85923	24.06003	23.46916	18.2075	21.34907
Intra-MERCOSUR exports, % of total exports	10.2	12.7	16	17.7	20	20	22.4	23.6	19	17.9
Intra-MERCOSUR exports, % of GRP	0.9	1.2	1.5	1.6	1.6	1.6	1.9	1.8	1.8	2

2001	2002	2003	2004	2005	2006	2007	2008	2009	2010	2011	2012	2015**
974.555	716.288	782.129	949.73	1235.071	1515.575	1894.661	2342.532	2303.654	2865.636	3306.237	3185.58	2486.09
114.6251	114.3457	132.9703	170.6967	219.7532	257.1706	295.46	375.3384	276.735	349.8292	448.489	437.0997	263.9119
18.74145	13.21016	15.07704	20.93713	25.95689	33.47434	41.32165	51.76943	40.56294	52.32751	63.37726	58.83228	35.36724
16.4	11.6	11.3	12.3	11.8	13	14	13.8	14.7	15	14.1	13.5	13.4
1.9	1.9	2	2.2	2.1	2.2	2.2	2.2	1.8	1.8	1.9	1.8	1.4

*LAIA, http://www.aladi.org/nsfaladi/indicado.nsf/9f813c3c0af78b100325749700746684/08dc4bc2bd4943b032567b4005cd7e9/$FILE/MERCOSUR.xls, 1.10.2014
**Comtrade data for MERCOSUR-4.

(Table 2.1.C), again below the average of 21% in the EU. In 2012 only 1.8% of total MERCOSUR production was exported intra-MERCOSUR: 0.5% of Venezuelan, 1.2% of Brazilian, 4.7% of Argentinean, 5.5% of Uruguayan, and 13.9% of Paraguayan (Tables 2.2 and 2.1.C). The relation of Brazilian intra-zonal exports to GDP (1.2%, Table 2.1.C) is particularly indicative of Brazil's low interest in the MERCOSUR's market.

The figures for investment are by far inferior to those of trade. Most Latin-American-sourced FDI comes from Argentina, Brazil, Chile, and Mexico. The volume of these outflows in relation to total FDI flows and GDPs is minimal: in the period from 1986 to 1997 regional FDI flows rarely surpassed 0.1% of global FDI flows and the total value of each country's resultant FDI stock did not surpass 1% of GDP until 1986 when Chile registered a level of 5.4%.[26] Intra- and extra-regional investment in Latin America is not efficiency promoting but resource and market seeking. It is focused on exploiting natural resources or circumventing market access restrictions by establishing branch plant operations.[27]

There are several factors explaining low economic interdependence among the MERCOSUR countries, of which protectionism and barriers to intra-regional exchange are of marginal importance. A more important cause is relative homogeneity of production patterns in member states due to the region's underdevelopment. MERCOSUR economies are not sufficiently diversified: the top ten export products of Paraguay, Uruguay, Argentina, and Brazil represent 91.2%, 77.4%, 69.7%, and 60.4% respectively of their total exports.[28] Even more significant causes of low interdependence within MERCOSUR come from the specific conditions of regional physical, economic, and political geography, and, particularly, the size of its member states. MERCOSUR countries have enormous territories, low population densities, and a natural deficit of cross-border infrastructure. Population density in MERCOSUR is five times lower than in the EU; an average MERCOSUR country is 16 times bigger than an average EU member in territory and 3.2 times in population.[29] In contrast to Europe, people in MERCOSUR live on the coast and not on the borders. European integration is a product of high economic concentration and short distances. These important conditions helped to sweep European borders away.

The MERCOSUR project confronts huge distances and scarcity of cross-border infrastructure. Good communications and infrastructure systems are crucial elements in the evaluation of the quality of economies. Conditions of MERCOSUR economic and physical geography have major implications on the lack of cross-border infrastructure. Infrastructure deficiency is both a result and a cause of low levels of physical interaction among the member countries. Historically, all transportation systems in the Southern Cone were built to connect national centres of production to national ports. Thus Argentinean operators run freight trains on 0.75-, 1-, 1.376-, 1.435-, and 1.676-metre gauge railway tracks; Brazilian trains move on 1-, 1.44-, and 1.6-metre gauges. This is the legacy of competing and privately built and operated rail lines. They were constructed for the transportation of extracted primary goods overseas and not for the facilitation of traffic among neighbouring nations or within them.[30] Brazilian and Argentinean railroads connect three times (between Corrientes and Rio Grande do Sul), but they have incompatible gauges. There is no connection between the Argentinean and Chilean rail systems. As a consequence, railways handle only 4% of cargo moved into Argentina and Brazil.[31]

About 75% of all terrestrial trade between Argentina and Brazil travels through just one bridge over the Uruguay River, while two other bridges do not accommodate significant flows of commercial traffic.[32] Despite 5,150 km of common border, some 90% of all commercial traffic between Argentina and Chile goes only through one road Santiago-Mendoza.[33] The Andes are a serious natural obstacle to exchange. They make road construction up to ten times more expensive than on the plain. The roads through the Andes are seldom operational in winters. Because of the mountains, Brazil and Paraguay lack exits towards the Pacific. Yet even maritime infrastructure is not sufficiently developed. A 1985 study indicated that the freight route Buenos Aires–Santos (São Paulo) was more expensive than New Orleans–Santos, even though the latter was four times longer.[34] The efficiency of the common market is highly conditional on the improvement of infrastructure. Because of the large distances, the amount of work to improve transport infrastructure is colossal, and so are the costs involved. Scarcity of public funds does not contribute to an easy solution of this problem.

If physical and economic geography point to infrastructure deficiencies and low demographic and economic concentration, MERCOSUR political geography indicates a variation in the number of parties to the unions: five against 28 participants in the EU. Because of the small size of the countries and their large number, many economic transactions within the EU are inter-state. MERCOSUR is comprised of relatively large countries, and a large share of commercial exchange in the region occurs within

Brazil and Argentina. This exchange is subject to domestic and not community regulations. It is administered through national regulations and is not directly dependent on intergovernmental measures at the regional level. Even if MERCOSUR economies were at the same level of economic development as European economies, EU-comparable figures of interdependence would be attainable only if Brazilian states and Argentinean provinces were treated as separate parties to MERCOSUR and the trade among them counted as intra-regional international trade.

In addition, MERCOSUR does not affect all the areas of Brazil and Argentina to the same extent. *MERCOSUR de facto* may be distinguished from *MERCOSUR de jure*. While *MERCOSUR de jure* encompasses complete territories of the member states, *MERCOSUR de facto* excludes practically unaffected territories of Northern Brazil, Southern Argentina, and parts of Paraguayan Chaco.[35] *MERCOSUR de facto* (the area from Belo Horizonte, São Paulo and Asunción to Córdoba, Neuquén and Bahía Blanca) accounts for 55% of the total regional population, 75% of GRP, and some 25% of the territory in MERCOSUR-4.[36] *MERCOSUR de facto* comprised by Paraguay, Uruguay, separate southern and southeastern Brazilian states and central and northeastern Argentinean provinces would be much more similar to the EU along a wide range of indicators: the number of member states, population density, production capabilities, GRP per capita, and standards of living.

Yet the reality is such that Argentinean provinces and Brazilian states do not conduct an independent commercial policy and are not subject to regulations at the MERCOSUR level. Though *MERCOSUR de facto* possesses more favourable population settlement patterns, improved infrastructure and better developed industrial capabilities than *MERCOSUR de jure*, the level of dependence of the EU on its common market is inherently unattainable for MERCOSUR due to the structural difference in the number of member states and their sizes. Liberal and neoliberal economists believe that larger volumes of trade serve a better allocation of resources. They blame MERCOSUR for inadequate policies, but it is clear that low intra-regional trade in MERCOSUR is not as much a result of inadequate economic policies and economic underdevelopment, but of physical, structural, geographic, and demographic characteristics of the bloc.

Despite the existence of literature dedicated to the role of interest groups in shaping regional integration process, it is possible to conclude that the neofunctionalist dynamic is missing in MERCOSUR, in the sense that regional interdependence is not growing in the long run, in accordance with neofunctionalist predictions. Table 2.2 provides an illustration. Intra-MERCOSUR trade peaked in 1998 and failed to reach this point again in the following 20 years.

Consequently, MERCOSUR and the EU have significant differences in their priorities in relation to internal and external markets. This difference is predetermined by the size of the share of regional exchanges in relation to extra-regional trade. The external market has greater importance for Argentina and Brazil as the absorber of a larger share of their exports and a provider of a greater volume of imports. Some other factors contribute to distinct attitudes in relation to internal and external markets. The EU process started in the 1950s before the golden age of neoliberalism when the ideas of protectionism were strong and provided fertile soil for projects like the high-impact CAP. The EC decreased internal tariffs but increased external tariffs.

The South American bloc functioned in a different way. As a child of *open regionalism*, MERCOSUR was born at least a couple of decades after disappointments about import-substitution policies. Its regional integration was considered a natural continuation of unilateral economic liberalization initiated by its key members earlier in the mid-1980s. Therefore MERCOSUR administered two types of opening: preferential liberalization within MERCOSUR and unilateral opening externally through a relatively low CET (12.5% on average). Designed from the perspective of open regionalism, the MERCOSUR process has never been referred to as 'Fortress' as in 'Fortress Europe.' While Europeans emphasized their unified internal market, MERCOSUR saw optimal insertion into the international economic system as its number one priority.

Another important factor that explained MERCOSUR's inclination towards the outward-looking model was the relative size of its economy. While the EU hosts some of the world's financial and industrial centres, MERCOSUR is a union of developing countries whose competitiveness in international markets is much lower. Currently, the size of the MERCOSUR economy represents less than a quarter of the EU economy (22.9%). While the EU accounts for 16.7% of the gross world product, MERCOSUR does for 3.8%.[37] The shares of the EU in global merchandise exports and exports of commercial services are 32.7% and 42%, while the shares of MERCOSUR are 1.8% and 1.1% only.[38] As a less self-sufficient bloc, MERCOSUR had more outward-looking policies. Its relatively small market size and limited economic capabilities have not been favourable for aspirations of self-sufficiency while the small share of trade in relation to GRP and the perception of trade as a source of growth compelled policy-makers to approach MERCOSUR as an instrument of external trade. This changed after the second half of the 1990s when economists and policy-makers reviewed the concepts of *open regionalism* and *global neoliberalism*, both of which entailed numerous negative consequences for less-developed countries. Current economic thought emphasizes the necessity of adequate protection and development of internal and regional markets, particularly in larger developing countries like Brazil.

2.2.2 *The Goals, Speed and Results of Economic Integration*

The varying levels of economic interdependence between the two regions have been responsible for the different perceptions of integration goals, the speed of their realization, and the overall integrity of the two regional market systems. The goals of integration are better judged as they are expressed in the concluded and ratified treaties rather than in random judgements of individual policy-makers and observers. The founding treaties of the EEC (the Treaty of Rome, 1957) and of MERCOSUR (the Treaty of Asunción, 1991) remain fundamental documents and crucial manifestations of the agreed objectives in economic integration. Both proclaimed common markets as their principal goal. Though similar in the overall objective in the free circulation of goods, services, and factors of production, the Treaties differed in the secondary objectives of attaining this target and in the schedules of initial trade liberalization.

Given the failures of preceding attempts of economic integration in Latin America (like LAFTA) and weaker incentives for intra-regional cooperation, the long-term proposals for integration in the Treaty of Asunción were less elaborate than those in the Treaty of Rome. Asunción sketched the goal of a common market in a generic and superficial way and suggested four instruments for its implementation: internal trade liberalization, the CET and common commercial policy in relation to third countries and blocs, the coordination of macroeconomic policy, and the adoption of sectoral agreements. Even though the goal of a common market was mentioned, there was no coordinated and detailed scheme directing and linking the negotiating groups. With exception of intra-regional trade liberalization, the Treaty gave no guidance on how these instruments should be implemented.

The original Treaty of Rome was more detailed and far-reaching in its projections and imposed more obligations for the implementation of the common market. Likewise, it operated with the notions of free trade and the CET, but in a different way. The CET and free intra-regional trade were perceived as insufficient for the definition of a true sense of a customs union. The customs union was approached as a base for the generation of a common trade policy, and the common policy was expected to require the participation of every country in collective decision-making. Article 9 of the Treaty stated that the EEC was based on a customs union. This already drew a structure of a community, linking it to projections of an economic and political union. Even at the preliminary stage of European integration, the ECSC implemented proposals for community organs, but these are still absent in MERCOSUR. Though Article 1 of the Treaty of Asunción defined the economic community through a common policy, it did not mention the word *community* in relation to MERCOSUR even once. The emphasis of Asunción was clearly on an FTA, an integration stage inferior to a customs union.

The limited outcomes of the Treaty on MERCOSUR reflected the understanding that any further-reaching commitments may not be adequate for tackling the specific problems to arise in the future. The drafters of the Treaty realized that the advance of integration would require provisional agreements, and they left space for future manoeuvres for agreements on MERCOSUR institutional structure and dispute resolution system. If in Europe the Treaty of Rome generally resolved these issues, the Asunción Treaty postponed them until subsequent normative statutes such as the 1994 Protocol of Ouro Preto (the basic document outlining MERCOSUR's institutional structure and establishing MERCOSUR as a customs union),[39] and the 2002 Protocol of Olivos (the main document for the MERCOSUR dispute resolution system).[40] It appears that in 1991, the drafters of the MERCOSUR Treaty felt that their countries were less prepared for longer-term economic commitments than the EEC was in 1957. The differences in the objectives and views of the future of MERCOSUR and the EEC appeared because the political decisions were made at different time, space, social, and economic realities, and reflected different intentions, aspirations, and past experiences of their countries.

The perceptions of a common market as a distant goal in MERCOSUR may have been explained by frustrations about preceding attempts at Latin American integration. Never before MERCOSUR had Latin American nations been able to launch an FTA, let alone a customs union.

The failures of LAFTA and the mixed success of other Latin American integration efforts kept expectations regarding MERCOSUR low. In Europe, on the contrary, there existed a successful project of the Benelux Economic Union.[41] Even though Benelux was made up of small countries, it produced important results. The union liberalized all internal trade prior to the Treaty of Rome, and soon thereafter it became a common market by 1960.

The results of Benelux contributed to the perception of European economic integration as a realistic project. In addition, during EU's earlier stages, functionalist ideas greatly stimulated European integration as a measure to increase interdependence among the countries in order to diminish chances of future wars. Clearly, from this perspective, the need to normalize intra-regional relations in MERCOSUR was not as pressing as the imperatives to cope with the 'German factor' in Europe. In addition, the late 1980s did not perceive globalization as a serious threat to developing countries; therefore regional integration was not seen as a dominant foreign policy goal of the MERCOSUR members.

While the differences in long-term objectives were dependent on expectations of the evolution of the initial processes, and the comparison of the stated integration goals revealed reservations of South Americans about their views of the distant future; the proper Treaties' agreements were the results of specific compromises, and the variations in the agreed schedules for intra-regional trade liberalization indicated a less cautious approach in MERCOSUR towards the speed of such liberalization. Thus the parties to Asunción agreed on a faster opening of national markets. Whereas the EEC needed eight years to form an FTA in 1965, 11 years to set up a customs union in 1968, and 35 years to set up a common market in 1992, MERCOSUR promised to liberalize internal trade and implemented the CET in less than four years (the Protocol of Ouro Preto proclaimed MERCOSUR an FTA and a customs union in late 1994), and after the agreements on free movement of citizens of 2002 MERCOSUR could be considered an imperfect common market for goods and labour 11 years after the Treaty of Asunción was signed. Thus intra-regional commercial liberalization in MERCOSUR occurred faster and despite its more modest initial goals. It took just a little more than half of the period that was originally planned by the initial 1986 agreements between Brazil and Argentina.[42] 'In the EU, to come where MERCOSUR is after one year, takes us four or five years.'[43]

Four years for setting up an FTA in MERCOSUR in accordance with the Treaty of Asunción seemed an ambitious project, even though MERCOSUR had such relative advantages over the EU as homogeneity of history, politics, culture and languages, a smaller number of member states, and weaker import-competing interests. The fast pace of integration in MERCOSUR was affected by the political dynamic of 'the electoral rhythm of presidential mandates in Brazil and Argentina.'[44] The goals of MERCOSUR were perceived as political and the scarce pattern of intra-MERCOSUR exchange allowed a rush in the set-up of an FTA and a customs union without a necessity to deal with a great number of conflicts arising from the speedy liberalization.

On the one hand, the initial economic liberalization was less pressing among the countries with low intensity of economic exchange. On the other hand, policy changes had limited implications, provoked fewer conflicts and were easier to implement due to the lack of strong resistance from domestic producers, who did not perceive threats of regional competitors as very serious. Initial compromise on the quick implementation of the reached agreements was possible because liberalization did not hurt too many production groups. Though the amount of intra-MERCOSUR trade increased four-fold from 1991 to 1998, this increase occurred from very low pre-MERCOSUR figures. In the 1960s and 1970s the European process passed through the stage referred to as *Eurosclerosis*. It was caused by the 'paradox of success' in which the growth of trade and deepening integration provoked the appearance of conflicts and clashes of interest. MERCOSUR witnessed a similar phenomenon after the mid-1990s, but it was provoked by financial crises and currency devaluations rather than by accumulation of grievances among import-competing sectors in regard to intra-regional commercial liberalization.

In spite of the impressive speed of achievement of formal agreements on integration, MERCOSUR economic regimes are characterized by a number of breaches and exceptions (Section 2.1). Rushed commercial liberalization has not produced a system as coherent and orderly as in the EU, because MERCOSUR left many sensitive products for special treatment (sugar, automobiles, telecommunications). In contrast to the EU, the MERCOSUR agricultural sector never required any special regimes like the CAP. However, a number of MERCOSUR agricultural goods have been treated as sensitive products of other categories. There were plans to abolish exceptions to the general treatment in 2006 with complete liberalization of internal trade and application of the CET on all items of the customs nomenclature. However, this has not been achieved yet.

The EC also met challenges in the application of the CET to many products: computers, automobiles, telecommunications and high-tech products, capital and agricultural goods. In spite of such deviations from the concept of free competition as the CAP, discriminatory treatment of Eastern European workers and products, partial memberships in the Schengen Agreement and the monetary union, the European single market is better consolidated than MERCOSUR's market. MERCOSUR has been successful in the liberalization of trade in goods and labour movement only (Section 2.1). In order to facilitate cross-border exchange and become a full-fledged common market like the EC after the SEA,[45] MERCOSUR needs to ensure macroeconomic stability, to improve transport links, to standardize customs regulations, technical and sanitary norms, to further open trade in services and financial services, to harmonize certain macroeconomic and tax policies, and to set a better balance between the state and common market institutions.

Importantly, if further economic integration remains on the agenda, the MERCOSUR legal order needs to be cleaned up from its two glaring deficiencies: the normative inconsistency (contradictions among the norms of equal status) and the internalization gap (inapplicability of the norms due to their non-incorporation into the domestic legal systems). The latter is particularly glaring, as in 2004 only half of the MERCOSUR legislation was in force.[46] As of 1 November 2017, out of 143 MERCOSUR agreements deposited at the Paraguayan Ministry of Foreign Affairs only 61 were in force in all MERCOSUR-4 members.[47] The optimism of dead agreements gives birth to political and academic discourses that sometimes create an excessively optimistic impression of the state of affairs in MERCOSUR. However, at times expressions like 'MERCOSUR's sterile dynamism'[48] or 'MERCOSUR only exists on paper'[49] do appear in the mouths or writings of the observers of the process.

The fast speed of integration reforms and their fragmented character fit well into the neofunctionalist explanation. With weaker business elites, MERCOSUR lacked serious domestic constituencies behind its economic initiatives. This resulted in cautious goals of integration, the seemingly high speed of intra-regional trade liberalization (due to minimal resistance of import-competing sectors), and partial and incomplete arrangements (due to insufficient influence of export-oriented private interests on governments to advance integration). The geographic and structural conditions of MERCOSUR predetermined low regional interdependence, low dependence and reliance on the regional market, weak mechanisms for the implementation and enforcement of common market policies, and less robust institutional structures managing intra-regional economic relations. With low intensity of intra-regional interactions and their limited implications, the potential for the expansion of regional exchange and a greater change in allocation of production resources is limited. The awareness of limitations of the MERCOSUR common market system should prevent excessive criticism of the MERCOSUR regimes and institutions, which is a tempting occupation for those who are familiar with the organization and operation of the EU.[50]

2.3 Divergences in Economic Performance

In addition to limited incentives for economic integration due to low interdependence, differences in production structures and performance among the MERCOSUR's national economies pose difficulties for integrating MERCOSUR through the homogenization of the varying national regulatory bases and the imposition of uniform economic policies. The divergence in macroeconomic performance among the MERCOSUR countries is greater than within the Eurozone (See Subsection 2.5.3). It is rooted in history and appeared as a result of different development strategies adopted by the governments in the previous century, and also by nonexistent or minimal interaction among the economies of the region prior to MERCOSUR.

Thus in the course of the twentieth century Brazil was encouraging industrial, scientific, and technological development while Argentina's military governments were demolishing industrial bases for the sake of vain efforts to restore the great agricultural power that Argentina had enjoyed in the late nineteenth and early twentieth centuries. If in the 1960s the Argentinean and Brazilian economies showed similar patterns of development and similar relative size and volumes of trade, the better economic performance during the 1970s caused Brazil to appear as a 'regional giant' with a strong and diverse industrial sector causing envy of developing countries. By the mid-1980s Brazil had experienced two decades of sustained growth and large investment in the basic sectors of its economy. During the 1990s three divergent factors strongly persisted in MERCOSUR, also to the disadvantage of Argentina. They were the pace of neoliberal reforms (more gradual in Brazil and more of a 'shock therapy' in Argentina), exchange policy (currency board in Argentina and partial and gradual adjustment in Brazil), and regional and sectoral policy (traditionally more activist in Brazil than in Argentina). Only recently has Argentina begun to crawl out from long decades of paralysis, outflows of investment, and the reduction of productive and technological capacity in absolute and relative terms.

Many contemporary difficulties of integration come from these different development strategies that have resulted in the varying levels of industrialization between the two countries. These strategies have exacerbated natural differences in relative size, production variation, factor endowment (capital, labour, natural resources), and the cost of production factors. All these are structural and permanent differences between the economies that cannot be adjusted by administrative or political decisions. Because of artificial and natural asymmetries there are fears that the costs of infrastructure and labour force, scale of production, and relatively developed industrial base will favour the commercial and industrial prevalence of Brazil. In Argentina there are fears that integration with Brazil would enforce a colonial or neocolonial relationship in which the smaller and less developed Argentinean economy would be compelled to import industrial goods from Brazil and to specialize in the export of primary commodities and agricultural goods.

These fears are even greater in the small countries, Uruguay and Paraguay. As early as August 1994, in the negotiations of Ouro Preto, Uruguay insisted on the maintenance of the preferential regimes granted by CAUCE and PEC while Paraguay demanded a special treatment for itself as of a less developed country. Paraguay in particular has not been successful in taking advantage of export opportunities to MERCOSUR while Brazil and Argentina have taken over the Paraguayan market causing damage to Paraguayan producers.[51] However, even Brazil has grievances in MERCOSUR: the Brazilian government often complains that the customs union, which imposes the necessity of a single policy, is very inconvenient for Brazil because Brazil has more developed industries and needs a higher level of protection than the neighbouring countries. The commitment to a CET with the countries that have diverging interests does not allow Brazil to maximize its necessities of protectionism as it has to receive the agreement of the partners whose competition capacity is dependent upon low tariff imports from third countries.[52]

MERCOSUR often praises the complementarity of Brazilian and Argentinean economies as a great virtue of the process, however uniform economic regimes are easier to impose on similar rather than dissimilar countries. Despite all the diversity of the EU, its national economies enjoy a somewhat higher level of macroeconomic convergence than MERCOSUR countries do (see Subsection 2.5.3). In conditions of a far better consolidated common market, variations in production structures and economic performance among individual EU members cause less controversy because the single European market is already perceived as given even in the current period of the financial turbulence. MERCOSUR, however, is still in its construction phase, and its economic divergences cause persistent arguments and disagreements thus presenting obstacles for the progress of economic integration.

The lack of convergence in economic performance is a common problem of all complex integration systems. Convergence is necessary for setting a common policy, the key goal of integration, but without convergence, the single policy has different (sometimes opposite) effects on the problems that require differentiated approaches. In absence of convergence a single policy may increase inequalities, cause tensions, exacerbate conflicts, exhaust the scope for collective action, and throw certain industries, territories, or countries into chronic incurable depression. Convergence requires exceptions, asymmetric policies, and concessions from more prosperous actors, all of which run contrary to the logic of integration.[53] Concessions are difficult to achieve, while privileged regimes delay integration and contradict the logic of equal treatment and homogenization for the sake of uniformity and reduced transaction costs.

2.4 MERCOSUR's Economic Effects

Even though economic forces play a less prominent role in the formation of MERCOSUR than of the EU, MERCOSUR is an obvious case of economic regionalism. Despite breaches in its common market system, managed trade in some important sectors, several remaining tariffs (Final Adjustment List) and NTBs in intra-regional trade, and applied antidumping actions on sensitive products, MERCOSUR has generally achieved the goals of free intra-bloc trade in goods through liberalization and harmonization in some NTBs and the elimination of tariffs in all sectors except sugar and automobiles. A number of studies have attributed both welfare and distributional effects to the bloc. These effects differ in the extent of their manifestation, but they are similar to what is generally expected from PTAs.

There are several views regarding the economic consequences of PTAs. Neoliberal economists believe that regionalism is an option inferior to non-discriminatory liberalization. Regional integration causes costs (especially trade diversion) for member countries and third countries, and restricts international trade. Other analysts emphasize economic liberalization promoted by regional integration, positive long-term effects on production transformation, investment, export activities, growth and less traditional effects such as modernization and the reform of political institutions and democratization. In either line of thinking, regional integration is expected to be a medium- and long-term process whose initial costs are compensated by benefits in the future. The third view emphasizes the social discrepancies of regional integration comparable to those that happen at the global level. If integration follows recipes of capitalism, it will inevitably sharpen inequalities across the region similar to the parallel processes going on at the national and global levels, adding to prosperity in dynamic areas and worsening stagnation in depressed areas, and increasing gaps in consumption and standards of life among various population groups.

The debate on the effects of regionalism has not been resolved. Economists present arguments and models emphasizing dynamic effects and non-traditional factors of political economy. Such models and non-quantitative changes are difficult to evaluate given the limitations of methodologies, available data, and methods of measuring. Empirical data might have limited persuasiveness and the results of such studies can be questioned by faults in the available information on preferences, rules of origin, costs, and profits of production. Assessment of the costs and benefits of regional integration is not easy because of the complex nature of the phenomenon. The calculations of aggregated impact of regional integration involve huge variations in different economic data. In most studies it is impossible to separate the impact of bloc formation from the effects of other simultaneous transformations such as technological development, unilateral trade liberalization, overvalued exchange rates, or macroeconomic interference.[54] All these variables can affect trade growth.[55] The coincident set of influences makes it difficult to isolate the effects of regional integration in MERCOSUR from other determinants of economic performance.

Regional liberalization involves trade in services, regulation of property rights, and licensing. Quantification of these notions is difficult. Also, regionalism is an integral part of profound structural reforms causing radical changes at all levels of national economies. The effects of integration are difficult to distinguish from the effects of unilateral liberalization, deregulation, privatization, macroeconomic changes, technological development, learning experiences, and various other externalities. These topics present difficulties for economic analysis even at the national level, not to mention studies dealing simultaneously with several economies. In addition, initial conditions and subsequent phases of integration present significant situational variations among the affected countries.

Integration is compared to what would have happened in its absence, but counterfactual suppositions cannot be verified through an experiment. The suppositions about integration effects have more chances to be persuasive if the process is simple, the period of time is short, analysed changes are minor and do not depend on many external variables.[56] Changes in the EU are certainly profound and long-standing for anyone to portray the economic reality of the EU countries in absence of the single market. The conclusions of studies of MERCOSUR's effects are all tentative not only because of the outlined methodological problems, but also because they often deal with relatively small quantitative manifestations.

2.4.1 Welfare Effects

The intensification of regionalism in the 1990s led to a great deal of empirical research on its results. Economists were interested in measuring changes in wellbeing, but given the difficulties in the definition of this parameter, they usually used a substitute expressed as a statistical summary reflecting economic and commercial growth. This posed certain problems for the validity of conclusions. Nevertheless, the results of most studies generally confirmed that PTAs generated welfare gains for member countries and losses in welfare for trading partners outside the unions. This conclusion held for MERCOSUR. The results of its integration policies were seen not only in the elimination of obstacles to trade and subsequent growth of trade, but also in the qualitative transformation of production.

MERCOSUR's CET and increased investments brought industrial and even agricultural specialization to the region. According to liberal economists, the qualitative transformation of production contributes to economic growth, as the growth of commercial exchange facilitates the increase of productivity through a better use of production capacity. However, MERCOSUR's impressive four-fold increase in intra-regional trade over the period from 1991 to 1998 was largely accounted for by 'export diversion' from non-members while the dramatic increase in FDI reflected the influence of large-scale privatization in Brazil and the consequences of the Asian crisis.[57] The welfare gains in MERCOSUR were largely achieved by the redistribution of gains from trade.

Behar computed overall welfare gains as changes in the sum of consumer welfare, profits, and tariff revenues. Concerning MERCOSUR as a whole, the loss in tariff revenues matched increases in consumer surpluses. Consequently, welfare gains were not quantitatively significant, amounting to 0.3% on average.[58] Zago de Azevedo's results based on different approaches suggested that from 1991 to 1998 the bloc impact on members' welfare was positive, though small, and negative, though negligible, for non-member countries.[59] It is hardly possible to predict the consequences of regional integration for aggregate world welfare.

Intra-MERCOSUR liberalization caused losses in economic welfare among non-members as they were forced to reduce their pre-tariff prices after the Treaty of Asunción cut members' intra-bloc tariffs by more than 50% of the most favoured nation rate. MERCOSUR significantly affected the prices for non-member exporters supplying to MERCOSUR. Crude estimations of losses on exports to Brazil in 1996 made US$624 million for the USA, 236 million for Germany, 58 million for Japan, 17 million for Chile, and 14 million for South Korea.[60] Thus empirical studies seemed to confirm general theoretical assumptions about PTAs causing welfare gains for bloc members and losses for non-member countries. Even if a PTA aims to facilitate intra-regional trade without raising barriers to outsiders, outsiders are still affected adversely.

In MERCOSUR trade liberalization proceeded in two directions, one for imports from the region and the other for imports from the rest of the world. Whereas intra-bloc liberalization had a limited impact on welfare gains and losses among member countries and outsiders, the effects of the MERCOSUR unified external policy had more far-reaching consequences. According to Benegas Cristaldo's evaluation, the changes in protection against the rest of the world were able to determine major gains of integration in MERCOSUR.[61] After isolating the effects of the bloc on intra-regional trade, Zago de Azevedo came to the conclusion that bloc formation did not have a significant impact on welfare, and that the effects of liberalization on a non-discriminatory basis exceeded those of bloc formation. They were positive before 1998, whereas implementation of the CET in 2006 and excessively low tariffs on imports from third countries suggested a likely improvement in welfare for the rest of the world and MERCOSUR becoming worse-off in comparison to 1995.[62]

As MERCOSUR leaders placed an excessive emphasis on the liberalization of the MERCOSUR external trade, members of MERCOSUR became more open to sources of imports from outside the bloc. The MERCOSUR CET on average was lower than the tariffs of each of the member state before MERCOSUR, and the bloc generated more trade in relative terms than any other integration group.[63] Over the period from 1991 to 1996 MERCOSUR external trade grew by 85%, compared with 75% in the Asian Tigers, 30% in NAFTA, and 28% in the EU.[64] A sharp increase in imports from the outside affected the performance of MERCOSUR economies more strongly than the policies targeting facilitation of intra-bloc exchange. The overall MERCOSUR trade balance changed from US$27.64-milliard surplus in 1990 to 13.59-milliard deficit in 1998.[65] Clearly, the MERCOSUR external trade policy was inadequate. Nevertheless, like other regions with a low potential for successful intra-regional cooperation, MERCOSUR could have used regionalism for a more efficient policy in relation to outsiders and industrialized countries in particular.

2.4.2 Distributional Effects

Many analysts emphasize the statistical effects of trade diversion and trade creation and ignore the social consequences of integration. Whereas the total welfare effects of PTAs are usually positive, the benefits of integration are spread unevenly among social groups, production sectors, and countries. Intra- and extra-regional trade is not always a source of economic efficiency. Economists use the Heckscher-Ohlin and Solper-Samuelson models to illustrate the benefits of economic openness and the resulting growth in welfare. However, empirical evidence does not support these predictions because market structures do not function in the conditions of perfect competition assumed by the models, the factors of production are not as mobile as believed, and the scope, speed, and costs of re-adaptation are not treated properly.[66] In the 1940s, the UN Economic Commission for Latin America suggested that liberalization could lead to deindustrialization, and this hypothesis has been confirmed in the relations of MERCOSUR with industrialized countries, CAN and MERCOSUR within UNASUR, and less industrialized Spanish-speaking countries and Brazil within MERCOSUR. The following paragraphs describe MERCOSUR's distributional effects among countries, sectors, subnational regions, and social groups.

Countries
Competition reveals the vulnerability of weaker economies whose less efficient enterprises are damaged by the inflow of foreign substitutes for domestic products. Less competitive industries face growing difficulties in

their efforts to modernize due to increased investment costs and elimination of subventions. As trade barriers fall and trade policies converge, similarity in consumption patterns and the scale of production matter more, but smaller countries' industries are unable to achieve a larger scale of production following the pace of policy reforms. Thus smaller economies see their position weaken relative to foreign competitors. In MERCOSUR the impact of intra-regional trade liberalization on economic activity is stronger for the Spanish-speaking countries than for Brazil. This is mainly due to the large size of Brazil's domestic market and the small weight of intra-regional trade in Brazilian consumption and production.

Regional integration raised questions about losing and winning countries in the very beginning. Policy-makers and academics were concerned with divergences in economic structure and policy, and pointed to inefficient reallocation of resources and consumption. Brazil is a more technologically advanced country, and the pattern of intra-regional trade in MERCOSUR indicates a markedly unequal division of labour within the bloc. Given the differences in the size of economy and growth dynamic, the fears that new asymmetries would introduce trade disequilibria of a structural type and that the patterns of exchange would reproduce traditional patterns of 'North–South' interaction began to worry Argentineans as early as in the mid-1980s.[67]

These fears were not unjustified. Brazilian firms became more competitive and had a greater ability to draw economies-of-scale gains from integration. Indiscriminate liberalization of trade between Argentina and Brazil launched in 1986 produced adjustment costs for Argentinean companies even before the Treaty of Asunción came into force in 1991.[68] The main implication of Argentina's and Brazil's market size for consumer and intermediate goods is that Argentina is unable to draw economies-of-scale gains from economic integration with Brazil and that economic integration in MERCOSUR enforces the position of Brazilian firms on the MERCOSUR market because of the higher likelihood for non-Brazilian firms to incur inefficiency costs due to suboptimal production scale.[69] Major production cutbacks and the largest adjustment costs are predicted for Uruguay primarily because of its undersized firms.[70]

Sectors
Several studies have attempted to provide an in-depth analysis of MERCOSUR effects on selected sectors.[71] These studies covered durable and non-durable consumer, intermediate and capital goods. The factors

taken into account to assess the sectoral impact of regional integration were the effects on intra- and extra-regional trade flows, FDI flows, competitive pressures, production restructuring, and business strategies. The results of these studies indicated that the sectors that had a competitive advantage prior to intra-regional trade liberalization consolidated their position at the expense of the weaker sectors in partner countries.

In most cases Brazilian sectors strengthened their competitiveness relative to their Argentinean counterparts.[72] However, in a few cases Argentinean producers did.[73] Nevertheless, observers predicted that despite the advantages of the Argentinean producers in few sectors, there was likelihood that Brazilians would outcompete Argentineans in the future. In a number of cases MERCOSUR was beneficial for Argentinean sectors due to the CET that increased the Argentinean national tariff and protected Argentinean industries against competitors from third countries. However, in such cases Argentinean producers were also losing to their Brazilian competitors.[74] Finally, in a few cases MERCOSUR proved beneficial to both national sectors that enjoyed relatively equal competitiveness prior to intra-regional liberalization.[75] This usually happened when Argentineans were able to obtain certain preferential treatment that compensated for their disadvantage of low scale.

The results of sectoral studies indicate that the benefits of regional integration are more obvious in cases where pre-integration discrepancies in economic parameters were not high. Only in such instances did MERCOSUR offer gains in productivity, quality, learning, the scale of production, and specialization. The conclusion for production sectors is in line with those in relation to national economies. Economic integration makes most sense among sectors or countries with similar levels of development and similar structures of supply and demand. Observers describe the effects of MERCOSUR on sectoral performance as modest. These effects were generally limited to intra-regional trade flows with limited effects on extra-regional exports. The effects on production structures were even more limited, especially the so-called dynamic effects of economic integration materialized in productivity gains from economies of scale and scope. Price competitive pressures were also insignificant.[76]

Sub-national Regions
Existing studies make tentative conclusions about adverse effects of MERCOSUR on disadvantageous territories. There are some indications that intra-regional liberalization has been aggravating the condition of the

Brazilian Northeast. The studies have also indicated that production specialization in the Northeast is partially a result of MERCOSUR.[77] Generally, studies of the Brazilian Northeast indicate its perpetuating disadvantaged position. From 1990 to 1995 the Northeast grew at an average rate of 2.6% per year whereas Brazil grew at 2.7%, Northeastern exports increased by 39% while Brazilian exports increased by 48%; in 1995 exports made 8.3% of Brazil's GDP and 4.7% of the gross Northeastern product.[78]

Social Groups
Many studies have confirmed that regional integration affected negatively vulnerable population groups, peasants and women in particular. In the Southern Cone only Argentina and Uruguay had agricultural business production in the 1970s. A marked deterioration in agricultural production in Latin America occurred in the 1970s in all the countries where peasant production prevailed over business production: the output of all important crops began to decrease relative to population growth while the dependence on imports from the exterior was growing everywhere except Uruguay, Argentina, and Chile. Inflows of North American imports aggravated agricultural production crisis in the 1990s. Already by that time peasants had lost any significant economic role and become excluded from public policy, programmes, credits, resources, and lands. Further specialization of Uruguay and Argentina as a result of MERCOSUR contributed to challenges to peasant life all over MERCOSUR, especially in Brazil and Paraguay. As in Bolivia and Peru, peasant production in these two countries was predominant and constituted more than half of the agricultural output. In Chile peasant production was also significant and reached 30%.[79]

MERCOSUR provoked resistance to agricultural trade liberalization in Brazil and Chile. The Brazilian Landless Movement became increasingly violent. The agricultural disadvantage of Brazil caused the government to allocate US$4 milliard for credits to support domestic production of grain. This measure was perceived as an obstacle to integration. In Chile 830,000 peasants blocked the Pan-American road on 29 March 1996 to protest against Chilean accession to MERCOSUR. They perceived the accession as 'the death of Chilean agriculture for the sake of a common market.' As a result of free trade with MERCOSUR, Chilean production of corn was calculated to fall by 9% between 1995 and 2006, and by 16% between 2007 and 2014 and of rice by 4% between 2006 and 2011.[80] The consequences of such shocks in agriculture cause damage to peasants and small farms, present threats to the survival of the indigenous population and contribute to disproportionate urban growth, excessive migration, and associated costs of urban readjustment.

In respect to the consequences of integration, Carlos Gasparri, the Uruguayan Minister of Agriculture and Fishing, made the following statement: 'In the case of Uruguay, it is certain that peasant migration will continue and that many agricultural producers have been expelled from their occupation because they were not profitable. However, the benefits of commercial integration in modernisation, volumes of production and consumer satisfaction are positive.'[81] Such view prioritizing markets over people may be compared to the idea in earlier US history that progress and development were impossible unless American Indians were exterminated.[82]

Studies identify another vulnerable group: women. In contrast to Western Europe, the Southern Cone countries have never had laws discriminating against women, but women's actual situation in MERCOSUR is worse than in the EU both in absolute terms and in relation to men. MERCOSUR has made women more vulnerable, as more of them became employed in disadvantaged and non-protected sectors.[83] The MERCOSUR studies echo the findings of Eastern European scholars who noticed a marked deterioration of women's position relative to that of men in their countries after the demolition of the socialist regimes and accession to the EU, as happened in Poland.[84]

The problem closely associated with achievement of economies of scale is the growth of unemployment as a result of the amalgamation of production. Growing unemployment affects both winning and losing countries. The growth of unemployment has been particularly significant in large metropolitan areas such as Greater Buenos Aires and Greater São Paulo where it rose from 7.3% and 6.7% to 17% and 16.6% between 1989 and 1997.[85] These rates of unemployment growth have been unprecedented for the two countries in the last 50 years, and MERCOSUR may be partially responsible for them. Another major trend in the MERCOSUR labour market has to do with declining security of jobs: the ratio of permanent jobs to temporary jobs has been in decline.[86]

2.4.3 Conclusion

Despite the increase in intra-MERCOSUR trade in the 1990s and the fact that intra-regional trade at some point exceeded all other trade flows, MERCOSUR's economic effects have not been strong enough due to limited volumes of exchange among the countries in relation to their total output. This is why welfare effects of MERCOSUR's intra-regional trade are uncertain, and so are MERCOSUR's distributional effects on subnational regions. The effects on countries, sectors and certain population groups have been more obvious, but many of the grievances attributed to MERCOSUR are rooted in pre-existing imbalances and the development trends unrelated to the construction of the regional market.

2.5 Case Study: Monetary Cooperation

The variation in economic cohesion between MERCOSUR and the EU is obvious in the extent of monetary cooperation among their members: the EU is a monetary union and MERCOSUR is not. In the late 1990s, however, there were debates discussing the US dollar, an external currency, as possible regional money for MERCOSUR. Dollarization was implemented partially at the sub-regional level when Argentina introduced a currency board with the peso pegged to the US dollar. The dissonance between the fixed peso and floating Brazilian *real* produced a number of asymmetric shocks and reduced the competitiveness of Argentinean exports to MERCOSUR in a situation in which Argentina's dependence on the MERCOSUR market was stronger than commercial ties with the USA. As an adjustment mechanism with an external currency, the Argentinean peso-dollar parity was incompatible with the desirable intra-union system and challenged sustainability of integration. The whole structure of MERCOSUR ended up by paying for the collapse of this system in 2001. With the Argentinean peso pegged to the dollar, the scope for monetary cooperation between Brazil and Argentina was limited. 'De-dollarization' of the Argentinean peso opened opportunities for attempts to harmonize the exchange rates of the MERCOSUR currencies and to bring them to a single currency.

Several factors and events have encouraged the idea of a monetary union in MERCOSUR. Devaluations of the *real* and peso intensified intra-union conflicts and showed the danger for integration posed by an unstable monetary system. The Asian and Russian crises also appealed to the belief that regional currencies were better. The introduction of the euro strengthened confidence of the proponents of a regional currency. Before 1998 and after 2004 MERCOSUR's intra-regional and intra-industry trade grew. The amount of goods crossing the borders increased and improved conditions for price arbitrage, raised efficiency, and created necessity of macroeconomic coordination.[87] In addition, Brazil, the most important country of MERCOSUR is displaying favourable macroeconomic development, while Argentina and Uruguay have achieved monetary stabilization. Both of the leading regional economies, Brazil and Argentina, have stabilized inflation: Their price fluctuation dynamics do not show serious explosions any longer. In addition to the relative stability, such factors as developed financial markets, lack of conflicts, and cultural affinity favour the idea of a monetary union.[88] However, in spite of a number of positive developments, in-depth studies of the prospects for a currency union in MERCOSUR reveal a number of problems. These problems will be identified following a review of the arguments for and against a single currency and a discussion of criteria for a monetary union.

2.5.1 Pros and Cons of Monetary Unions

The necessity of cooperation in the monetary sphere arises from the quest for stability in commercial exchange and investment movement. There is a coherent political-economy logic for a customs union to contemplate a monetary union, as it is a basic solution for the major inconsistency 'one market – several currencies.' A monetary union can become a base for generation of more effective policies for economic management and can have a number of positive implications such as:

1) Elimination of transaction costs. A monetary union eliminates psychological and technical barriers to exchanges, border taxes, and exchange control barriers to factor mobility in the product, capital, and labour markets. Reduction of transaction costs facilitates intraregional exchange, and allows a better exploitation of the benefits of a common market.

2) Reduction of risks for regional exchanges.[89] A monetary union diminishes the risks of regional exchanges through the reduction of discretion and uncertainty caused by exchange rates. The lack of norms in the monetary sphere is fraught by turning cooperation efforts in areas like trade, investment, and production into disaster by an administrative decision of competitive devaluation of one of the system's currencies. Consecutive *real* and peso devaluations have already caused trade wars in MERCOSUR. Importantly, a

monetary union in MERCOSUR can reduce 'Brazil-dependency' for Argentinean exports after diminishing the uncertainty about Brazil's exchange rates.[90]
3) Reduction of dependence on domestic politics. A monetary union can centralize and strengthen institutional environment by taking control over monetary affairs away from national politicians. Democratic regimes cannot be trusted with monetary policy formation, as they tend to make decisions favouring short-term effects (reducing unemployment) with adverse consequences in the long-term (rising inflation) whereas regional central banks are not subject to domestic political pressures. They take responsibility for unpopular measures and discipline national governments by isolating policy-making from the demands of political cycles.
4) Reduction of consequences of external shocks. A monetary union strengthens the political and economic standing of the bloc in relation to outside competitors. The challenges of globalization and the threat of external shocks compel countries with substantial market integration to undertake measures for a higher degree of monetary cooperation to reduce the consequences of the external shocks that affect member countries in similar ways.[91]
5) Other macro-economic benefits. Monetary unions reduce the risks of external and regional shocks through the commitment of economies to satisfy minimum prerequisites of economic stability.[92] Economic growth resulting from stabilization policies further decreases the chances for economic crises. The common policies target convergence and stability. They decrease inflation, promote full employment, nurture long-term price stabilization and more constant purchasing power, decrease interest rates, promote increases in financial assets, prevent capital volatility through anti-speculative mechanisms, and offer incentives for investment. Economic stabilization and amalgamation of the currency units stimulate aggregate demand for the MERCOSUR means of payment.

For all of the mentioned reasons, a monetary union secures greater monetary and financial credibility, prevents reverses in integration and intra-regional currency crises, and brings economic efficiency. In addition, a monetary union is a stimulus for further integration development and the creation of supranational institutions, as it requires considerable central government involvement to operate fiscal and social security policies. It may stimulate convergence in business cycles and decrease the possibility of asymmetrical shocks. All these are important benefits for MERCOSUR as divergence in economic performance of its economies is not being reduced, reversibility of integration is still a possibility, and the financial credibility of MERCOSUR is low because its countries have had long histories of financial shocks and high inflation.[93]

Despite the listed benefits of a single currency, it cannot be easily resolved at the domestic level. Recent crises and fears of greater financial instability make MERCOSUR leaders avoid serious attempts at financial and monetary integration. The Brazilian *real* is unable to guarantee the stability of the common currency in the way the German *mark* conditioned the somewhat successful euro. As MERCOSUR countries are weaker and poorer, a deflationary bias can impose greater costs of a single currency than in Europe.[94] The criticism of monetary unions is centred on the deprivation of countries of adequate means to deal with regional discrepancies through monetary mechanisms to confront regional shocks, unemployment, low productivity, and low competitiveness. Governments in a monetary union lose sovereignty in the budgetary sphere and the ability to promote individual growth, to secure balance of payments stability, to stimulate effective demand and affect unemployment through optimal country-specific monetary policy. A single currency imposes central policies that may not be suitable for countries with varying economic conditions or at different stages of the business cycle. The history of trade conflicts within MERCOSUR shows that the growth of intra-regional trade has sharpened the differences and asymmetries of macroeconomic performance of individual economies.

Empirical studies confirm that the logic of the market implies inequality rather than convergence in growth rates. Monetary unions can cause huge problems if undertaken in systems containing deep structural inequalities.[95] Differences in economic structures may generate vicious circles deepening the gap of development among integrating countries. This is especially true when financial liberalization of capital accounts is pursued. Financial liberalization is a prerequisite for a monetary union. As Spanish-speaking countries have less developed financial systems, financial integration will move the flux of liquidity to Brazil.[96] The core country will have a financial concentration that promises concentration of economic growth, greater regional discrepancies, and more disadvantaged position of peripheral territories.

2.5.2 Criteria for Optimum Currency Area

Proposals for a single currency are evaluated against the assumptions of the Theory of OCA. This theory integrated a number of studies since the 1960s.[97] It lists the following basic criteria:

1) *Economic openness and high factor mobility.* Countries entering a monetary union should have no restrictions on the flow of goods and services and should have flexible factors of production: unrestricted labour movement and fiscal transfers allowing adjustment for shocks in order to avoid economic disturbances. The cost of a single currency can be low only if prices are stable, and salaries and factors of production are flexible.
2) *Strong economic interdependence.* It is preferable that the countries have large economies with diversified production. These two conditions ensure high levels of intra-regional exchange. If there is no intra-regional exchange, there are no incentives for a single currency. The benefits of a single currency are greatest when the volumes of trade are large and adequate for effective price arbitrage.
3) *Convergence in macroeconomic performance.* Studies of monetary unions indicate that in the absence of a political union, convergence in economic performance has paramount importance to ensure that the common monetary policy is appropriate for all members of a monetary union.[98] This is why indicators like inflation, fiscal deficit, deficit of the public sector, deficit of the current account, public debt, GDP growth, GDP per capita, and unemployment rates should be similar. The countries should display identical patterns of cyclical development and should be vulnerable to symmetric shocks. These conditions hold when national economies' production patterns are homogeneous. If countries experience asymmetrical shocks that affect them in opposite ways, and if there are significant obstacles to the movement of factors, the countries will need separate currencies to adjust the consequences of the shocks.[99]

2.5.3 Monetary Union Criteria in MERCOSUR and the Eurozone

There are no strict criteria to determine pass/failure conditions for a monetary union.[100] Relative to the USA, an indivisible market with a single currency, the Eurozone lags behind in all the conditions of OCA. EU volumes of intra-regional exchange are significantly lower than those within the USA. When the euro was launched, unemployment varied from 3% in Oberösterreich (Austria) to 37% in Réunion (France), and the output gap as a sign of the stage of the business cycle was +2% in Ireland and −2% in Italy.[101] There are legal, economic, and cultural limitations to labour mobility. Labour immobility and the lack of fiscal policy are the most obvious weaknesses of the EMU. There is very little evidence of macroeconomic convergence in Western Europe. In contrast to the USA, the EU budget does not operate as a stabiliser. Evidently, the OCA theory played little role in the deliberations over the introduction of the euro. Still Eurozone's indicators are much closer to the satisfaction of the OCA criteria than those of MERCOSUR.

Economic Openness and Factor Mobility
The degree of economic integration in MERCOSUR is inferior to European integration, and MERCOSUR factor markets are unified to a lesser degree. Compared to the EU, MERCOSUR commercial liberalization is limited. There are exceptions to free intra-regional trade that do not allow us to consider MERCOSUR even a complete FTA. Regional labour mobility is minimal. National labour markets are heavily regulated and their requirements differ substantially. MERCOSUR's financial integration is low, and capital mobility is asymmetric because Uruguay, Argentina, and Paraguay have open markets while Brazil retains capital controls.[102] The European experience shows that integration should be gradual, from commercial to the financial sphere and only then to a monetary union.[103]

Economic Interdependence
Within MERCOSUR, the volumes of intra-regional exchange are much lower in relation to total international trade and investment than in the Eurozone due to the factors examined in Subsection 2.2.1. Intra-regional trade in MERCOSUR is only 13% of all total trade versus 63% in the EU (Table 2.1.B); the relation of trade to GRP is very low, intra-regional exports make only 1.2% and 0.5% of Brazilian and Venezuelan GDPs (Table 2.1.C); intra-regional investment is 6% of the total FDI to the region.[104] Thus the incentives for a monetary union in MERCOSUR to facilitate regional exchange are much lower than in the Eurozone, and the benefits in the reduction of transaction costs will be far from equally significant. In spite of the low interdependence of the MERCOSUR

countries in general, Paraguayan and Uruguayan extreme exchange rates for *real* and peso generate burdens because of their proximity to Brazil and Argentina and the high costs of transport for extra-regional trade.[105] If small countries have perceivable gains from the monetary union, the gains for Brazil are negligible because it has the lowest degree of dependence on MERCOSUR. If one country dominates in the region in terms of size, its incentives to enter a monetary union diminish.[106] This is truer for Brazil in MERCOSUR than for Germany and France in the EU.

Macroeconomic Convergence
The MERCOSUR countries' macroeconomic variables are further away from convergence than those of the Eurozone members. Though trends towards convergence occurred over the period from 1991 to 1998 and confronted MERCOSUR countries with similar problems such as vulnerability to external shocks and social disequilibria—rates of inflation, nominal interest rates, economic growth, and employment are not moving in the same direction.[107] Difficulties in monetary integration are caused by severe discrepancies in incomes per capita that are larger than within the Eurozone.[108] Thus Paraguayan income per capita is 3.7 times lower than the Uruguayan, whereas in the Eurozone the difference between the highest (the Netherlands) and lowest (Latvia) GDP per capita is 3.2 times.[109]

MERCOSUR needs to reduce divergence in unemployment rates and incomes. Disparities in unemployment and average incomes need to be addressed by a fiscal policy involving significant transfers among the countries and sub-national regions after the national governments lose the ability to adjust macroeconomic problems through exchange rates. While the Eurozone does not use mechanisms of fiscal transfers for the reduction of disparities, the EU implements a symbolic structural programme pretending to address socio-economic problems. MERCOSUR's funds and institutional capacity to deal with regional inequalities is symbolic even in relation to the respective EU initiative.[110]

Further, co-movement in MERCOSUR business cycles is non-existent: in 2000 the Brazilian and Paraguayan economies were growing while Argentina and Uruguay were in recession.[111] MERCOSUR shocks are neither asymmetrical, nor do they display any identifiable pattern in contrast to the shocks among the leading European economies.[112] The lack of any patterns for shocks is not unexpected between the countries with production structures as different as Argentinean and Brazilian. However, there is no identifiable correlation even between Argentinean and Uruguayan shocks.[113] In addition, shocks affecting MERCOSUR are much stronger than those affecting Europe. Economic integration and similar stabilization policies might cause shocks to become a little more similar, but hardly enough to introduce a currency zone. In terms of shock adjustment, a small open country like Uruguay has most to lose if it drops its national currency.[114]

Extra-OCA Considerations
In the 1990s the FTAA and universal liberalization seemed viable projects, and it was believed that MERCOSUR would eventually become a segment of the FTAA or a universal FTA. In such an instance a single currency was thought to be the only feature that would distinguish MERCOSUR from other peripheral countries. Therefore, a monetary union was perceived as an important policy-making instrument vis-à-vis global centres of power and multinational corporations.[115] Also, upgrading MERCOSUR to a monetary union seemed a warranted initiative as a means of protection against external disruptions. They were the major stimuli for the introduction of the euro. As demonstrated by Henning, there was a direct causality between disrupting policies of the USA and the advances of the EU monetary cooperation. Every consecutive step to increase monetary cooperation in Europe followed the consequences of disruptions caused by the US Federal Reserve. European cooperation in the monetary sphere stalled when the USA was not affecting Europe in a destabilizing way.[116]

MERCOSUR has also suffered from external shocks such as the consequences of the Mexican, Asian, and Russian crises resulting in the devaluation of the *real* in 1999. Though MERCOSUR is more vulnerable to external shocks than Europe, shocks do not affect the countries of the bloc in a uniform way. While leading Western European economies had a high level of interdependence with the US economy and saw the US dollar as the biggest threat to their monetary stability, MERCOSUR equally depends on the stability of the dollar, euro, and the aggregate of remaining external currencies. Thus the sources of MERCOSUR external shocks are more diffused. Besides, shocks affect each of the countries of the union in a different way; and leaps in exchange rates for the dollar and euro have different implications for individual economies. Brazil is more dependent on the US market and the dollar, while Argentina is more dependent on the euro. The smaller countries of MERCOSUR are more affected by monetary instability in Brazil and Argentina than instability overseas. Thus the lowest common denominator for the MERCOSUR members' common monetary policy in relation to the rest of the world is very low.

2.5.4 Conclusion

It is natural that the differences in the economic cohesion of Western European and the Southern Cone countries have produced dissimilar results of monetary integration: a monetary union in the EU and a zone of monetary influence in MERCOSUR.[117] According to the literature, a single currency is good for a highly integrated regional market, which MERCOSUR is not. There are many reasons to believe that a monetary union is inappropriate for MERCOSUR at the current stage of its development. The bloc does not respond well to the OCA criteria: its common market is not complete and not open enough, mobility within factor markets is restricted, the volumes of trade are low, macroeconomic variables indicate that the convergence of macroeconomic performance cannot be achieved soon, relative price flexibility and fiscal transfers are hardly in evidence. Under such conditions the gains of a single currency for the sake of minimizing transaction costs are negligible, while the risks and uncertainties associated with the loss of national sovereignty in the monetary policy are perceived as very high.

Before monetary union is implemented, MERCOSUR might want to advance economic and social integration: improve the mobility of labour and capital, intensify commercial and financial integration, and move macroeconomic variables of the countries in a similar direction. Though monetary union is not yet advisable, empirical evidence is against the option of no macroeconomic coordination.[118] Fiscal and monetary policies conducted by a regional board are required to regulate foreign reserves, maintain a stable exchange rate system, eliminate external imbalances, monitor and prevent market failures, and reduce economic divergences among the member countries.

2.6 CONCLUSION

Integration theorists acknowledge that high interdependence is a prerequisite for integration, but they seldom resort to the analysis of regional demographic, physical, and economic geography. However, these factors determine economic density and interdependence levels. Compared to

Western Europe, MERCOSUR has limited motivation for integration because of low intra-regional cross-border exchange. The low exchange levels are conditioned by geographic, demographic, and structural features of the bloc. The later have to do with the large size of the countries. With low exchange levels, few regional transactors are affected by integration. On the one hand, this helps the process: as there is no resistance from affected import-competing sectors, agreements on intra-regional commercial liberalization may be fast and easy to achieve. On the other hand, limited numbers of export-oriented agents and the lack of sufficient pragmatic interest in integration explain member states' low motivation for securing and facilitating intra-regional exchanges. As a result, MERCOSUR's common market remains rigid and partial. Structurally conditioned low interdependence and divergences in economic performance among the member states explain existing difficulties and the slow progress in MERCOSUR's economic integration.

As a regional market is relatively unimportant for national economies and regional development, the respective governments have never seen the common market as their topmost integration priority. The implementation of the common market has not been taken with the declared rigour, and the limited measures have resulted in weak enforcement mechanisms, ununiformed regimes, and the preservation of many exceptions to general rules. Higher levels of economic interdependence have enabled 19 EU countries to adopt the euro. MERCOSUR does not have a regional currency. It is far behind the Eurozone in all OCA criteria such as economic interdependence, economic openness, and macroeconomic convergence. Other important differences of MERCOSUR from the European system deal with limited liberalization in the capital and services markets, the lack of a central judiciary for dispute settlements, and the remaining distinction between national markets and regional market in the regional competition law.

There are two sources of changes regional groups inflict on members' economies. These changes come from intra-bloc liberalization and from the common economic policy in relation to third countries. Studies of MERCOSUR effects ascribe more serious consequences not to the changes from protectionism and liberalization at the intra-regional level, but to the changes coming from external liberalization and globalization. The gains of intra-regional liberalization in MERCOSUR were smaller than the changes resulting from the implementation of the CET. The CET regulates the exchange with the external market, and this market retains a larger share of exports and imports of the MERCOSUR countries than the regional market.

The results of empirical studies confirm that the effects of MERCOSUR's intra-regional liberalization on amalgamation of production, bloc's welfare gains, and changes in aggregate non-members' welfare are weak and consistent with the assumption of limitations of the MERCOSUR's common market. Studies of MERCOSUR's distributional effects highlight growing inequalities and divergence in economic performance caused by MERCOSUR and the market tactics it adopted. MERCOSUR favours stronger producers and richer countries. In a few cases intra-MERCOSUR liberalization caused social disturbance akin in character to that attributed to globalization. Such consequences along with the initial discrepancies in the level of development of the member economies make integration harder. However, even though MERCOSUR's distributional results may seem more visible than welfare effects, the studies usually find it difficult to attribute growing social inequalities exclusively to the consequences of intra-regional liberalization.

In relation to third countries MERCOSUR's initial policy was self-damaging, as a wrong balance between liberalization and protectionism was chosen in favour of liberalization. The erroneous strategy converted MERCOSUR's trade balance from US$27.64-milliard surplus to 13.59-milliard deficit between 1990 and 1998. Clearly, this was not a problem of MERCOSUR's inherent incurable defects, but of policies implemented. As protectionism and governmental intervention are crucial for the survival of MERCOSUR's industrial sectors, there is an argument about MERCOSUR's important role in the protection of regional production from the competition of powerful transnational companies, countries and blocs in the era of globalization. This argument has empirical backing.[119]

However, it is worth noting that MERCOSUR members per se do not need MERCOSUR to provide protectionism at the regional level as they can do so themselves relying not on the CET, but on optimal national tariffs that are more responsive to the needs of each individual economy. Another argument is that the value of MERCOSUR stands in being an instrument of external commercial policy in relations with large external traders and an important bargaining chip in international negotiations on the terms of trade. Even though MERCOSUR is unable to offer a CET as efficient as the optimal national tariffs, it is able to provide a framework for the type of external commercial policy that the small, poorer, and dependent countries dare not pursue individually. Thus the importance of MERCOSUR is not as much economic, as geoeconomic and geostrategic, and this is a topic of discussion in Chapter 5.

NOTES

1. WTO, http://www.wto.org/english/tratop_e/region_e/region_e.htm, 1.11.2017. As of 15 June 2015, these numbers were even larger, 585 and 379 (Idem, 1.10.2015).
2. Gardini, Gian Luca. 2011. MERCOSUR: What You See Is Not (Always) What You Get. *European Law Journal*, 17:5, pp 683–700. p 695.
3. This description is partially based on Bouzas, Roberto, da Motta Veiga, Pedro and Torrent, Ramón. 2002. *Analysis of MERCOSUR integration, its prospects and effects on the market access of EU goods, services and investment*. Report presented to the European Commission. University of Barcelona, Barcelona. pp 129–138. It is updated where necessary.
4. Gardini, 2011. p 695.
5. Protocolo relativo al Código Aduanero del Mercosur, 16.12.1994.
6. Bouzas et al, 2002. p 131.
7. Decisión 27/2010 and Decisión 10/2010.
8. As of 1 November 2017 the customs code was not in force. SM, http://www.mercosur.int/innovaportal/v/5837/11/innova.front/preguntas-frecuentes#codigo, 1.11.2017.
9. Decisión 32/2000.
10. Protocolo de Montevideo sobre el Comercio de Servicios del MERCOSUR, 15.12.1997.
11. The Paraguayan Ministry of Foreign Affairs, http://www.mre.gov.py/tratados/public_web/DetallesTratado.aspx?id=1RzZPEFh9pQPghDrS5IZow==&em=lc4aLYHVB0dF+kNrtEvsmZ96BovjLlz0mcrZruYPcn8=, 1.11.2017.
12. Quijano, José Manuel. 2011. El MERCOSUR 20 años después. In *MERCOSUR: 20 años*, edited by Gerardo Caetano. pp 89–127. Centro de Formación para la Integración Regional, Montevideo, Uruguay. p 103.
13. Acordo Multilateral de Seguridade Social do Mercado Comum do Sul, 15.12.1997.
14. Acuerdo sobre Residencia para Nacionales de los Estados Partes del Mercosur, 6.12.2002; Acuerdo sobre Residencia para Nacionales de los Estados Partes del Mercosur, Bolivia y Chile, 6.12.2002.
15. Treaty establishing a Constitution for Europe, 29.10.2004.
16. Margheritis, Ana. 2013. Piecemeal regional integration in the post-neoliberal era: Negotiating migration policies within Mercosur. *Review of International Political Economy*, 20(3), pp 541–575. p 548.
17. The Schengen Agreement, 14.6.1985; Convention Implementing the Schengen Agreement, 19.6.1990.
18. Margheritis, 2003.
19. Protocolo de Colonia para la Promoción y Protección Recíproca de Inversiones en el MERCOSUR, 17.1.1994.

20. 'Commercial presence' is having an office, branch, or subsidiary in a foreign country.
21. Protocolo de Cooperación y Facilitación de Inversiones Intra-MERCOSUR, 7.4.2016.
22. Protocolo de Olivos para la Solución de Controversias en el Mercosur, 28.2.2002; Protocolo de Brasília para a Solução de Controvérsias, 17.12.1991.
23. Protocolo de Defesa da Concorrência do Mercosul, 17.12.1996.
24. Velasco San Pedro, Luis Antonio. 1998. La defensa de la competencia en la Unión Europea y en MERCOSUR. In *MERCOSUR y la Unión Europea: Dos modelos de integración económica*, edited by Luis Antonio Velasco San Pedro, 171–191. Lex Nova, Valladolid. p 184.
25. The ruling affects Argentina and Brazil, as Paraguay and Uruguay do not have national antitrust laws.
26. Chudnovsky, Daniel, Kosacoff, Bernardo and López Andrés. 1999. *Las multinacionales Latinoamericanas: Sus Estrategias en un Mundo Globalizado*. FCE, BsAs.
27. Burges, Sean. 2005. Bounded by the Reality of Trade: Practical Limits to a South American Region. *Cambridge Review of International Affairs*, 18:3, pp 437–454. p 446.
28. http://www.worldstopexports.com, 1 November 2017.
29. Based on CIA population and territory data for 2017.
30. Le Gras, Gilbert. 2002. *The New New World: The re-emerging market in South America*. Reuters, New York. pp 200–201.
31. Ibidem.
32. The Economist, 1996. p S3.
33. Idem, p S19.
34. Basco, Carlos. 1988. El costo de transporte: una barrera más al comercio. *Integración Latinoamericana*, 132, pp 3–15.
35. It is indicative that out of 16 Brazilian representatives to the MERCOSUR Joint Parliamentary Commission, 13 were from the three states of the South: Rio Grande do Sul (5 representatives), Paraná (4), and Santa Catarina (4). The remaining three representatives came from Mato Grosso do Sul, São Paulo, and Roraima (Pasquariello Mariano, Karina, Vigevani, Tullo, and Fernandes de Oliveira, Marcelo. 2000. Democracia e atores políticos no Mercosul. In *O Mercosul no limiar do século XXI*, edited by Marcos Costa Lima and Marcelo de Almeida Medeiros, pp 250–285. Cortez Editora, São Paulo. p 263).
36. Simonsen Associados. 1992. *MERCOSUL: O Desafio do Marketing de Integração*. McGraw-Hill, São Paulo. pp 58–59.
37. Based on CIA GDP data for 2016.
38. WTO. 2016. International Trade Statistics 2016. Figures for 2015 showing both intra- and extra-regional trade.

39. Protocolo Adicional ao Tratado de Assunção sobre a Estrutura Institucional do Mercosul, 17.12.1994.
40. Article 44 of the Treaty of Asunción reads: 'Before finalising the convergence process with the common external tariff, the States will undertake a revision of the current MERCOSUR dispute resolution system geared towards adopting a permanent system.' Article 18 of the Treaty says: 'The nations involved will convoke an extraordinary reunion in order to define the final institutional structure of the administrative organs of MERCOSUR as well as the specific attributes of each organ.'
41. The Benelux process started in 1921 with the Convention of Brussels between Belgium and Luxembourg. The Netherlands joined the process after WW2. Benelux faced a number of difficulties caused by competitiveness rather than complementarity of the Dutch and Belgian economies and different degrees of liberalization of the economic systems of the two countries. The customs convention among the three countries entered in force in 1948. Prior to the Treaty of Rome nearly all internal trade in Benelux was tariff-free. The Treaty of the Benelux Economic Union of 1958 came into operation in 1960. Benelux became the first free international labour market; the movement of capital and services was also made free. Postal and transport rates were standardized, and welfare policies were coordinated. In 1970 border controls were abolished. The present agreement provides for an economic union. The importance of Benelux lies in the opportunity it gave to gain experience in certain forms of integration that proved useful for the EU. The fact that the Benelux countries are small and share a long history of relations made their goals of integration relatively easy to achieve.
42. Vizentini, Paulo G. F. 2000. Mercosul: dimensões estratégicas e geoeconômicas. In *O Mercosul no limiar do século XXI*, edited by Marcos Costa Lima and Marcelo de Almeida Medeiros, pp 27–41. Cortez Editora, São Paulo. p 31.
43. Chancellor of Spain Javier Solana in 1995 as cited as in Campbell, Jorge, Rozemberg, Ricardo, and Svarzman, Gustavo. 2000. O Mercosul na década de 1990: da abertura à globalização. In *Mercosul: entre a realidade e a utopia*, edited by Jorge Campbell, pp 99–180. Relume Dumará, Rio de Janeiro.
44. Guilhon Albuquerque, José Augusto. 1999. Mercosur: Democratic Stability and Economic integration in South America. In *Regional Integration and Democracy: Expanding on the European Experience*, edited by Jeffrey J. Anderson, pp 261–283. Rowman and Littlefield, Lanham. pp 266–267.
45. The Single European Act, 17.2.1986 & 28.2.1986.
46. SM. 2004. *Un Foco para el Proceso de Integración Regional. Primer Informe Semestral*. SM. Montevideo. p 9.

47. http://www.mre.gov.py/tratados/public_web/ConsultaMercosur.aspx, 1.11.2017.
48. Bouzas et al, 2002. p 159.
49. Compare with the quote: '90% of the books dealing with the WTO are speaking of something that does not exist. I have already seen a similar phenomenon with regard to MERCOSUR—people discuss and criticise a MERCOSUR that only exists in their heads. And nobody is speaking about what really exists.' Luiz Olavo Baptista (professor of law at the University of São Paulo and arbiter in MERCOSUR dispute settlements), cited as in Malamud, Andrés. 2005. Mercosur Turns 15: Between Rising Rhetoric and Declining Achievement. *Cambridge Review of International Affairs*, 18:3, pp 421–436. p 421.
50. For example, according to Uruguayan Minister of Foreign Affairs Álvaro Ramos, the more appropriate administration of trade and cooperation in production requires 'adequate legal and institutional arrangements' able 'to define procedures for the resolution of problems at the supranational level.' 'To frustrate the economic growth due to the lack of an appropriate regulatory framework would be to neglect to learn the historical lessons of 40 years of European integration' (Ramos Trigo, Álvaro. 1996. In *Latin America – European Union. Forum 1996. Europe and Latin America: Two Ways of Integration for the 21st Century*, pp 88–91. European Commission, Brussels. p 90).
51. Fleitas, Ovidio. 2004. *Integraciones Regionales, el Mercosur y Paraguay*. El Lector, Asunción. p 14.
52. Ginesta, Jacques. 2000. *El Mercosur en tiempos de crisis*. Instituto de Estudios Políticos e Internacionales, Montevideo. p 76.
53. For example, producers in small countries are able to increase output and make gains only in cases of high tariff differentials and low cost differentials. These require the enforcement of a variation in the degree of economic openness among members. At the same time, the variation does not strengthen the position of smaller countries in negotiations on an economic policy and reinforces the propensity of larger economies to individually establish policy parameters.
54. A 5% depreciation of the Argentinean currency is calculated to increase Argentina's output by 2% to 25%. Disparities in exchange rates have detrimental effects on the conditions of competition. It is clear that discrepancies in exchange rates can undermine the efforts of MERCOSUR to achieve the objective of a common market (Behar, Jaime. 2000. *Cooperation and Competition in a Common Market: Studies on the Formation of MERCOSUR*. Physica-Verlag, Heidelberg. p 102).
55. Campos Filho, Leonardo. 1999. *New Regionalism and Latin America: The Case of MERCOSUL*. Institute of Latin American Studies, London.

56. Garay Salamanca, Luis Jorge, Devlin, Robert and Taccone, Juan José. 1999. Nota Editorial. In *Impacto sectorial de la integración en el MERCOSUR*, edited by Luis Jorge Garay Salamanca, Robert Delvin and Juan José Taccone, pp i-ix. Banco Interamericano de Desarrollo, Departamento de Integración y Programas Regionales, INTAL, BsAs.
57. Carrera, Jorge and Sturzenegger, Federico. 2000. Capítulo 1. Los resultados de la integración en el Mercosur. In *Coordinación de políticas macroeconómicas en el Mercosur*, edited by Jorge Carrera and Federico Sturzenegger, pp 11–60. FCE, BsAs.
58. The publication came in 2000. The author does not specify the period of calculation. Behar, 2000. p 101.
59. Zago de Azevedo, André Filipe. 2001. *The Economic Effects of MERCOSUR: An Empirical Analysis*. Doctoral Thesis, University of Sussex, Brighton. p 159.
60. Chang, Won and Winters, L. Alan. 1999. *How regional blocs affect excluded countries: The price effects of MERCOSUR*. Centre for Economic Policy Research, London. p 32.
61. Benegas Cristaldo, Gladys S. 1994. *A la búsqueda de un Mercado Común: Mercosur. Creación de Comercio, Desviación de Comercio e Implicancias de Políticas Públicas*. Universidad Católica 'Nuestra Señora la Asunción', Asunción.
62. Zago de Azevedo, 2001. p 163.
63. Mosca Sobrero, Luis. 1996. In *Latin America – European Union. Forum 1996. Europe and Latin America: Two Ways of Integration for the 21st Century*, pp 91–92. European Commission, Brussels. p 91.
64. Campbell, Jorge. 1996. In *Latin America – European Union. Forum 1996. Europe and Latin America: Two Ways of Integration for the 21st Century*, pp 92–95. European Commission, Brussels. p 95.
65. LAIA, http://www.aladi.org/nsfaladi/indicado.nsf/vvindicadoresweb/Mercosur, 1.10.2014.
66. Jacobs, Gerardo. 1999. Conclusión: los retos de globalización. In *Procesos de integración en América Latina: Perspectivas y experiencias latinoamericanas y europeas*, edited by Raymond Buve and Marianne Wiesebron, pp 178–184. Universidad Iberoamericana, México.
67. According to *Jornal do Brasil*, several days before signing the agreements on PICE, Brazilian foreign minister Abreu Sodré said: 'Brazil has interest in wheat at a price that satisfies the Brazilian consumer and meat at prices competitive with those of the European single market' and that Argentina 'can import Brazilian manufactures.' Commenting the observation of a journalist that this type of exchange resembles relations between first- and third-world countries, and that internally the Argentinean government may be accused of victimizing Argentina by 'Brazilian imperialism,' Abreu

Sodré responded that Brazil did not have an imperialist vocation. Being afraid of negative comments and consequences in Argentina, on the following day the negotiators released a communiqué reinforcing already stated comments about the spirit, mechanisms and criteria that inspired the integration process between the two countries. On a similar occasion, the chairman of the Federation of Industries of São Paulo noticed in 1986: 'It is very important that the accounts of [bilateral] exchange are balanced. It is clear that one cannot make integration buying wheat and selling airplanes' (Cited as in Campbell, Jorge, Rozemberg, Ricardo, and Svarzman, Gustavo. 2000. Argentina e Brasil na década de 1980: entre a cornija e a integração. In *Mercosul: entre a realidade e a utopia*, edited by Jorge Campbell, pp 31–98. Relume Dumará, Rio de Janeiro. pp 89–90 and 91). At the same time the attitude that 'the only beneficiaries of the agreement are Argentineans' prevailed in Brazil. Government bureaucrats and non-governmental opinion-formers were emphasizing 'natural' complementarity of Brazilian-Argentinean partnership in which Argentina supplied energy resources to Brazil. In its turn Brazil 'pleased' Argentina with the supply of manufacturers of more powerful and efficient industries of São Paulo (Idem, pp 61 and 62).
68. Behar, 2000. p 27.
69. Idem, p 27.
70. Idem, p 101.
71. These studies include the following: Nofal, María Beatriz and Wilkinson, John. 1999. La producción y el comercio de productos lácteos en el Mercosur. In *Impacto sectorial de la integración en el MERCOSUR*, edited by Luis Jorge Garay Salamanca, Robert Delvin and Juan José Taccone, pp 235–394. Banco Interamericano de Desarrollo, Departamento de Integración y Programas Regionales, INTAL, BsAs. Chudnovsky, Daniel and Erber, Fabio. 1999. El impacto del Mercosur sobre la dinámica del sector de maquinas-herramienta. In *Impacto sectorial...*, pp 573–667. Bastos Tigre, Paulo, Lapalne, Mariano, Lugones, Gustavo, Porta, Fernando and Sarti, Fernando. 1999. Impacto del Mercosur en la dinámica del sector automotor. In *Impacto sectorial...*, pp 1–234. Hasenclever, Lía, López, Andrés and de Oliveira, José Clemente. 1999. Impacto del Mercosur sobre la dinámica del sector petroquímico. In *Impacto sectorial...*, pp 395–572. Bekerman, Marta and Sirlin, Pablo. 2001. Impactos estáticos y dinámicos del Mercosur. El caso del sector farmacéutico. *Revista de la CEPAL*, 75, pp 227–243. ECLAC, Santiago de Chile.
72. *Example 1. Brazilian sector gains advantage over Argentinean sector.* In most sectors where administered trade arrangements have not been used (such as footwear and textiles) the liberalization of intra-regional trade

led to sizeable regional trade imbalances resulting in Brazilian trade surpluses. These imbalances have reflected structural asymmetries between Brazil and smaller partners. Thus intra-regional liberalization has promoted strong growth of trade in footwear with large Brazilian surpluses (Bouzas et al, 2002. pp 129–138 and 34–40). Resulting trade diversion from extra-regional trade has benefited Brazilian exporters. Even though any special effects on FDI have not been observed, intra-regional trade exerted downward pressure on prices in Argentina. There occurred specialization of production in Argentina, which was based on static comparative advantages. The Argentinean firms have been compelled to undertake defensive strategies.

73. *Example 2. Argentinean sector gains advantage but it is likely to lose to Brazilian sector in the future.* Regionalism gave benefits to Argentinean and Uruguayan agricultural producers relative to their Brazilian and Paraguayan counterparts. For example, changes in milk production have been typical of the rest of agriculture (Nofal and Wilkinson, 1999). Prior to the Treaty of Asunción, milk production differed substantially across the MERCOSUR countries. In the early 1990s there were 1 million milk producers in Brazil, 140,000 in Paraguay, 20,000 in Argentina and 8,000 in Uruguay. The Argentinean producers gave the output equal to half of the Brazilian output whereas Uruguayan farmers produced 5% of Brazilian or 200% of the Paraguayan output. Over the period from 1987 to 1995 Argentina sharply increased diary exports and decreased imports while Brazil displayed the opposite trend. Sectoral liberalization gave advantages to Argentina and Uruguay compensating their losses in industrial production. Though MERCOSUR has helped Argentina and Uruguay to become successful exporters of milk products intra-MERCOSUR and internationally, and compelled Brazil to dramatically increase diary imports, analysts predicted a tendency for Brazil to become self-sufficient in the future and to convert to an exporter. Despite current advantages, Argentina and Uruguay will probably need to look for new markets competing with more efficient producers from Australia and New Zealand. Amalgamation of milk production has drastically deteriorated the situation of small domestic producers not only in Brazil and Paraguay, but also in the benefiting Argentina and Uruguay. Multinationals ruined small farms and took control over domestic markets. Whereas single multinational *Parlamat* absorbed the whole Paraguayan industry, *Sancor* monopolized supplies to the Argentinean market, and *Conaprole* became responsible for the collection of 80% of all Uruguayan milk.

74. *Example 3. Argentinean sector benefits from the MERCOSUR CET but it is unlikely to withstand competition with Brazilian sector in the future.* PICE and MERCOSUR delayed the agony of Argentinean machinery

tools (Chudnovsky and Erber, 1999). By 1997 the output of machinery tools in Argentina was 22 times smaller than in Brazil and the range of production was much narrower. The Argentinean industry was highly disadvantaged due to its size, ownership, accumulation of production and technological capacity, and long exposure to detrimental macroeconomic and sectoral policies of the Argentinean government. Brazilian protectionism, on the contrary, strengthened Brazilian companies and helped them to develop the capacity to export to industrialized countries and to enter the electronic sector. The access for Argentinean goods to the regional market was an escape from an earlier collapse, and even more so was the CET that compelled Argentina to reject its zero tariff to harmonize with the Brazilian external tariff. The adverse effect of entrance of the Brazilian tools on the Argentinean market was less appreciable as sectoral imports already made 90% of the Argentinean consumption.
75. *Example 4. Argentinean and Brazilian sectors equally benefit from MERCOSUR due to compensatory treatment offered to Argentinean sector.* Positive trends have been observed in the automobile and petrochemical sectors. One is an important source of economic growth; the other is a major provider of inputs for a vast number of applications in many goods and services. The petrochemical sector was comprised by small firms in both Brazil and Argentina. Both the countries witnessed serious employment cuts and amalgamation of production. Yet the competitiveness of Argentinean and Brazilian industries has remained equal, and the shares of Brazilian and Argentinean sectoral exports to each other and to third countries have increased proportionately (Hasenclever et al, 1999). The automobile market, in spite of the regulatory asymmetries, observes a tendency for convergence towards the common automobile regime (Bastos Tigre et al, 1999). Though deregulation in this sector has been delayed, it has transformed to a semi-open market. The volumes of production and estimated flows of investment to Brazilian and Argentinean automobile sectors are in relation four to one. This roughly corresponds to sizes of the national automobile industries and sizes of the national markets.
76. Bouzas et al, 2002. pp 38–39.
77. Benzaquen Sicsú, Abraham and Katz, Frederico Jayme. 2000. Nordeste e Mercosul: reflexões iniciais sobre conjuntura e perspectives. In *O Mercosul no limiar do século XXI*, edited by Marcos Costa Lima and Marcelo de Almeida Medeiros, pp 289–299. Cortez Editora, São Paulo. Lima, João Policarpo R. and Meira de Oliveira, Enildo. 2000. Integração regional, Mercosul e os bens intermediaries do Nordeste. In *O Mercosul...*, pp 300–228.
78. Lima, João Policarpo R. and Katz, Frederico Jayme. 1997. Comércio Externo e Estratégias de Crescimento: uma Visão a Partir do Nordeste. In *Anais do XXV Encontro Nacional de Economia*', pp 435–456. ANPEC, Recife.

79. Rubio, Blanca. 1999. Las consecuencias de los tratados comerciales sobre los campesinos latinoamericanos: los casos del TLC y el MERCOSUR. In *Procesos de integración en América Latina: Perspectivas y experiencias latinoamericanas y europeas*, edited by Raymond Buve and Marianne Wiesebron, pp 97–113. Universidad Iberoamericana, México.
80. Daher, Antonio. 1997. El Mercosur y la agricultura tradicional en Chile. *Comercio Exterior*, 47:5, pp 355–366.
81. El Financiero, 14.11.1997.
82. Rubio, 1999. p 112.
83. Wiesebron, Marianne. 1999. La mujer y las consecuencias de la integración: la situación en la Unión Europea y en el MERCOSUR. In *Procesos de integración en América Latina: Perspectivas y experiencias latinoamericanas y europeas*, edited by Raymond Buve and Marianne Wiesebron, pp 114–133. Universidad Iberoamericana, México.
84. Plomien, Ania. 2006. Women and the labor market in Poland: from socialism to capitalism. In *Globalization, Uncertainty and Women's Careers: An International Comparison*, edited by Hans-Peter Blossfeld and Heather Hofmeister, pp 247–275. Edward Elgar Publishing, Cheltham.
85. Pochman, Marcio. 2000. Novas dinâmicas produtivas do emprego e do sindicalismo no Mercosul. In *O Mercosul no limiar do século XXI*, edited by Marcos Costa Lima and Marcelo de Almeida Medeiros, pp 120–134. Cortez Editora, São Paulo. p 124.
86. Idem, pp 125–128.
87. Fanelli, José María, González Rozada, Martín and Keifman, Saúl. 2001. Comercio, régimen cambiario y volatilidad. Una visión desde la Argentina de la coordinación macroeconómica en el Mercosur. In *Coordinación de políticas macroeconómicas en el Mercosur*, edited by José María Fanelli, pp 25–70. Siglo Veintiuno de Argentina Editores, BsAs.
88. Arestis, Philip and de Paula, Luiz Fernando. 2003. Introduction. In *Monetary Union in South America: Lessons from EMU*, edited by Philip Arestis and Luiz Fernando de Paula, pp 1–18, Edward Elgar Publishing, Cheltenham.
89. Asymmetrical shocks can present quite tangible costs to MERCOSUR. Intra-industry trade is particularly sensitive to fluctuations in interest rates. Intra-industry trade makes up between 13% and 23% of the Argentinean trade with MERCOSUR, between 4% and 7% of the Argentinean total trade and up to 2% of the country's GDP (Fanelli et al, 2001).
90. Giabiagi, Fabio. 2003. MERCOSUR: why does monetary union make sense in the long term? In *Monetary Union in South America: Lessons from EMU*, edited by Philip Arestis and Luiz Fernando de Paula, pp 39–66. Edward Elgar Publishing, Cheltenham.

91. Henning, C. Randall. 1998. Systematic Conflict and Regional Monetary Integration: The case of Europe. *International Organization*, 52:3, pp 537-573.
92. Giabiagi, 2003.
93. Idem.
94. Arestis, Philip, Ferrari-Filho, Fernando, de Paula, Luiz Fernando and Sawyer, Malcolm. 2003. The euro and the EMU: lessons for MERCOSUR. In *Monetary Union in South America: Lessons from EMU*, edited by Philip Arestis and Luiz Fernando de Paula, pp 11-36, Edward Elgar Publishing, Cheltenham.
95. Moreiera Amado, Adriana and Simoens da Silva, Luiz Afonso. 2003. Some issues on the financial/monetary integration of MERCOSUR. In *Monetary Union in South America: Lessons from EMU*, edited by Philip Arestis and Luiz Fernando de Paula, pp 104-127. Edward Elgar Publishing, Cheltenham.
96. Arestis and de Paula, 2003.
97. Since Mundell, Robert A. 1961. A theory of optimum currency areas. *American Economic Review*, 51, pp 657-664. American Economic Association, Nashville.
98. Arestis et al, 2003.
99. Mundell, 1961.
100. Licardo Ferrando, Gerardo. 2000. Capítulo 5 ¿Una área monetaria para el Mercosur? In *Coordinación de políticas macroeconómicas en el Mercosur*, edited by Jorge Carrera and Federico Sturzenegger, pp 183-222. FCE, BsAs.
101. Arestis et al, 2003.
102. Ferrari-Filho, Fernando. 2001. *Monetary Union in Mercosur? A Keynesian alternative proposal.* Working Paper CBS-23-01. University of Oxford Centre for Brazilian Studies, Oxford.
103. Heymann, Daniel and Navajas, Fernando. 2000. Capítulo 3. Coordinación de políticas macroeconómicas en el Mercosur: algunas reflexiones. In *Coordinación de políticas macroeconómicas en el Mercosur*, edited by Jorge Carrera and Federico Sturzenegger, pp 101-128. FCE, BsAs.
104. de la Balze, Felipe. Comentarios. In *Coordinación de políticas macroeconómicas en el Mercosur*, edited by Jorge Carrera and Federico Sturzenegger, pp 231-233. FCE, BsAs.
105. Licardo Ferrando, 2000.
106. Idem.
107. GDP growth has been slowly converging since 1980, inflation rates since 1993, and external debt is about 40% in Brazil and Argentina. Thus there is no need to generate compensatory primary results in the country with higher debt level through taxes that would negatively affect the inflow of capitals, making the implementation of a monetary union more difficult (Giabiagi, 2003. pp 48, 50 and 51).

108. Carrera, Jorge, Levy Yeyati, Eduard and Sturzenegger, Federico. 2000. Capítulo 2. Las perspectivas de la coordinación macroeconómica en el Mercosur. In *Coordinación de políticas macroeconómicas en el Mercosur*, edited by Jorge Carrera and Federico Sturzenegger, pp 61–99. FCE, BsAs.
109. Outliers Luxembourg and Ireland are disregarded as cases of financial parasitism. Based on WB data for 2016.
110. The CAP and structural funds constituted 86,000 million euros in the EU in 2006 while MERCOSUR structural funds made up only US$100 million in 2008. German net contribution to the EU budget made up 8,000 million euros or 0.39% of GDP in 2005 and Brazilian contribution to MERCOSUR constituted only US$60 million or 0.007% of GDP in 2008.
111. Arestis et al, 2003.
112. Licardo Ferrando, 2000.
113. Idem.
114. Idem.
115. Giabiagi, 2003.
116. Henning, 1998.
117. Out of the four possible stages: monetary autonomy, zone of monetary influence, monetary coordination, and monetary union (Carrera and Sturzenegger, 2000).
118. Fanelli, José María. 2001. Coordinación macroeconómica en el Mercosur. Marco analítico y hechos estilizados. In *Coordinación de políticas macroeconómicas en el Mercosur*, edited by José María Fanelli, pp 1–24. Siglo Veintiuno de Argentina Editores, BsAs.
119. For example, even though intra-regional trade liberalization strengthened the position of many Brazilian industries vis-à-vis their Argentinean counterparts causing damage to Argentina, the CET saved a number of Argentinean industries from extinction. Previously, these Argentinean industries did not withstand competition with extra-regional competitors in the highly open pre-MERCOSUR economy and were disappearing. See Garay Salamanca, Luis Jorge, Delvin, Robert and Taccone, Juan José (editors). 1999. *Impacto sectorial de la integración en el MERCOSUR*. Banco Interamericano de Desarrollo, Departamento de Integración y Programas Regionales, INTAL, BsAs.

CHAPTER 3

Structural Factors of Regional Integration

So far everywhere in the world regionalism has revealed itself most in the standardization of economic practices. Examples of many integration schemes are stalled at the stage of FTA formation despite growing levels of regional interdependence as a result of their operation. The case of MERCOSUR on the contrary illustrates that integration may sometimes proceed under conditions of decreasing interdependence. Clearly, the neofunctionalist account alone with its emphasis on economic interdependence and interests of economic groups is unable to explain all instances of development and stagnation of regionalism, and the examination of political factors at play in MERCOSUR is needed to substantially complement the understanding of this process.

Discussions of politics of regional integration deal with circumstances, actors, and aspects of decision-making invariably involved in integration in any societal domain: economics, culture, security, foreign policy, social sphere, and so on. Definitions of what constitutes politics vary. 'But whereas economic or economistic accounts lay primary emphasis on interests (of states, of private actors, of bureaucracies), political accounts are concerned with the relationship between three dimensions: power, interest and values.'[1] In his analysis of 'the politics of regional integration' Hurrell singles out four dimensions of politics: *interest groups*, *institutions*, *identity*, and *power and state interest*.[2] The focus of this chapter is more restrictive. As states are the major actors in integration, the discussion of politics of integration is centred primarily on the structural differences between MERCOSUR and the EU, which are asymmetries of size, power, and interest among their member states. These asymmetries provide the omnipresent context for decision-making across all integration dimensions. Consequently, intergovernmentalism, the approach emphasizing differences and similarities among the interacting countries, is used to explain difficulties of the MERCOSUR process.

Identity and values as aspects of politics are excluded from the analysis below. They are contingent on culture and discussed in Chapter 4 on cultural integration. Neither do interest groups receive a separate coverage. It is understood that the most influential interest groups in the integration process are those whose economic interests are at stake. Powerful groups define state interest in economic matters, which is further pursued by the governments. For the purposes of this chapter the consideration of economic interests of different states in relation to integration issues is sufficient for the understanding of difficulties of integration, without looking in detail at how this interest is formed at the domestic level in each country.

Lastly, as in the case of the economic analysis of the preceding chapter, the book distinguishes between political factors at work for integration in intra-regional context from those in external context. The discussion of regional economics in the preceding chapter was centred on the regional market and intra-regional economic topics, and it left extra-regional themes for Chapter 5 on geopolitics and geoeconomics. Likewise, this chapter focuses on political aspects of integration in relation to intra-regional matters, while Chapter 5 deals with geopolitical interests in relation to interaction with external actors. However, intra-regional contradictions and difficulties in formulating a common international position on extra-regional matters are the two constants characterizing any example of regionalism and affecting any regional order. Therefore, differences in foreign policy approaches are discussed in this chapter to the extent that they are relevant for the understanding of the difficulties in consolidating the regional system. Whereas Chapter 5 discusses the standing of MERCOSUR and the EU vis-à-vis the hegemonic system and their interaction with the system, this chapter is interested in the differences between the individual member states' approaches towards foreign policy, and it explains how these differences stem out from the variation in the size, power, and interest of the particular countries.

The chapter focuses on such structural characteristic of MERCOSUR as size asymmetry among the member states. This asymmetry has a lot to say about each state power, interest, and behaviour, and it has major effects on the strength of institutional and legal cohesion of the bloc and the degree of divergence among national foreign policies. The chapter demonstrates that MERCOSUR has far greater imbalances of size, power, and interest among its members than the EU, and that these imbalances restrict the development of regional institutions. The following variables are identified and discussed throughout the chapter: (a) the number of participant countries, (b) peculiarities of regional decision-making, (c) size asymmetries among the member states, (d) average size of the member states, (e) image of the regions' core countries, (f) the character of regional leadership, (g) the quality of the regional institutional system, and (h) principles of operation of the regional law.

3.1 Number of Member States and Challenges of Enlargement

The most visible structural difference between MERCOSUR and the EU is in the number of participant countries: 5 versus 28. This difference affects a significant variation in the principles of decision-making between the two blocs. While MERCOSUR's only decision-making mechanism is consensual agreement among the member governments, the EU makes decisions by simple majority, qualified majority, or consensus depending on the nature of the issue. Decisions by consensus are far more difficult to achieve among 28 actors. The goal of cooperation and enforcement of uniform regimes compels the EU to resort to majoritarian voting procedures. These procedures force undesired policies and generate disappointments due to the democratic deficit and the lack of transparency. Systematic disappointments can become a source of instability for the whole system. Undeniably, the small number of member states is a virtue of MERCOSUR. It allows members to use consensus in the adoption of decisions on common policy in every situation. As MERCOSUR countries may veto any proposal in any policy area, they are able to adjust a common policy to their individual interests in a better way.

The ability to take common decisions and formulate common policies is increasingly challenged by the unions' enlargements. Enlargements have been an important issue in the agenda of both blocs, particularly in the EU where they also caused significant institutional changes. After several successive waves of the EC/EU enlargements, several more countries (Turkey,

Serbia, Albania, Macedonia, and Montenegro) are aspiring to membership while MERCOSUR has admitted Venezuela and is on the way to incorporating Bolivia, following the completion of the ratification process by its member states.[3] MERCOSUR is also consolidating SAFTA with its seven associate members (Bolivia, Chile, Peru, Ecuador, Colombia, Suriname, and Guyana). To an extent, enlargements are indicators of success as they show that neighbouring countries feel that staying out of the two blocs and membership in alternative clubs are less attractive options.

However, enlargements destabilize existing intra-bloc relations and pose difficulties for policy formation and regional self-identification. Definitions of the EC/EU changed with every consecutive enlargement, and the perceptions of *Europeanness* continue to vary from a collection of a few wealthy states of the North–West to a vision of Europe including Turkey and Israel and stretching to as far as the Russian Pacific to include all whiter people of Eurasia. These changes and pluralism cause a lot of confusion about who friends, enemies, bosses, and younger brothers are and what holds them together. As the costs and benefits of the acquisition of new members are different for the existing members, the latter articulate varying positions on the issue. Similar to the Eastern enlargement in the EU that gave geopolitical advantages to Germany over France, the incorporation of Venezuela reduced the significance of Buenos Aires in favour of Brasília.

Expanding regional borders pose new political divisions and create the necessity to adjust the community policy and institutions towards new members, their neighbours, and new areas of cooperation. Enlargement promises to bring in countries that are less politically and economically stable. Incorporation of a poorer country and stabilizing participation in its economy and politics is a way to secure regional stability. However, this creates difficulties, and scepticism has often arisen from the fears that the acceptance of new members can hurt the development of relations among the existing members and frustrate further cooperation efforts.

As consequence of adding new countries with different capabilities, needs, and visions of themselves, the enlargements have been accompanied by a spread of flexibility mechanisms allowing or requesting certain countries to abstain from various cooperation policies, such as the monetary union and the Schengen Agreement. The Schengen Agreement excludes Britain and Ireland, and the EMU excludes Britain, Sweden, Denmark, and some Eastern European countries. Other regimes treat members in different ways: the CAP, and goods and labour markets disadvantage the poorer eastern accession sates in the EU. The regional authorities may characterize such optional or partial regimes as adaptation measures optimizing performance of the union, but they can also be perceived as discriminatory and undermining regional unity by those whom they disadvantage.

The EU's discriminatory regimes in which countries have different privileges, rights, and obligations are referred to as 'multispeed Europe.' The phenomenon is quite clearly linked to the union's operation in a diverse cultural setting where conflicts of interest are present among the countries with substantial socio-political and economic divisions. The EU is at a risk of being victimized by its unrestricted ambition to digest its own diversity and to enforce the political and economic will of the core countries on the large conglomerate of peripheral and semi-peripheral nations without being particularly sensitive to their needs and concerns.

MERCOSUR is bound for similar problems. The participation of Paraguay in the trilateral process among Argentina, Brazil, and Uruguay was inevitable for historic fairness, geographic integrity, and political solidarity with the nation facing serious political, social, and economic challenges.[4] Yet this inclusion brought in a much poorer country with a distinct non-white cultural profile. Incorporation of societies as different as Venezuela and Bolivia further dissolves the original Creole composition of the region. Thus Venezuela's membership in MERCOSUR makes it no longer possible to refer to MERCOSUR as a union of Southern Cone countries of which Venezuela is not. The Southern Cone is not simply a geographic term, as there are historical, demographic, geopolitical, and geocultural features that make this sub-region of Latin America distinct from other sub-regions of the continent.

MERCOSUR's fifth member Venezuela is distant from MERCOSUR's core production and population area. This distance and Venezuela's low commercial exchange with MERCOSUR (See Table 2.1.C) clearly indicate to political rather than economic reasons of the bloc's first enlargement. Even though Venezuela is a wealthy country by Latin American standards, its incorporation into MERCOSUR caused a great deal of disruption. Caracas is nearly three times closer to Miami than to Buenos Aires. Venezuela brought a peculiar ideology and perspective on the USA that divided MERCOSUR and resulted in the suspension of Paraguay whose Congress had been refusing to approve Venezuela's membership.[5] Besides, Venezuela entered MERCOSUR without previous adaptation to any of MERCOSUR's regimes. This set a bad example to the existing members about how to ignore MERCOSUR's rules in a situation when non-compliance had already been a huge problem. If MERCOSUR expands substantially by incorporating its associate members or through merging with UNASUR, it may require the necessity of deep structural changes, especially in terms of the supranationalization of political decision-making, as consensual agreements would be more difficult to achieve among ten or more governments.

3.2 Intra-Bloc Size, Power and Interest Asymmetries

In terms of institutional development MERCOSUR is a shallower process than the EU despite its more manageable number of participating governments. Evidently, the mere number of member states is not a decisive factor determining the quality of integration. Intergovernmentalist analyses of differences among the South American countries in relation to MERCOSUR reveal that motivation for integration in this union is weaker than in the EU. Intergovernmentalism approaches integration as a series of rational choices by national governments that reflect state interest and relative power. An agreed integration policy is a result of negotiations that comes from the aggregate of individual states' actions based on their preferences and power potential. States calculate the utility of all possible courses of action and choose the action maximizing their utility under given circumstances. Many intergovernmentalist accounts are about small states bargaining with large states, reconciling divergent interests stemming out from the size of the states and the exercise of different kinds of power by the states. Intergovernmentalism operates with the notions of interest and power, and integration propensity is contingent upon the presence of common interests within the system. As state power and interests often depend on the size of the state (in terms of market power and population numbers), this section compares the sizes of MERCOSUR and EU countries and discusses how intra-bloc size and power imbalances among the states reduce occurrences of mutual interest, and, therefore, of integration progress.

Both MERCOSUR and the EU are characterized by an uneven distribution of power among their members with Brazil and Germany standing out as dominant countries. The largest states of the blocs shape regional politics in a significant way as their goals and strategies often coincide.

However, there is a significant difference in the relative size of the two countries, which has important implications for regional cohesion. Power asymmetries in the American group are extremely sharp due to the absolute predominance of Brazil, which accounts for about three-quarters of total MERCOSUR-4 assets such territory, population, and GRP.[6] The imbalance of power in the EU is less pronounced as its regional hegemon Germany did not constitute more than one-third in either of the three assets even in the EU-15. The EC was launched as a project of equally sized France, West Germany, and Italy. All of them were seriously undermined by WW2 consequences to the extent that none could claim the leadership role. Similar economic capabilities and equal sizes gave them a greater scope for mutually acceptable concessions and compromises. Today the balance of power within the EU is uneven, but Britain, Italy, Spain, and Poland are able to counterbalance Germany and France.

Big power and size differentials among participant countries impede integration. Policy harmonization is difficult to achieve in a group where one country, Brazil, differs so much from the rest in terms of size and where smaller countries are very anxious about preserving their sovereignty. Even the incorporation of Venezuela has been unable to significantly alleviate the huge power imbalance in favour of Brazil. For a country like Brazil, whose size does not differ from the size of the region by far, it is very difficult to match the loss of national control over domestic policies with the gains of participation in regional decision-making. The existing literature offers numerous accounts illustrating this point.

For example, despite recognition of the high dependence of the MERCOSUR countries on Brazil, the Brazilian Ministry of Economy abandoned the practice of consultation and coordination at the MERCOSUR level and took a discreet decision to devalue the *real* in 1999, clearly prioritizing national economic interests over the interests of the MERCOSUR partners.[7] This action reflected the low priority of the MERCOSUR-related issues on the Brazilian political agenda in the moment of crisis. As the Brazilian economy recovered, a more considerate approach towards Buenos Aires was adopted. President Cardoso claimed that his country was a 'responsible hegemon' in relation to MERCOSUR and instituted the position of Extraordinary Ambassador for MERCOSUR Affairs. Yet the fact remained clear that from the national perspective, the interests of MERCOSUR associates for the Brazilian Ministry of Economy are marginal compared to the interests of the southern domestic elites.[8]

This view echoes the statement of Argentinean ambassador Roberto Lavagna: 'Brazil is mistaken in not differentiating between its partners and the rest of the world. Integration requires that we get used to the idea that there are three types of interests: national, of the integrating region and of the rest of the world. The interests of MERCOSUR have to be increasingly assimilated with the national interests.'[9] According to Brazilian political economist da Motta Veiga, MERCOSUR's medium- and long-term agenda is entirely dominated by Brazil. MERCOSUR became possible only because of the convergence of the interests of the Brazilian powerful import-competing industrial sectors with the objectives of regional integration.[10] The Brazilian industrial oligarchy supported MERCOSUR because their satisfaction with the potential growth of exports and the new opportunities of access to external markets exceeded their concerns about losing the domestic market to weaker competitors from Argentina and Uruguay.

Nevertheless, economic incentives for Brazil to prioritize the interests of the small countries are low as 'for a regional big power surrounded by small or very small states, the advantages of scale accruing from regionalism are marginal.'[11] In terms of market expansion, Brazilian businesses have a relatively weak motivation for expansion into MERCOSUR, as the MERCOSUR market is not much larger than their domestic market. For Brazilian economic actors, the capture of 80% of the Argentinean market is equivalent to expansion into just 20% of the domestic market without the necessity to deal with foreign regulatory obstacles and cultural adjustment of their products. Adaptation to the Uruguayan market is more costly. Saturation of 90% of the Uruguayan market is equivalent to the revenue from operation in just a 2% segment of the Brazilian market.[12]

Asymmetry of size impedes policy harmonization. Certainly, the opening of the huge Brazilian market for a country like Paraguay is not equivalent to the return service of Paraguay in offering Brazilian products the access to its much smaller market. Concurrently, reciprocal measures of investment liberalization are resulting in all profitable industries of the smaller countries being taken over by the Brazilian capital. Capital-scarce Paraguay is unable to use this policy to its advantage as it cannot compete with either Brazilian or third-country capital on the Brazilian market. As consequence, measures of financial market liberalization agreed upon in 1994 in the Protocol of Colonia are not implemented even a quarter of a century after it was signed (Subsection 2.1.4). Clearly, the size of the Brazilian market makes it easier for Brazil to negotiate extra-regional commercial agreements unilaterally than to seek the consensus among its MERCOSUR partners over a common commercial policy.

Many studies indicate that Brazil is primarily responsible for the preservation of the intergovernmental structure of MERCOSUR.[13] In reality, the lack of supranationality is not Brazil's, but the system's fault. Any attempts to introduce supranational decision-making in MERCOSUR would lead to a stalemate. Argentina, Paraguay, Uruguay, and Venezuela cannot agree on proportionate powers, as this will automatically assume uncontested dictatorship of Brazil. Understandably, Brazil cannot put up with the degree of discrimination of its size that would be acceptable to its partners:

> Probably the most important problem of consolidation of MERCOSUR has to deal with heterogeneity of power among its constituent parties and consequently with the disequilibrium that comes from it. Since foundation, MERCOSUR has seen two types of attitudes. From one side, Argentina, Paraguay and Uruguay tried to condition the process of decision-making in Brasília in relation to MERCOSUR, insisting that the logic 'one country – one vote' were observed in the design of supranational institutions. On the other hand, for understandable reasons Brazil is looking to secure intergovernmentalism, and supranationalism can only be taken seriously if it is proportional to the size of the country. For obvious reasons such supranationalism is not acceptable for the smaller countries.[14]

Disparities of economic and social indicators among the MERCOSUR members do not allow conditions under which policies adequate for Brazil were possible or advisable in smaller countries. Because of its size and more complex social problems Brazil cannot abandon sovereignty over its domestic policies. Its inclinations to preserve autonomy are derived not only from its relative size, but also from historic views of the necessity of autonomous development and consolidation of regional power. Such aspirations in Brazil are stronger than anywhere else in Europe, especially taking into consideration the historic tradition of inward-looking development. Thus Brazil displays stronger resistance to deepening integration and changing the quality of relations among the member states than does Germany. The Brazilian government has been particularly resistant to the ideas of political supranationality and the monetary union.

If large countries are generally less interested in regionalism, small countries, on the contrary, are more eager to accept integration and commercial liberalism. Relatively, they lose in integration, as their industries do not enjoy the advantage of scale in competition with large countries.[15] However, their costs of non-participation are even higher. They involve greater retardation and sharper divergence in productivity rates relative to large national industries that are exposed to the competition of each other. As the production potentials of small countries are limited, they are less self-sufficient and need to rely on imports more heavily. Integration is necessary to facilitate their exports and enhance production specialization in order to pay for imports. Universally, small countries have higher shares of trade in proportion to GDP, more open economies and governments that are more experienced in foreign trade. In addition, small countries are more committed to formal rules, institution-led methods of law-making, and strict legal order as they have less bargaining power for negotiations and re-negotiations. Because of their natural desire to reduce the discretion of large countries, they tend to be stronger supporters of supranationality. It is easier for them to reconcile with supranational authority as they have less political sovereignty anyway.

The behaviour of the Benelux countries and Uruguay illustrate small countries' greater interest in integration. The Benelux Union became a model of reference and inspiration for the designers of the EEC. Not only did the Benelux countries find themselves in the centre of European integration developments, but they also tried to accelerate this process. The first proposals of a common Western European market in industry repeatedly came from the Dutch government since the early 1950s. The Benelux became a common market in 1960, 26 years before the SEA with analogous provisions was adopted in the EC.

In MERCOSUR it was Uruguay that pioneered economic liberalization with Argentina and Brazil through the bilateral agreements of CAUCE (1974), PEC (1975), the Act of Colonia (1985), and the Act of Economic Cooperation Uruguay-Brazil (1986).[16] All these agreements preceded PICE (1986), the bilateral Argentinean-Brazilian initiative that resulted in the formation of MERCOSUR. In both Europe and MERCOSUR agreements involving small countries have been easier and faster to achieve compared to instances where large countries were involved. Negotiations on the EEC and PICE were slower than negotiations on the Benelux or bilateral Uruguayan-Argentinean and Uruguayan-Brazilian programmes. Both Paraguay and Uruguay joined the Treaty of Asunción almost without any preceding negotiation process.[17] This was very similar to the way small Eastern European countries rushed into the

STRUCTURAL FACTORS OF REGIONAL INTEGRATION 97

embrace of the EU. The large number of small countries in the EU and their bigger share in relation to the rest of the union is one of the key reasons for the dynamism of the European process.

Chapter 2 explains low interdependence in MERCOSUR by the large size of its members. In average, a MERCOSUR country is 16 times bigger in territory and 3.2 times in population than an EU member. The chapter indicates that if MERCOSUR were composed by separate Brazilian states and Argentinean provinces, its regional dynamic would be much stronger because MERCOSUR would be responsible for facilitating the regional exchange among the federated states and provinces, which in real life is happening domestically without the involvement of the regional institutions. Compared to Europe, the share and, correspondingly, the influence of small countries in MERCOSUR is negligible. The bloc's balance of power has reflected itself in common Argentinean-Brazilian decisions being imposed on Uruguay and Paraguay.[18] Size imbalances reduce the prospects of integration development in MERCOSUR, even though MERCOSUR has a smaller number of negotiators over a common policy relative to the EU.

Literature on the EU often emphasizes the positive significance of the cooperative French–German relationship and leadership for the development of European integration. The French–German commitments to mutual cooperation found reflection not only in the dual leadership in European integration, but also in the bilateral *Élysée Treaty* (1963) that institutionalized strong ties between the two countries. The relationship between Brazil and Argentina is fundamental to MERCOSUR not only because the two countries represent 87.6% of the region's economy (in MERCOSUR-4),[19] but also historically because the bloc was born out of bilateral PICE and the bilateral Treaty of Buenos Aires (1990). Parallels are often drawn to the necessity of appeasement of the two pairs of countries Germany/France and Brazil/Argentina as an essential consideration and condition for the formation of the two integration blocs in functionalist terms, even though Brazil and Argentina have never fought with each other unlike Germany and France. MERCOSUR observer concludes that 'The bilateral ties in both cases give strong impulse to integration. The evolution of the projects will depend to a large extent on the level of stability reached by these two axes of integration.'[20]

While stability in Brazilian–Argentinean relations is possible, parity between the two countries is unattainable in principle. Whereas in the EC France stopped being an equal partner of Germany only after the German reunification (in 1990), Brazilian leadership in MERCOSUR has never been doubted. Though the French sometimes talk about their fears of becoming 'a francophone province of a new Third Reich,'[21] the fears of 'Brazil-dependency' in Argentina are much stronger and more constraining of the cooperation between the two countries. Brazilian-Argentinean parity is unthinkable in a situation when the single Brazilian state of São Paulo exceeds Argentina in both population and economy.

There are fears in Argentina that a deeper MERCOSUR and the growth of Brazilian power will convert the country into a new Brazilian federal state. Such fears are even stronger in Uruguay and Paraguay. The power structure of MERCOSUR is similar to the power structures of NAFTA, the SACU, the CIS, and the SAARC with the presence of undisputed regional hegemonic leaders: the USA, South Africa, Russia, and India. Moreover, MERCOSUR represents a more extreme example of these groups in terms of the overwhelming power imbalance in favour of just one member state. The presence of the hegemonic leader reduces attractiveness and credibility of the bloc.

Not only is Brazil more hegemonic than Germany in terms of relative size, it is also poorer in relative terms as its income per capita is lower than in Argentina, Uruguay, and pre-crisis Venezuela. Brazil's acute social problems do not contribute to its favourable image as a leader. An important disadvantage of MERCOSUR over the EU is that MERCOSUR is a club of poorer countries. A club of the rich is easier to sustain because membership in such a club is more prestigious. No matter what the wrongs and evils of the EU are, many citizens in peripheral countries remain eager to associate themselves with this relatively prosperous entity, whereas a great deal of Argentineans, Uruguayans, Paraguayans, and Venezuelans perceive Western Europe and North America more favourably than Brazil.

Importantly, wealth allows the EU to allocate greater resources for the promotion of its positive image and supporting peripheral countries and regions through the Regional Cohesion Programme. Even though structural cohesion funds are quantitatively unimportant to stimulate development, they proved sufficient for good publicity and bribes to politicians from the peripheral countries. However, financial transfers are not simply aid to poorer members. They are a compensation mechanism of redistribution of the unequal gains of integration, because integration undermines the periphery to the benefit of more competitive operators from the core areas. Less developed countries need to be supplied with a safety net in order to expand their social capital to ensure against possible disruptions of the whole system.

MERCOSUR started the implementation of financial transfers in 2004 under the scheme called *El Fondo para la Convergencia Estructural.* However, these funds are miniscule even in comparison with the symbolic EU funds. Brazil is the main beneficiary of integration, but it is sensitive to the costs of leadership given great discrepancies in its social and regional development. The burdens to sustain MERCOSUR in luxury and style may subject Brazil to excessive demands, as the choice confronting Brazil between sponsoring MERCOSUR and fighting poverty is not theoretical.[22] The mobilization of resources necessary for the construction of the region is more difficult for MERCOSUR than for the richer Western European economies.

As a consequence of poverty and underdevelopment, over the 1990s Brazil was significantly constrained by US hegemony and had fewer opportunities to exert unilateral leadership in MERCOSUR through coercive actions the way the leading European countries did in the EU. Brazilian leadership in MERCOSUR has been possible through the more rational and equitable administration of the system and suggestions of measures of general interest to all members. Although structural funds were not implemented in MERCOSUR at that time, Brazil made concessions to the smaller states. It reconciled itself to the fact that its trade surpluses in pre-MERCOSUR trade with Argentina turned into systematic deficits because of recessions and shocks in Argentina.

Both Brazil and Argentina agreed to lengthier adaptation to the common market for a long list of Uruguayan and Paraguayan products. The phase for transition to the FTA for Uruguay and Paraguay (until 2006) lasted five years longer than for Brazil and Argentina (until 2001). At present, Brazil unilaterally gives concessions to Uruguay and Paraguay in rules of origin. This is different from the EU where Eastern European governments rushed to accept conditions that heavily discriminated against their workers, products, and capital in a situation when their less competitive economies actually needed privileged regimes for their gradual adaptation to the single market. Such unwise conduct of the new member states was possible only because the EU enjoyed elevated levels of popularity among their populations. Never in history has MERCOSUR caused similar enthusiasm among the general public of its members and neighbouring countries.

3.3 FOREIGN POLICY DIVERGENCE

Membership in MERCOSUR and the EU embraces countries different not only in size, geography, wealth, integration performance, and integration history, but also in economic ideology and geopolitics. These varying characteristics account for disunity of political views and policies and different perceptions of what constitutes national interest. The difference in the relative size of the member states alone explains significant divergences in individual commercial and foreign policy agendas and therefore the behaviour of the states. The mere figures of intra-regional exports alone (2% for Venezuela, 12% for Brazil, 28% for Argentina, 32% for Uruguay, and 50% for Paraguay in 2012, Table 2.1.C) explain national governments' varying incentives to constrain national policy discretion and the variation in interests and approaches towards MERCOSUR and third countries. The figures clearly indicate the greater commercial importance of MERCOSUR for Argentina and the small countries.

Acknowledgment of the MERCOSUR members' different expectations from integration is essential for the understanding of the existing difficulties in the bloc. Brazil's low level of commercial dependence on the region combined with the long-standing tradition of policy independence is a major factor behind Brazil's reluctance to 'deepen' integration. As a big country with complex foreign policy objectives, Brazil has exploited MERCOSUR for strategic non-commercial purposes to consolidate its role as a regional and international power. Expansion of Brazil's international influence is the primary theme that preoccupies the minds in the Brazilian Ministry of Foreign Affairs. Whereas the size of Brazil compels the country to the affirmation of its regional power status, Argentina, constrained by size, has to search for multiple suitable alliances to consolidate its international position and the one in relation to Brazil. Throughout the 1990s Buenos Aires wanted to maximize its political utility through a strategic partnership with the USA and approached MERCOSUR exclusively as a conveniently located export market. Modernization and reliance on the market exceeding one's own by several times were the main considerations for integration with Brazil.[23]

Geopolitical differences in MERCOSUR are immense: while Brazil has borders with all the countries in South America except Ecuador and Chile, Argentina only borders the countries of the Cone. While Argentinean policy-makers thought they were in a world order dominated by the triumph of the western alliance and global capitalism whose consequences were the disappearance of East–West axes, ideas about globalization aggravating the North–South conflict dominated in Brazil. Argentina valued the neoliberal ideology whereas Brazil was more responsive to dependency theories.[24] Even though MERCOSUR became a policy of the state, the strategic choice of Argentina in the 1990s was not integration in MERCOSUR but rapprochement with the USA and NATO.

Whereas Brazil preferred autonomy in foreign affairs and resisted Washington's attempts to expand US leadership prerogatives in Latin America, Argentina's special partnership with NATO sought to emphasize Argentina's commitment to US regional and international initiatives. Brazil avoided NATO and unwanted US influence and military presence in the region; Argentina offered its territory for the allocation of a US military base. For Argentina, participation in MERCOSUR and the FTAA were complementary processes while for Brazil, the FTAA and NAFTA undermined MERCOSUR, and hemispheric negotiations were possible only after the consolidation of SAFTA. While Argentina was negotiating a special partnership with NATO, Brazil was trying to advance its candidacy for a permanent seat in the UNSC. Both parties were displeased by each other's initiatives. Brazilian officials considered the USA–Argentinean accord an undesired motive for the US military presence in the region while Argentineans were against the Brazilian candidacy to the UNSC, expressing a preference for a rotating seat among Latin American nations. In the Brazilian view, the USA intended to weaken MERCOSUR through USA–Argentinean relations, but Argentineans felt uneasy with Brazil's growing relative power and believed that an Argentina–Brazil–USA triangle balanced power distribution in the Americas.[25]

Many Argentineans believed that Brazil's active participation on the international arena was useful for Argentina as long as common interests were pursued: Brazil could share its expanded power with Argentina in exchange for Argentinean support. Thus a Brazilian seat on the UNSC was an asset for MERCOSUR, and alignment with the USA was a wrong strategic option. Others feared dependence on Brazil and considered alignment with the USA necessary to counterbalance the expansion of the Brazilian economy. In both instances, relations with Brazil were viewed as an indispensable factor in domestic and external matters. Though differences to foreign policy approaches were less relevant for Brazil than for Argentina, both countries had to deal with each other's unilateral agenda. Argentina never easily yielded to Brazilian aspirations, but the inability to control Brazil through competition was somehow compensated by the ability to influence Brazil in cooperation.

The Argentinean erratic search for preferential agreements with the USA accentuated the weakness of the strategies for intra-regional cooperation. When the financial crisis hit Brazil in 1999, the Argentinean and Uruguayan governments did not think twice about demanding the demolition of the CET for the sake of the ability to conclude individual commercial agreements with third parties. Some observers believe that if in 1994, Argentina had been promised trade deals with the USA, it would have left MERCOSUR because of preoccupations about hyperinflation in Brazil and the fears of leftist Lula approaching the Brazilian presidency.[26] From 1999 to 2002, the prospects for Argentina to withdraw from MERCOSUR were particularly viable when the Argentinean government was insisting on downgrading MERCOSUR to an FTA for the sake of an ability to strike unilateral trade deals with the USA and the EU.

In 1999 the USA invited Argentina to cooperate with NATO. This gesture was not accidental as Washington was planning an intervention to Colombia that constituted 'a national security issue' in words of President Clinton. President Menem promised to send troops to Colombia to assist the US intervention and agreed to host a military base in Misiones. He offered a national border territory with Brazil for US forces to carry out military training. As the Argentinean constitution prohibited the establishment of foreign military bases in Argentina, he labelled the base a 'delegation.' The US flag near the Brazilian border irritated the Brazilian government and caused protests. President Cardoso considered Menem's application to NATO without consulting MERCOSUR partners 'savage' and publicly asked against whom Argentina was allying with the USA. Geraldo Cavagnari, director of the Centre for Strategic Studies at the University of Campinas, noticed that it was impossible to be a strategic ally of both the USA and Brazil at the same time.[27] Argentina's alignment policy with the USA undermined MERCOSUR, and Argentinean strivings for NATO and NAFTA membership reinforced Brazilian position against supranationality.[28] With Menem's government opposing Brazilian membership in the UNSC, Brazil perceived Argentinean government's deliberations about a common currency in MERCOSUR as pure demagogy.[29]

Concurrently, the MERCOSUR's precious deal regarding the CET was not successfully maintained and this questioned the mere idea of the customs union. While in Brazil there was a growing perception that the political benefits expected from MERCOSUR were not materializing (particularly the alignment of the smaller countries behind Brazil's international priorities), the rest of the region had the prevailing view that Brazil was reluctant to relinquish its unilateralism to provide constructive leadership to the region. Since foreign policy considerations played a key role in Brazil's engagement in MERCOSUR, the emergence of different views with Argentina over foreign policy priorities reduced Brazil's perception of gains to be derived from regional integration. With the expected trade-off between Argentina's greater access to the Brazilian market and its alignment with Brazilian views on foreign policy failing to materialize, Brazilian policy-makers found few reasons to reduce policy discretion or abide by collective disciplines.

EU politics are generally more complicated than those of MERCOSUR because the EU is a more complex entity. 'The "European perspective" on just about anything resembles a colourful Scottish tartan with lines of various hues criss-crossing and intersecting.'[30] In essence though, similar mechanisms dominate the paradigms of relations between Brazil and smaller countries in MERCOSUR, and of Germany and France with the rest of the EU. Like Argentina, Britain and smaller EU members tend to side with the USA and support Washington's vision of transatlantic relations. Germany and France are trying to enforce their order on the smaller members and to subordinate the union to the needs of their own national economies and foreign policy goals. In contending the more independent Franco–German alliance, the smaller countries are constantly trying to reduce their dependence on France and Germany and to reduce the collective Franco–German influence on the union's politics. This is why they are often subservient to the wishes of the US administration. Even though their multiple favours to Washington undermine regional cohesion, they are an effective means to make the union's core more sensitive towards the interests of the periphery.

In both cases the divergence in foreign policy orientation among the member states is damaging to the intra-union relations. The EU is experiencing a persistent dissonance caused by the 'English factor.' Britain has not been part to many important agreements and has often blackmailed the union with threats to withdraw in order to receive concessions. In 2016 it finally took the irreversible decision to leave the union. There were moments in MERCOSUR's history when Argentina was close to secession as well. However, without Britain, the EU may actually end up being better off while the withdrawal of Argentina would question the mere continuation of MERCOSUR's existence. In time when the EU has a relatively stable core of confident France and Germany, MERCOSUR is dependent on the dynamic of relationship between self-assured Brazil and Argentina, a typical medium-sized country whose great power ambitions are in conflict with low potency. Even though much has changed since the 1990s, and the two countries' views on economic development and policy towards the US now converge, Argentina continues to refuse to support the Brazilian claim to the UNSC permanent seat. Argentineans are still not sure if a stronger Brazil is good for them. That they are not ready to support Brazil in the key issue of its foreign policy is not adding stimulus to regional integration.

3.4 INSTITUTIONAL AND LEGAL ORDER

At first glance, MERCOSUR and the EU have parallel institutional systems. Their institutions correspond to each other in their major functions.[31] Thus, the supreme agenda-setting organs, the Council of the EU and the MERCOSUR Common Market Council, are comprised of representatives at the ministerial level (prime ministers in the EU and ministers of economy and international affairs in MERCOSUR). The Councils are responsible for the definition of the overall integration policy insuring the involvement of sufficient political mechanisms necessary for the implementation of the defined general course of integration. The MERCOSUR Common Market Group is the analogue of the European Comission. Both have executive control over common market affairs and are responsible for the implementation and supervision of community policies. The Commission and the Group observe compliance of the undertaken measures with the concluded agreements and the objectives set by the main treaties of the unions. They set work programmes, propose measures in the domain of the common market, and suggest proposals on policy coordination that are seen as beneficial for the unions as a whole and for the advance of integration. The two bodies administer the implementation of the principal agreements and their subsidiary acts, and negotiate with third countries, blocs, and international organizations on behalf of the unions by the authority granted by the respective Councils. The resolutions of the executive bodies are binding for the member states.

The two unions have judicial and legislative powers, but these are rudimentary in MERCOSUR. The PCA is a simplified version of the ECJ. It has consultative functions and the power to review the decisions of the MERCOSUR arbitration tribunals. The MERCOSUR Joint Parliamentary

Commission acted as a chain between the executive power of MERCOSUR and the national parliaments. Its functions were purely consultative as those of the European Parliament in the past, and limited to the formulation of proposals. Sixteen parliamentary members from the four countries were expected to offer suggestions to the Common Market Group and to accelerate the adoption of national legislation that was necessary for the implementation of the decisions of the Common Market Group and the Trade Commission. The Joint Parliamentary Commission has been replaced by the regional Parliament, but its functions and membership have not been defined.

Both unions possess institutional mechanisms of political cooperation. The EU has institutionalized the CFSP and MERCOSUR has developed a framework called *El MERCOSUR Político* in which full and associate members take part in political consultations with equal rights.[32] MERCOSUR and EU political institutions are fairly amorphous as they operate on a consultation basis and have a limited capacity for efficient decision-making and problem-solution. While the CFSP is a permanent mechanism, *El MERCOSUR Político* meets only on the occasion of general MERCOSUR meetings. MERCOSUR and the EU have also instituted consultation bodies that represent interests of business and social groups (the Economic and Social Committee and the Economic and Social Consultative Forum), and supporting structures (the MERCOSUR Secretariat and the General Secretariat of the EU Council of Ministers). The level of MERCOSUR bureaucratization is much lower: the Secretariat employs only about 50 people, and has no need to maintain a monstrous EU-like army of translators and interpreters.

The unions have chosen similar patterns for the location of their institutions. Their main headquarters are placed in the capitals of the smaller member states (Brussels and Montevideo) as a compromise among the bigger states and a symbolic recognition of the importance of the small countries. The organs for judiciary are set up in different capitals (Luxembourg and Asunción) to diminish pressures over the courts and tribunals exercised by the executive branch and lobbyists who settle around the executive powers. To finalize shaping MERCOSUR's institutional framework in the style of the European system the South American bloc needs to launch its operational Parliament and to establish a centralized Court and uniform legislation. If this happens, among the most important institutions only the European Central Bank will not find its match in the MERCOSUR institutional structure because MERCOSUR has not consolidated itself as a monetary union.

Even though the overall institutional structure of MERCOSUR is built upon the European model, MERCOSUR does not copy European institutions and procedures, and the institutions between the two blocs are far from being identical. The major difference is the lack of supranational competences among MERCOSUR's bodies. Western Europe's first regional institutions and the EU's immediate predecessors—the ECSC, EURATOM, and the EEC—were all given supranational authority from the moment of their foundation. In contrast, MERCOSUR has not created a supranational executive authority capable of producing binding decisions on the member states in 26 years since foundation. After 1991 its institutional functions and responsibilities were defined more precisely and new organs were created, but the major intergovernmental principle of decision-making through consensual agreement has not been altered.

One of the significant institutional differences has to do with the set up and the principles of operation of the regional executive branches. The European Commission's key functionaries, the commissioners, are appointed by member states. They represent their states, but are formally independent from their governments. Commissioners are instructed to work in community rather than national interests. Even though they are subject to strong pressures from home, they need to deal with such pressures trying not to jeopardize their status and not to undermine the work of the Commission as a common institution.

The MERCOSUR Common Market Group, on the contrary, is run by representatives of ministries of foreign affairs and economy and of central banks. The most important body of the Group, the Trade Commission (a technical body in charge of implementation of the commercial policy), is also comprised of functionaries reporting to the members of the Group who are their ministers or central bankers. Thus hierarchical relations between the MERCOSUR Common Market Council and the Common Market Group are in place of the dualism of the Council of the EU and the European Commission. The MERCOSUR Group is an executive appendix to the MERCOSUR Council. The intergovernmental nature of MERCOSUR restricts the ability of the Group to act as an impartial intermediary among the member states and reduces the Group's autonomy. In contrast to the European Commission, the Group does not have supranational prerogatives that place the common interest above interests of the member states even at the rhetorical level.

The dependence of MERCOSUR's executive authority on the respective governments makes it more difficult to pursue common interests vis-à-vis individual state interests. In contrast to the European Commission, the Group does not have a right for monopoly in starting initiatives at the community level, does not have the capacity to take non-compliant parties to court for dispute resolution, and is not granted absolute powers of a sole negotiator in international trade in goods. Its employees have a lower level of employment stability. In order to achieve a stronger institutional cohesion, MERCOSUR would have to grant certain supranational authority to the executive power and to make its functionaries less dependent on the ministries and presidents of the member states.[33] This could help the MERCOSUR Group to control the observance of reached agreements and norms derived from them more impartially, though not necessarily more efficiently.

Another factor testifying to the weaker institutional cohesion of MERCOSUR is the lack of an operational supranational parliament. The 1994 Protocol of Ouro Preto set up a joint parliamentary commission. In contrast to the European Parliament, the MERCOSUR Joint Parliamentary Commission did not exercise any control over the activities of the MERCOSUR Council and the Common Market Group.[34] It had purely consultative functions, but formally it was not consulted even once. In 2007 a protocol establishing PARLASUR, the MERCOSUR's parliament, was ratified.[35] Its earlier drafts suggested that PARLASUR would have control over MERCOSUR's budget and would have powers to appoint the Director of the MERCOSUR Technical Secretariat. However, the national authorities promptly removed these provisions, as they were clearly reluctant to give significant powers to the regional parliament and to lose their control over the integration process.

The Protocol on PARLASUR stated the goal to launch a fully operational parliament with deputies elected simultaneously by population of all member states since 2015. However, in 2014 the transition stage for PARLASUR was extended until 1 January 2021.[36] At first, PARLASUR continued with 18 members appointed by each country as was the case in the Joint Parliamentary Commission. However, the permanent ratio of deputies from each county became difficult to agree on. Proportional distribution of seats in PARLASUR was rejected from the very beginning, as this would have given exclusive decision-making powers to representatives from Brazil. 'Diluted proportionality'—a system combining a fixed number of seats with additional seats calculated from population numbers—still gave too many deputies to Brazil. Finally, a compromise on such a system was achieved internally in PARLASUR, but the Common Market Council refused to approve it.[37] As of 1 November 2017, the PARLASUR web-site listed 42 members from Argentina, 37 from Brazil, 18 from Venezuela, Paraguay, and Uruguay each.[38] That powers and composition of PARLASUR are taking long to agree on is a reflection of the dramatic structural imbalances among the member states discussed in Section 3.2.

It is not clear if PARLASUR is a necessary undertaking for MERCOSUR at all. The supporters of PARLASUR are under the impression that a regional parliament would secure democratic control and provide civil participation in union affairs. They believe that such a parliament could strengthen political and democratic aspects of integration and provide better coordination between the legislative and executive branches. However, imported from the EU, the debate on democratic deficit is not pertinent to MERCOSUR as its decisions are taken by representative authorities of the states.[39] The idea of a parliament in MERCOSUR is premature given the lack of an independent executive. Decisions in MERCOSUR are taken by the governments that are accountable to the national parliaments. In the EU, the Commission is not accountable to national parliaments. If there were no European Parliament, the Commission would not be subject to any external control.[40] There are also justifiable concerns that PARLASUR might become nothing more than an expensive cruise destination for politicians.

In contrast to the EU, MERCOSUR also lacks a single centralized judiciary to observe and enforce implementation of the union's norms such as the ECJ in Luxembourg. In 80% of cases EC law affects economic operators.[41] A common market can hardly become a reality if economic actors and citizens are not allowed to protect their interests obstructed by conflicting domestic laws. Thus individuals and economic actors have a right of appeal to the ECJ. The court has proven efficient in the protection of the rights affected by the operation of the single market. In a situation when enforcement sources are few and weak, complaints from individuals and economic actors are important. Decisions on such claims accelerated economic integration and insured its irreversibility. The role of the legal system was particularly important for integration when the EC political process was paralyzed in the 1960s and 1970s. 'Judicial activism' of the ECJ served as a catalyst to European integration. Without it, the integration efforts would not have been as profound and sustainable.[42] The original Treaty of Rome did not envisage individual claims to the ECJ and few people could have thought about the role of the Court's decisions on individual cases for the advancement and consolidation of integration before the process in the EC started to deal with such claims.

In MERCOSUR individual parties are allowed to submit claims to different arbitration bodies such as MERCOSUR Ad-hoc Arbitration Tribunals, or courts of the WTO, LAIA, or any other PTA in which the parties of the dispute participate. The decisions of all external courts are final and binding, and they need to be enforced by the respective member states. The 2002 Protocol of Olivos established a permanent judicial authority, the PCA, which was inaugurated in 2004. This Court may revise the decisions of the MERCOSUR Ad Hoc Arbitration Tribunals. However, if parties to a dispute decide to use arbitration courts outside MERCOSUR, the whole arbitration system of the union is by-passed. With the PCA's failure to become the absolute superior authority in MERCOSUR law, the MERCOSUR arbitration system lacks the centralization that is crucial for the performance in the legal sphere. Therefore, the PCA is just a compromise between the desire for a firmer legal system and forces resisting supranationality.[43]

As a result of this compromise, norms and laws generated by the whole system are not interpreted systematically and in a uniform way. This produces dissatisfaction among individuals and enterprises subjected to the MERCOSUR law. The original Treaty of Rome established the ECJ and prescribed a *preliminary judgment* mechanism according to which any court in the Community could consult Luxemburg about a Community norm or regulation that caused doubt. A PCA in Asunción with similar consulting functions was instituted 13 years after the goal of the common market was proclaimed in 1991. The early Treaty of Rome already distinguished between community norms from derived law (regulations that had direct applicability) and norms that required incorporation into the legislation of the member states. The Treaty of Asunción, on the contrary, was silent about regional law. The Treaty of Rome made direct effect the basic principle characterizing the EC law. This means that the EC law creates not only obligations for member states, but also rights for private parties that they can enforce against the member states. The 1994 Protocol of Ouro Preto failed to enforce the principle of direct effect in the MERCOSUR legal system in an unambiguous way.[44]

Because of the lack of tight norms, the legal system of MERCOSUR favours flexibility over legal security. There are complaints all the time that Brazil and Argentina engage into negotiations and re-negotiations instead of staying within the strict boundaries of the legal system. This reduces legal security and gives suspicions that assumed guarantees can be re-negotiated. Businessmen and investors working in the union are unlikely to operate their businesses in a small market if they have doubts about the integrity of the bloc. In a union where rules are imperfect and their enforcement is uncertain, a large market is preferable to a small market. Thus smaller countries have all the more reasons to be discontented.

Another disadvantage of MERCOSUR is that its common norms become effective only 30 days after every member state informs the Secretariat about the incorporation of the norm into its domestic system. Such a practice can cause lethargy and non-fulfilment of the common law. A number of MERCOSUR agreements from the early 1990s are still not in force because they have not been 'internalized' by the member states. In the EU all countries have adjusted their constitutions to the EC law and have eliminated contradictions between their domestic legislation and the community law. In MERCOSUR only Argentina and Paraguay have done so. Deepening and consolidating MERCOSUR would require a broad national consensus at the level of national parliaments of Brazil, Uruguay, and Venezuela to amend their national constitutions. This might become a very difficult task for domestic politics especially in Brazil.[45]

Clearly, the overall cohesion of the MERCOSUR judiciary lags behind that of the EU. The MERCOSUR countries do not rely on the common market system as heavily as the European countries do because the volumes of intra-MERCOSUR exchange are much lower and intra-zonal disputes are less frequent.

> Whereas the European Court has produced hundreds of rulings every year since its creation, the MERCOSUR dispute-settlement mechanism has been used 9 times in 14 years! There appears to be no official or social demand for an empowered court or for the judicialisation of regional procedures.[46]

> The Ouro Preto Protocol also established a general procedure to make claims before the Trade Commission aimed to speed up trade-related complaints raised either by member states or by private sector. Between 1995 and 1999 the mechanism was used 11 times, most frequently by Argentina (nine times as against two by Brazil).[47]

At one time MERCOSUR commercial disputes were solved through negotiations between national presidents, a situation impossible to imagine in the context of the EU. Given the lack of great importance of the regional order in MERCOSUR, the flaws of the MERCOSUR legal system do not appear critical. The need for a consolidated legal system and a centralized court is not compelling not only because of the low number of cases they would need to handle, but also because of the small number of MERCOSUR members, which also makes it easier to enforce the implementation of the MERCOSUR law and to monitor its application. With low levels of economic transactions within MERCOSUR, the MERCOSUR court could hardly play a role comparable to that of the ECJ in European integration.

Obviously, the EU has a more supranational and centralized set-up with stronger central entities such as the Commission, the Parliament, and formally impartial Court whose decisions are binding for private and corporate parties and for the governments. The lack of a supranational executive, of the operational parliament, and of the court is the feature that importantly distinguishes MERCOSUR institutional system from that of the EU. The institutions of MERCOSUR are less autonomous, less centralized, and less independent from national governments. They are entirely intergovernmental in character whereas EU institutions represent a mixture of supranational and intergovernmental elements. EU institutions have legal primacy over national authorities in certain areas, but MERCOSUR bodies are always subordinate to national sovereignty.

Both MERCOSUR and the EU appear to be concerned predominantly with economic matters, and their most prominent and powerful institutions operate in the economic sphere. The discussion in Chapter 2 suggested that scarce intra-bloc economic exchanges and low economic interdependence reduced the motivation for economic integration, and therefore limited the institutionalization of commercial relations. This is particularly evident in the case of the MERCOSUR arbitration system and underdeveloped judiciary. However, the younger age of the South American process and the much lower levels of interdependence among the MERCOSUR countries are not the only reasons of MERCOSUR's integration difficulties and limited institutionalization of the region. These limitations clearly relate also to the size and interest asymmetry among the member states. These asymmetries significantly reduce the scope of the common policy and make heavy institutions redundant.

The importance of a structural balance as of a factor of integration is not just a theoretical observation. It finds empirical backing in the comparison of MERCOSUR with CAN. As a bloc of equal-sized countries with a much weaker economic interdependence than that of MERCOSUR, CAN established a supranational parliament and a centralized court at a very early stage of its integration. In Europe as well, the Treaty of Rome provided for the supranational institutions at the birth of the EEC, but these are still lacking in the 26-year-old MERCOSUR.

3.5 Conclusion

The features of MERCOSUR's institutional system and of regional law suggest that MERCOSUR lags behind the EU in institutional and legal development. MERCOSUR's institutions are weak and lack competences in relation to their EU counterparts. This chapter attributed limited institutional development of MERCOSUR to the inherent structural characteristics of the region such as great size and interest asymmetry among the member states. Primarily because of the size asymmetry, the countries' interests and strategies in relation to integration vary substantially. The asymmetry reduces the scope of the common interest, causes divergence in policy choices, and prevents institutional development. All of these circumstances impede integration.

Another disadvantage of MERCOSUR relative to the EU is in being a club of poorer countries dependent on financial resources and political conditioning of rich countries. Even though Latin American governments are much more confident now than in the 1990s, perceptions of inferiority remain shared by significant numbers of individuals both inside and outside the region. The only structural advantage of MERCOSUR's integration is in the smaller number of members, which, with everything else being equal, would have made the implementation of common policies easier among the 5 countries than among 28. Table 3.1 summarizes the chapter's discussion of the two unions' properties that affect the strength of their consolidation in relation to each other.

Even though the EU process has advantages in most of the above criteria, the EU's deeper unity should not be taken for granted. The EU has a vast potential for corruption, a complicated non-transparent mechanism of decision-making, and dubious policies towards the periphery that have accumulated negative consequences for its economic development. The union's expansion through coercive means may be met with increasing resistance and growing nationalism causing not only disruption, but also ungovernablility, paralysis, delusion and disintegration of the whole system. At the same time, prior to the Venezuelan crisis, Brazilian, Argentinean, Venezuelan, and Uruguayan governments shared a consensus regarding social development priorities. Restoration of such consensus and converging foreign policy goals may contribute to the strengthening and deepening of MERCOSUR in the future.

Because of relatively rigid legal and institutional systems, many observers consider MERCOSUR institutions too weak to successfully perform their functions. They say that MERCOSUR needs stronger institutions if

Table 3.1 Political variables and their effect on regional consolidation

Criteria	The EU	MERCOSUR
1. The number of participant states	**Disadvantageous** The number of national delegations involved in decision-making is too big. It is difficult to come to a genuinely common decision among representatives of 28 governments	**Advantageous** It is easier to negotiate among 5 negotiators than among 28
2. Peculiarities of decision-making	**Arguably disadvantageous** **Majoritarian and consensual** Decision-making lacks transparency. Accumulated negative outcomes for specific countries may ultimately frustrate the whole system	**Arguably advantageous** **Consensual** Consensual decision-making allows a better adaptation of the integration policy for each country but is fraught with deadlocks preventing the conclusion of any decisions
3. Size asymmetries among the member states	**Advantageous** With four equally sized large members (Germany, France, Britain, Italy) and two somewhat smaller countries (Spain and Poland) size asymmetries in the EU are not as strongly pronounced as in MERCOSUR	**Disadvantageous** Power asymmetries are very sharp. As Brazil alone represents 71% of regional population and 69 % of economy, it is difficult to build a balanced system of inter-state relations in the bloc
4. The quality of the regional institutional system	**Arguably favourable** **Supranational and intergovernmental** Supranational institutions may be faster and more efficient in introducing integration measures and enforcing compliance with regional regimes. However, they are less sensitive to individual countries' needs. There are risks that they produce undesirable and unsustainable outcomes	**Arguably unfavourable** **Intergovernmental** Intergovernmental institutions are criticized for guarding sovereignty rather than advancing integration. However, they may safeguard against adoption of unsuitable and undesired policies and obligations by individual countries. Therefore, they may be beneficial for the stability of the regional system
5. Principles of operation of the regional law	**Favourable** **Superiority over national laws. Direct applicability** These principles ensure quick introduction of community norms and their uniform interpretation and application	**Unfavourable** Community law is understood as a system of norms generated by MERCOSUR. To become effective the norms must be fully incorporated into domestic legal systems. Therefore, the community law operating as a distinct body of law from domestic law does not exist. Community norms often take too long to 'internalize.' They may be interpreted in different ways in different countries, which feeds the potential of dissatisfaction and conflicts among the concerned parties

it wants a stronger integration dynamic; they argue that institutions in the EU played an important role in sustaining integration in difficult times when member governments were unwilling to do so; and they call for institutional reforms copying European procedures. Nevertheless, it is unlikely that EU-like institutions would be able to perform well in MERCOSUR. If supranational institutions had been created in MERCOSUR, they would have soon caused disappointment because of their inability to sustain adequate levels of performance. Given the great asymmetries in the size of the four countries, it was decided from the very beginning that the decision-making in MERCOSUR would be intergovernmental and based on consensus. The intergovernmental structure provides the best framework that is acceptable to everybody in the process. Consensus implies restriction of Brazil's ability to impose its unilateral decisions on the bloc through the powers of veto of the other members.

Thus a greater institutional integrity would not necessarily be a virtue for MERCOSUR. Flexibility and the lack of a heavy institutional structure might have helped MERCOSUR to survive the periods of Brazilian and Argentinean defaults in 1999 and 2002. On the contrary, tighter institutional connections among the countries may be responsible for severe systematic crises, as in 2000 when Austria refused to vote on issues requiring unanimity and paralyzed the work of the EU. The specific institutional arrangements in MERCOSUR and the EU have developed to serve the particular groups of countries in a given historic period and, therefore, are not transferable between the two regions. This does not mean that the MERCOSUR institutions should not develop and change in dealing with the bloc's problems and conflicts. The change may occur as functions of intergovernmentalism are further explored without the necessity of the supranationalization of the process.[48]

Notes

1. Hurrell, Andrew. 2001. The Politics of Regional Integration in MERCOSUR. In *Regional Integration in Latin America and the Caribbean: The Political Economy of Open Regionalism*, edited by Victor Bulmer-Thomas, pp 194–211. Institute of Latin American Studies, University of London, London. p 194.
2. Idem.
3. Protocolo de Adhesión del Estado Plurinacional de Bolivia al Mercosur, 17.7.2015.

4. The War of the Triple Alliance of Brazil, Argentina, and Uruguay against Paraguay between 1865 and 1870 killed up to 90% of the Paraguayan male population and up to 75% of the total population. As a result of the war, Paraguay lost up to half of its territory of that time. The war brought this formerly prosperous country into chronic poverty that has not been overcome.
5. Decision of the Presidents of Argentina, Brazil and Uruguay of 29 June 2012.
6. Brazil makes up 72% of the territory, 75% of the GRP, and 79% of the population in MERCOSUR-4, and 67% of the territory, 69% of the GRP, and 71% of the population in MERCOSUR-5. The figures are based on CIA data for 2017.
7. de Almeida Medeiros, Marcelo. 2000. A hegemonia brasileira no Mercosul: O efeito samba e suas conseqüências no processo institucional de integração. In *O Mercosul no limiar do século XXI*, edited by Marcos Costa Lima and Marcelo de Almeida Medeiros, pp 190–205. Cortez Editora, São Paulo. pp 200–201.
8. Idem, p 200.
9. Ambassador Roberto Lavagna as cited in Campbell, Jorge, Rozemberg, Ricardo, and Svarzman, Gustavo. 2000. O Mercosul na década de 1990: da abertura à globalização. In *Mercosul: entre a realidade e a utopia*, edited by Jorge Campbell, pp 99–180. Relume Dumará, Rio de Janeiro. p 166.
10. da Motta Veiga, Pedro. 2000. O Brasil no Mercosul: política e economia em um projeto de integração. In *Mercosul: entre a realidade e a utopia*, edited by Jorge Campbell, pp 237–294. Relume Dumará, Rio de Janeiro.
11. Pedersen, Thomas. 2002. Cooperative hegemony: power, ideas and institutions in regional integration. *Review of International Studies*, 28, pp 677–696.
12. Simonsen Associados. 1992. *MERCOSUL: O Desafio do Marketing de Integração*. McGraw-Hill, São Paulo.
13. de Almeida, Paulo Roberto. 2000. O futuro do Mercosul: os desafios da agenda interna e da liberalização hemisférica. In *O Mercosul no limiar do século XXI*, edited by Marcos Costa Lima and Marcelo de Almeida Medeiros, pp 17–26. Cortez Editora, São Paulo. p 23.
14. de Almeida Medeiros, 2000. p 202.
15. Behar, Jaime. 2000. *Cooperation and Competition in a Common Market: Studies on the Formation of MERCOSUR*. Physica-Verlag, Heidelberg.
16. Convenio de cooperación económica y Protocolo adicional, 20.8.1974; Protocolo de Expansão Comercial, 12.6.1975; Acta de Colonia, 19.5.1985; Ata de Cooperação Econômica Brasil-Uruguai, 13.8.1986. Because of chronic deficits in trade with Argentina, Brazil, and LAIA, the Uruguayan government hoped that CAUCE and PEC agreements with

Argentina and Brazil were a way to expand, diversify, and balance Uruguayan trade. Both agreements established lists of products (normally excluding agriculture) free from duties in Uruguay in the amount of 5% of their production in the preceding year in Argentina and Brazil. In their turn, Argentina and Brazil allowed the proportionate amount of Uruguayan exports in duty free. These measures coincided with the overall liberalisation of the Uruguayan economy and decreased Uruguayan deficit in trade with Brazil and Argentina. As the Uruguayan government expected to further improve the country's position in the system of regional exchange, it prepared additional agreements, the Act of Colonia and the Act of Economic Cooperation Uruguay-Brazil that deepened and widened the respective CAUCE and PEC. Even though the application of the Act of Colonia turned out difficult because of the ambiguities that allowed defensive measures by affected industrial sectors in Argentina, the new agreement with Brazil was beneficial. It emphasised the ability of Uruguay to export agricultural products free of duties and gave concessions to Brazil in the financial sector. It also gave equal rights to Brazilian and Uruguayan companies engaged in the Uruguayan infrastructure projects (Simonsen Associados, 1992. pp. 7–8).

17. de Sierra, Gerónimo. 2000. Uruguay: limitaciones y potencialidades de un pequeño país frente al Mercosur. In *O Mercosul no limiar do século XXI*, edited by Marcos Costa Lima and Marcelo de Almeida Medeiros, pp 206–224. Cortez Editora, São Paulo. p 214.
18. 'A small country is defined in MERCOSUR as a country that can say 'no' in some discussions, regarding very few things and only when the large countries listen to it. In small countries there are very few policy areas that are not conditioned on what the others do. Everything we do in macroeconomics is conditioned on what Argentina and Brazil do. This is why we enthusiastically support macroeconomic cooperation, exchanges of information, and discussions' (Vaz, Daniel [of the Central Bank of Uruguay]. 2000. Comentarios. In *Coordinación de políticas macroeconómicas en el Mercosur*, edited by Jorge Carrera and Federico Sturzenegger, pp 303–304. FCE, BsAs).
19. Based on CIA GDP data for 2016.
20. Gratius, Susanne. 1993. *El MERCOSUR y la Comunidad Europea: Una Guía para la Investigación*. Working Paper, Instituto de Relaciones Europeo-Latinoamericanas, Madrid. p 3.
21. Attali, Jacques. 1996. In *Latin America – European Union. Forum 1996. Europe and Latin America: Two Ways of Integration for the 21st Century*, pp 95–98. European Commission, Brussels. p 96.
22. Markwald, Ricardo Andrés. 2003. Mercosul: Beyond 2000. In *The European Union, Mercosul and the New World Order*, edited by Helio Jaguaribe and Álvaro de Vasconcelos, pp 62–91. Frank Cass, London.

23. Caputo, Dante Mario. 1992. *América Latina y las democracias pobres*. Ediciones del Quinto Centenario. Madrid.
24. Bernal-Meza, Raúl. 2000. Políticas exteriores comparadas de Argentina y Brasil hacia el Mercosur. In *O Mercosul no limiar do século XXI*, edited by Marcos Costa Lima and Marcelo de Almeida Medeiros, pp 42–52. Cortez Editora, São Paulo.
25. On Brazilian and Argentinean foreign policy in the 1990s see Hirst, Mônica. 1999. Mercosur's Complex Political Agenda. In *MERCOSUR: Regional Integration, World Markets*, edited by Riordan Roett, pp 35–47. Lynne Rienner, Boulder.
26. Luiz Inácio da Silva had participated in four presidential campaigns before he was elected president in 2002.
27. Moniz Bandeira, Luiz Alberto. 2003. Brasil, Argentina e Estados Unidos – Conflicto e Integração na América do Sul (Da Triple Aliança ao Mercosul 1870–2003). Editora Revan, Rio de Janeiro. p 541.
28. Guedes de Oliveira, Marcos Aurelio. 2005. Mercosur: Political Development and Comparative Issues with the European Union. Jean Monnet/Robert Schuman Paper Series, 5/19. p 246.
29. Ibidem.
30. Peterson, John. 2002. Europe, America and 11 September. *Irish Studies in International Affairs*, 13, pp 23–42. p 25.
31. MERCOSUR's institutions are discussed in: González-Oldekop, Florencia. 1997. *La Integración y Sus Instituciones: Los Casos de la Comunidad Europea y el MERCOSUR*. Ediciones Ciudad Argentina, BsAs. Bouzas, Roberto and Soltz, Hernán. 2001. Institutions and regional integration: The case of MERCOSUR. In *Regional Integration in Latin America and the Caribbean: The Political Economy of Open Regionalism*, edited by Victor Bulmer-Thomas, pp 95–118. Institute of Latin American Studies, University of London, London.
32. Mecanismo de Consulta y Concertación Política del MERCOSUR, Chile y Bolivia.
33. In 2003 MERCOSUR created the Commission of Permanent Representatives that is a permanent body of the Council of the Common Market. It is comprised of representatives from each state and presided by a distinguished politician. The body's general responsibility is to present the initiatives on integration to the Council, to conduct external negotiations, and to monitor the operation of the common market.
34. Pasquariello Mariano, Karina, Vigevani, Tullo, and Fernandes de Oliveira, Marcelo. 2000. Democracia e atores políticos no Mercosul. In *O Mercosul no limiar do século XXI*, edited by Marcos Costa Lima and Marcelo de Almeida Medeiros, pp 250–285. Cortez Editora, São Paulo. p 274.
35. Protocolo constitutivo del Parlamento del Mercosur, 9.12.2005.

36. Decisión 11/2014.
37. Gardini, Gian Luca. 2011. MERCOSUR: What You See Is Not (Always) What You Get. *European Law Journal*, 17:5, pp 683–700. p 694.
38. https://www.parlamentomercosur.org, 1.11.2017.
39. Dabène, Olivier. 2000 ¿Todavía tiene un proyecto el Mercosur? In *O Mercosul no limiar do século XXI*, edited by Marcos Costa Lima and Marcelo de Almeida Medeiros, pp 151–162. Editora Cortez, São Paulo. p 159.
40. Florêncio, Sérgio and Araújo, Ernesto. 1997. *MERCOSUR: proyecto, realidad y perspectivas*. Brasília.
41. Martínez Lage, Santiago. 1996. In *Latin America – European Union. Forum 1996. Europe and Latin America: Two Ways of Integration for the 21st Century*, pp 119–123. European Commission, Brussels. p 121.
42. Rozo, Carlos. 1997. Judicial activism and regional integration: Lessons from the European Court of Justice. *Integration and Trade*, 1:2, pp 27–45.
43. Other criticisms of the MERCOSUR legal system include the difficulty of access to the Asunción Court and Tribunals, the lack of transparency and high susceptibility to the influence of lobbying and other external influences. Arbitration is ineffective in terms of enforcement. It is also time-consuming and redundant in a number of cases. The procedure in the EU allows the non-complying parties to change their behaviour prior to the legal action, making the legal action unnecessary. According to González-Oldekop, because of this rule, only 6% of disputes go to the ECJ. The mere possibility of legal consequences prevents conflicts among states and non-state parties (González-Oldekop, 1997. pp 118–119 and 293).
44. Martínez Lage, 1996. p 120.
45. Bohomoletz de Abreu Dallari, Pedro. 1997. O MERCOSUL perante o sistema constitucional brasileiro. In *MERCOSUL: seus efeitos jurídicos, econômicos e políticos nos estados-membros*, edited by Maristela Basso, pp 102–116. Livraria do Advogado, Porto Alegre. Delpiazzo, Carlos E. 1999. El Derecho de la Integracíon frente a la Constitución Uruguaya. In *El Derecho de la Integración del MERCOSUR*, edited by Héctor Gros Espiell, pp 61–66. Universidad de Montevideo, Facultad de Derecho, Montevideo, 1999.
46. Malamud, Andrés. 2005. Mercosur Turns 15: Between Rising Rhetoric and Declining Achievement. *Cambridge Review of International Affairs*, 18:3, p 430.
47. Bouzas and Soltz, 2001. p 109.
48. Guedes de Oliveira, 2005. p 9.

CHAPTER 4

Cultural Diversity and Community-Building

Most approaches to regional integration share an emphasis on evolving economic and political interests as the driving force of integration. Political scientists and political economists address the structural and developmental character of integration blocs, theorize the internal and external dynamics, the 'invisible' hand of integration, and the 'prerequisites' and 'spillovers' that punctuate the stages of the process. They have also produced a debate on specific outcomes of the transfer of competences and powers from states to regional institutions. The emergence of permanent regional institutions capable of making decisions binding on member states is the focal theme of interest in EU studies: 'Anything less than this—increasing trade flows, encouraging contacts among elites, making it easier for persons to communicate or meet with each other across national borders, promoting symbols of common identity—may make it more likely that integration will occur, but none of them is "the real thing."'[1]

Therefore, many authors are sceptical about the study of culture in conjunction with regionalism:

> Some of the clusters of national states that share the most in terms of language, religion, culture and historical experience have been the least successful in creating and developing organizations for regional integration, e.g. the Middle East and North Africa, West and East Africa, Central and South America. Ironically, it has been Europe with its multiple languages,

firmly entrenched national cultures and dreadful experience with armed conflict that has proceeded the furthest [...]. If nothing else, the EU demonstrates that it has been possible 'to make Europe without Europeans.'[2]

Europe is divided by language and religion, but united by regionally similar social and economic conditions and institutions: Latin America is united merely by language and religion.[3]

Several scholars fail to appreciate the nature of the phenomenon [regional integration] by focusing on the adjective, regional, rather than the noun, integration. The former indicates scope, not substance. The conventional usage of the word Europe to refer to the EU tends to misdirect observers from politics toward geography, culture or identity: this is a mistake, especially when applied to 'regions' that are not organizations. For, as Latin America teaches us, 'natural' regions can be dysfunctional for regional integration.[4]

These authors overlook the abiding social character of integration and its preoccupation with the society. Politicians, on the contrary, at least at the rhetorical level, interpret the ultimate goals of integration as humanitarian and perceive regionalism as the project of people and for people:

The integration we are looking for is not limited to the elimination of tariffs and customs barriers, and is not about trade only. It is about integrating the spirit, peoples, cultures, opening social and political space for the process of communion among all of us to put forward together what we are, what we have, and what we can do. (MERCOSUR, Fernando Cardoso, 1996)[5]

We are uniting people, not forming coalitions of states. (the EU, Jean Monnet, 1952)[6]

This dimension of integration lends itself to a wide-ranging ethnographic analysis linking the study of regional organizations to a wider consideration of regional societies.[7] A number of reasons make the study of ethnocultural characteristics of regions an integral part of regionalism studies.

Integration is certainly stronger if it has both vertical and horizontal dimensions: the polity is conceived as a set of relations of citizens with the polity, and of relations among citizens themselves.[8] The participation in a polity is not just a civic project based on an abstraction of citizenship and the involvement with the respective institutions. It can be founded on ethnic elements such as common language, common culture, and particular historical memories shared by citizens.[9] The possibility of interactions among citizens assumes the necessity of linguistic homogeneity. Thus linguistic, or some kind of ethnic and cultural homogeneity is the only possible base for a community with horizontal relations.[10] Certainly, cultural affinities favour the positive image of neighbours and partners and generate a significant premium for the public support of integration.[11] Importantly, such support provides legitimacy for redistribution. Economic integration has distributional effects, and it produces winners and losers within and outside regional borders.[12] In the unions where different groups have a sense of community, the losers are less likely to hinder and sabotage the process and the winners may find themselves more eager to provide compensations.

Some political scientists prioritize culture over economics and believe that people's actions and interests depend on the meanings provided by their identities: 'The behaviour of states in international relations is not exclusively determined by relations of power: ideas and sentiments influence the decisions of international actors.'[13] Decision-makers are receptive to demands and ideas of dominant domestic groups and incorporate their values into the foreign policy that promotes integration. Whenever identities and interests are established as a stable set of rules, an institution is born. The institutionalization of an international process, such as signing a multilateral agreement, is possible only when new visions of oneself and the others are internalized by the collective national being.[14] Concurrently, the relationship between identity and power may be reverse when institutions and powerful groups shape discourse on identities. Regional polities need legitimacy, and greater legitimacy is provided by a consolidated regional society where most members feel that the polity somehow represents their interests. Therefore, greater societal consolidation is attempted through manipulations with mass consciousness and the promotion of elements of a regional identity.[15]

In Europe the construction of a multicultural regional identity is based on various national, sub-national, indigenous, and immigrant cultures. Limited progress, if any, is achieved in this enterprise, as EU societies are extremely heterogeneous historically, culturally, and socially. Social constructivists believe that existing social relations condition and constrain human agents' behaviour. As integration policies target standardization and homogenization, diversity poses resistance to the process. Therefore, multicultural regions integrate with greater difficulty than culturally homogeneous regions, at least in cultural spheres. Thus the central theme of the comparison of MERCOSUR with the EU in cultural domains is that of cultural homogeneity and heterogeneity, in which the two blocs are fairly different. The comparison of the regions along the criteria of cultural diversity offers useful projections on intra-union relations, past and currently undertaken policies, and further integration development. Therefore, Section 4.1 identifies key cultural variables relevant for integration and compares the degree of cultural homogeneity of MERCOSUR with that of the EU along the identified variables.

Cultural similarities alone cannot sustain integration, particularly in situations where no political meaning is attached to interactions among the groups or where such interactions are missing. This is why Section 4.2 looks into the history of the two regions and compares the dominant discourses that link history to imagined regional identities. These discourses serve well in identifying the particular elements of regional unity emphasized by politicians and intellectuals. Their juxtaposition highlights a greater civilizational unity of MERCOSUR and reveals the political essence of 'united' Europe, which is often disguised in cultural rhetoric. In addition, Section 4.3 offers a survey of intra-regional relations among the Southern Cone countries prior the Treaty of Asunción. Section 4.4 discusses linguistic policies implemented by MERCOSUR and the EU. The two cases of regional policies illustrate that as a linguistically more homogeneous entity MERCOSUR has a greater capacity for integration in cultural spheres than the EU. Section 4.5 lists specific areas of cultural work supported by MERCOSUR and compares them with the corresponding activities in the EU. In contrast to MERCOSUR, most cultural and educational work in the EU remains in the sphere of competence of member states, therefore MERCOSUR may outperform the EU in cultural integration.

4.1 Cultural Homogeneity and Heterogeneity

The ideas about a united Latin America are rooted in the pre-independence period. Discourses on regional unity have come from a vision and desire of a shared future based on the common language and colonial heritage. Latin American solidarity has always played an important role in both internal and external politics. However, all Hispanic countries of the region were mobilized only once, and for disintegration purposes, when they fought against their colonial empire Spain in independence wars. Apart from these wars, there have been no significant realistic projects or events making use of the continental cultural affinity. This affinity has served Latin American integration well only at the sub-regional level, of which MERCOSUR is an example.

In contrast to Latin America, historic discourses on the necessity of political unity in Europe have never centred on a language or common cultural heritage. Europeans defined themselves through opposition to enemies rather than through a search of kinship among themselves. The reasons beyond Pan-Europeanism are rooted in one of the three objectives: collective defence against external challengers like Ottomans, Soviet communists, or Islamic terrorists (since *the Treaty of Universal Peace* of 1518); prevention of never-ending intra-regional conflicts (since William Penn, *An Essay toward the present and future peace of Europe*, 1693); and the consolidation of domination over colonial empires (since Duc de Sully, *Grand Design*, 1638).[16] These projects assumed a certain commonality inherited from Western Christianity and usually excluded the involvement of Turks and Russians. They addressed Western Christianity as the only cultural factor able to mobilize intra-regional cooperation for political purposes. However, as a cohesive force for pan-Europeanism, Western Christianity lost its function after the Reformation's divisions between Catholicism and Protestantism and the subsequent secularization of the region.

In the contemporary period the cultural definition of Europe runs next to its institutional definition. The EU is more easily identified with the places where its treaties were signed or with the number of states before every enlargement.[17] The moral and behavioural norms of contemporary Europeans differ as they are shaped by different Catholic, Protestant, Orthodox, Jewish, and Muslim traditions. Neither do Europeans have a uniform linguistic identity. They use Germanic, Romance, Slavic, Ugric, Finnish, Baltic, Celtic, and other languages. Linguistic divisions expose Europeans to different literary, philosophic, and media discourses. These divisions cause numerous misunderstandings and problems of communication. Even EU institutions are often unable to provide adequate translations.[18] When they do offer good translations, many communicated concepts are still understood differently, so there is a need for compromises in meanings.

Multiethnicity and the complexity of the governing system cause many problems. Not only does the EU need to reconcile the incompatibilities of its kingdoms, archduchies, presidential, and parliamentarian republics; it is divided by the heritage of two different systems of socio-economic organization, capitalism, and socialism that produced different types of societies. East/West divisions are complemented by North/South divisions that set apart semi-peripheral Mediterranean countries from the wealthier core. The special character of two 'Northern' sub-regions, the

British Isles and the Nordic countries, has always been recognized, particularly in the foreign policy area. The incongruity of the 28 different cultural systems is noticed in attitudes regarding the role of money and state regulation, the divide between private and public spheres and the use of time and space. Twenty-eight EU member states cannot simply make one Europe.

MERCOSUR has important advantages over the European project. The foundations of the MERCOSUR societies are quite similar as they were inherited from their former colonial metropolises Spain and Portugal. These foundations are the two mutually intelligible languages Spanish and Portuguese (there are 24 official languages in the EU); the uniform legal tradition based on the Roman law (national legal systems in the EU are based on the English and Roman law); and Roman Catholicism, which has contributed to a more or less uniform understanding of morals. All MERCOSUR countries have similar administrative and government systems that are based on the model of a presidential republican state. MERCOSUR's linguistic affinities facilitate: intra-regional tourism; the administration of joint educational and artistic programmes; scientific and research cooperation; maintenance of archive, library, and mass media networks; and the interpenetration of products of cultural industries (radio, television, music, books, press, cinema and video). Even though existing studies do not say much about the effects of cultural affinity on MERCOSUR's political and economic integration, at least at the level of working relations among bureaucrats, they point to 'excellent' and warm inter-personal relations among negotiators that help them to solve conflicts.[19]

The relative cultural heterogeneity of the EU is effectively illustrated by the comparison of MERCOSUR with the Iberian Peninsula of the EU along linguistic, ethnic, racial, and religious criteria. Language, religion, ethnicity, and race are the most important notions affecting separatist and unification claims at all levels: national, sub-national, and supranational. Certainly, the chosen elements give a far from exhaustive picture of cultural multiplicity in the two regions. However, they represent significant divisions within the two regional communities. It is convenient to compare MERCOSUR-4 with Spain and Portugal for two reasons. On the one hand, Iberian culture was transplanted into the Americas and became the most important component in the formation of the Latin American civilization after the Americas underwent complete geocultural rearrangement in the colonial era. On the other hand, the two regions have similar proportions in ethno-cultural composition. Their population consists of five major ethno-linguistic or ethno-racial groups and is equally divided between the domains of Spanish and Portuguese (4:1 and 1:4). The two regions seem equally heterogeneous in terms of the mentioned criteria, but the Peninsula is just a small segment of the EU, which is a much more culturally heterogeneous entity.

Table 4.1 demonstrates that Spain and Brazil make up four-fifths of the regional population. The remaining fifth is formed by Portugal in 'Iberia' and by three Spanish-speaking countries in MERCOSUR. Even though Argentina, Paraguay, and Uruguay have strong perceptions of national identity, they share a common language in opposition to Brazilian Portuguese, and they originate from the same political entity of the Spanish Viceroyalty of the Río de la Plata. The two regions display identically reversed proportions of Spanish- and Portuguese-speakers. Additional linguistic divisions exist in both the regions. The Southern Cone countries possess a greater diversity of indigenous and immigrant languages. There are 195 indigenous languages in Brazil and 25 in Argentina. Yet, the Amerindian communities in MERCOSUR countries are tiny (nil in Uruguay, 0.17% of the Brazilian population, about 1% of the Argentinean population, and 2–3% of the Paraguayan population). The only well-established language in MERCOSUR other than Spanish and Portuguese is Guaraní. It is an important element of the Paraguayan identity.

Ethno-social divisions are marked by languages in racially homogeneous Spain and by race in monolinguistic Brazil. Added to linguistically and racially homogeneous national groups of Argentina, Paraguay, Uruguay, and Portugal, they produce five major population groups in each of the regions (Tables 4.1 and 4.2). Most people in the two regions identify themselves with Roman Catholicism. Similar levels of cultural heterogeneity are also reflected in the presence of social conflicts, even though their nature is different. Spain has regional conflicts accompanied by terrorism in the Basque Country. Brazil has social conflicts reflected in the violence of urban crime and landless peasants' movement. The latter occurs despite lower levels of rural population. The correlations of rural and urban population are included as life in urban communities differs much from the life of peasantry and farmers. Spain and Portugal have higher shares of rural population, which is a feature of more parochial societies.

It is sometimes argued that Europe is better consolidated than Latin America as a geocultural region because Western European wealth, technology, and communication allow a greater mobility of citizens and more frequent exposure to the lives of each other. However, poverty expressed

Table 4.1 Cultural diversity in MERCOSUR-4 and the Iberian sub-region of the EU

	Spain and Portugal	*Brazil, Argentina, Paraguay and Uruguay*
Ethno-national groups[a]	Spaniards (81.9%), the Portuguese (18.1%)	Brazilians (79.2%), Argentineans (16.9%), Paraguayans (2.6 %), Uruguayans (1.3%)
National languages[a]	Spanish (81.9 %), Portuguese (18.1%)	Portuguese (79.2%), Spanish (20.8%)
Major ethno-linguistic and ethno-racial groups[a]	Spanish-speakers (60.6%), the Portuguese (18.1%), Catalan-speakers (13.9%), Galicians (5.7%), Basques (1.6%)	Afro-Brazilians (40.1%), White Brazilians (37.8%), Argentineans (16.9%), Paraguayans (2.6%), Uruguayans (1.3%), others (1.3%)
Local languages[a]	Catalan (13.9%), Galician (5.7%), Basque (1.6%)	Guaraní (2.6%)
Nominal self-identification with the predominant religion[a]	Roman Catholicism: Spain (67.8%), Portugal (81%)	Roman Catholicism: Brazil (64.6%), Argentina (92%), Paraguay (89.6%), Uruguay (47.1%)
Conflicts	Regional conflicts in Spain	Social conflicts in Brazil
Urban population[b]	Spain (79.8%), Portugal (64%)	Brazil (85.9%), Argentina (91.9%), Paraguay (59.9%), Uruguay (95.5%)

[a]Based on CIA data for 2016; [b]Based on WB data for 2016

Table 4.2 Five ethno-social groups in MERCOSUR-4 and the Iberian Peninsula

Ethno-social group	National identity	Language	Racial type
'Iberia'			
1. Spanish-speakers	Spain	Spanish	White
2. the Portuguese	Portugal	Portuguese	White
3. Catalan-speakers	Spain or Catalonia	Catalan	White
4. Galicians	Spain	Spanish, Galician	White
5. Basques	Spain or Basque Country	Basque	White
MERCOSUR			
1. Afro-Brazilians	Brazil	Portuguese	Black and *mulatto*
2. White Brazilians	Brazil	Portuguese	White
3. Argentineans	Argentina	Spanish	Mostly white
4. Paraguayans	Paraguay	Spanish, Guaraní	Mostly *mestizo*
5. Uruguayans	Uruguay	Spanish	Mostly white

in subsistence farming or begging on the street homogenizes opportunities and life-styles of millions of people all over the world; therefore a higher GDP per capita is not a factor of integration. Other observers argue that Latin American collective identity is weaker than the European identity because Latin American civilization is much younger and because many Latin American countries (Colombia, Peru, Brazil, Mexico) lack sufficient internal consolidation. However, a number of European nations have acute integrity problems due to nationalism and separatism (Spain, Belgium, Britain, Romania). Other countries have territorial problems (Hungary, Cyprus). The historic maturity of Europe has not been able to secure it against the emergence and re-emergence of nations younger than any Latin American country. They appeared as a result of the processes that redrew European maps after WW1, WW2, the Cold War, and the Balkan crises in the 1910s, 1930s, 1940s, 1980s, 1990s and even the 2000s (Montenegro and Kosovo).

4.2 HISTORICAL PERSPECTIVES ON REGIONAL UNITY

Language, ethnicity, and religion are often emphasized as key components of a territorial identity. However, cultural affinities alone are unable to provide a sufficient base for cooperation without viable socio-economic and political underpinnings. On the contrary, culturally integrated societies sometimes break apart (Czechoslovakia, the Koreas, segments of the

USSR). In Serbia, Croatia, and Bosnia, which shared the same language, fragmentation was accompanied by bloodshed. Also, mistrust and competition characterized relations both between Brazil and Argentina and between Spain and Portugal over significant historic periods.[20] Neither do intensifying social interactions consolidate territorial integrity by default. In MERCOSUR, the construction of the Bridge of Friendship between Encarnación (Paraguay) and Posadas (Argentina) led to emergence of conflicts, which resulted in violent fights among local residents.[21] Thus cultural affinity and growing interdependence do not guarantee stability. Much depends on how they interact with political contexts. In order to identify the role of cultural factors in integration, it is important to look into how cultural diversity has operated on the soil of the two regions historically, as history is one of the most important aspects of people's culture and identity.

4.2.1 *Questioning* Europeanness

As textbooks frequently note, 'since the Middle Ages there has been virtually no period in which statesmen or philosophers did not point to the common European heritage and the necessity for more "political" unity in Europe.'[22] Visions of a united Europe have a long legacy and considerable ideological potency. Many attempts have been made throughout history to unify Europe, from Romans and Charlemagne's Holy Roman Empire, to Napoleon and Hitler's Third Reich. Yet far from uniting Europe, the result has been 'not unity but a fragmentation verging on near-total self-destruction.'[23] Europe is home to powerful concepts of the nation-state, nationalism, and sovereignty. The effect of the two opposed ideas of European unity and the nation state 'has been to set up lasting tension which the two "world" wars only partially dispelled.'[24]

Convention, however, suggests that history of the European civilization starts in about 900 BC in Crete. About 300 BC the Greek civilization primacy was superseded by Rome. Rome gave way to Byzantine around 300 AD. Another centre of high culture appears in Muslim Spain in about 900. Three other centres important to European political history, the Carolingian Empire (~800), the Danish Empire (~1000) and Kiev (~1000), are more amorphous states that do not survive long and do not leave evidence of high culture. In Eastern Europe the Golden Horde flourishes in about 1200. At that time Granada and Byzantine yield their political and cultural supremacy to Italy (~1300). Italy returns them to the

Iberian Peninsula and Bosphorus when the Spanish, Portuguese, and Ottoman Empires rise in about 1500. By 1700 the dynamic centres in Europe shift towards north-western Europe when the Low Countries emerge as the most influential centre. It is superseded by France (~1800), Britain (~1850), Germany (~1900), and the Soviet Union (~1970).[25] By no means does conventional European history make a history of a single civilization. It is a sequence of rivalries, conflicts, conquests, rises, and declines of territories with autonomous or semi-autonomous development. There are a number of problems associated with the conventional view of the European history and the concept of *Europeanness* that serve to legitimize the dominance of the EU. Several of them are outlined below.

(1) It is arbitrary that Greece and not any other preceding or subsequent civilization is chosen as the beginning of Europe. It is true that it was Greek seamen who introduced the word *Europe*, which they used to refer to the territory west of the Aegean Sea counterposing it to *Asia* in the east and *Africa* in the south. These terms received political configurations and were preserved only because Greek autonomy was challenged from the east, west, and south. Apart from this casual factor, there are no reasons to see Ancient Greece as the beginning of the European civilization as Greece had a relation to the preceding Mediterranean and Near Eastern civilizations in no way different from that of Rome and Byzantine to Ancient Greece.

(2) Between 900 BC and 1600 AD 'European' history is focused exclusively on the Mediterranean region, which today is peripheral to the notion of *Europeanness*. It was not before the seventeenth and eighteenth centuries that Europe became a system linking to the North-West. In this system Poland, Sweden, and Ottoman Turkey were vying for dominance only in the periphery of this order. Russia, a system outsider like Turkey, displaced Sweden and Poland and even transferred its capital to the western coast while pursuing a deliberate policy of 'Westernization.' 'Western Christendom' as the major basis of identification of Europe gave way to the secular concept of 'the civilized world' in 'the West.' German unification further sharpened the concentration of power in the west of Europe after Germany became the central economy essential for the support of European economies in the east, north, and west.

As for the EU Mediterranean region (Spain, Portugal, Greece, Southern Italy), its truly European character is often disputed. Paradoxically, it was particularly difficult for the ideologists of the Mediterranean enlargement to persuade themselves in the Western character of Greece, the 'cradle' of the European civilization, as it happened to have an Orthodox Christian profile, Ottoman history, 'authoritarian' habits, and swarthy population. Spain and Portugal were not identified as part of Western civilization before Spain joined NATO in 1982 (See Maps 4.1, 4.2 and 4.3). Informally, in northwestern Europe Spain was considered 'the beginning of Africa.' North Americans happened to classify Spain and Portugal together with Latin America as 'regressive' Iberian civilization different from Western civilization. For example, according to Russett, Argentina, Japan, and Papua New Guinea belong to the 'Western Community' while Spain and Portugal do not. In this system, the Western community is opposed to such breath-taking socio-cultural groupings as 'Brazzaville Africans,' 'Conservative Arabs,' 'Afro-Asians,' 'Semi-developed Latins,' and 'Communists' (See Maps 4.1 and 4.2).[26]

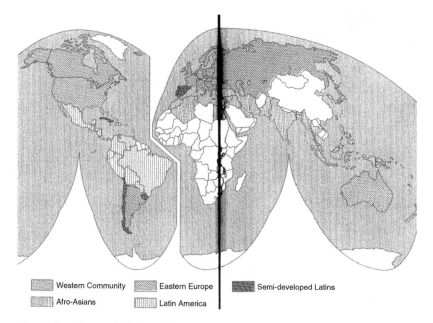

Map 4.1 The world before the Spanish accession to NATO.
Source: Russett, 1975, pp 26–27

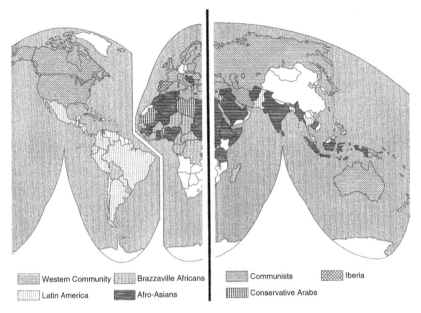

Map 4.2 The world before the Spanish accession to NATO.
Source: Russett, 1975, pp 72–73

(3) The concept of *Europeanness* claims to embrace Christianity as historico-cultural legacy. If Protestantism and Catholicism as descendants of Latin Christianity may coexist under a single umbrella with a few tensions, *Europeanness* hardly accommodates Eastern Christendom. Byzantine, Greece, the Balkans, and Russia are considered peripheral to European history even though Greek, Byzantine, and Russian cultural centres in certain periods of history by far exceeded anything existing in Western Europe at the same time. Throughout history, the Orthodox countries have been regularly invaded by Latinists, which compelled their alliances with the Muslim neighbours against the aggressors from the West. Russian and Greek elites had a conscious preference to subdue to the Mongol and Ottoman rule rather than to seek the cooperation of Latin Christians against the eastern powers. Muslims and the Orthodox are bearers of civilizations different in many ways from the West. They are shaped by Greco-Roman and ancient Near Eastern elements and share a lot in common despite certain doctrinal differences.

132 M. MUKHAMETDINOV

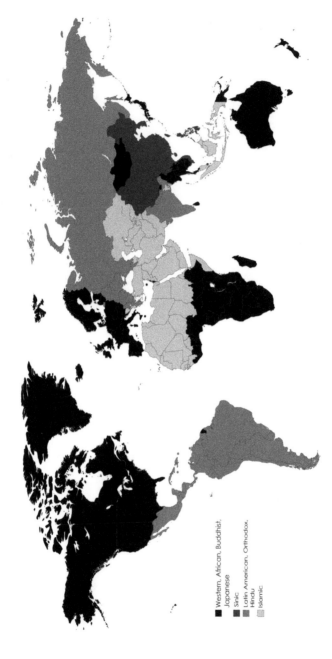

Map 4.3 The world after the fall of communism.
Source: Based on Huntington, 1997, pp 26–27

(4) Convention fully excludes Islamic history and civilization as part of European heritage. Muslim Spain, Islamic Steppe culture of ancient Ukraine, Golden Horde, and the Ottoman Empire are considered non-European, despite the undeniable fact that they existed for many centuries on the soil that is conventionally defined as Europe. This exclusion reflects a religious prejudice of very long standing, which identified everything admirable with Christianity and abhorred Islam as infidelity and persistently denigrated it. Yet the contribution of Islamic civilizations to the formation of subsequent cultures in Europe is not insignificant. Islam gave a strong impetus to the development of European science. Muslim Spain achieved the highest level of prosperity, civilization, and religious tolerance. Its level of development was rivalled or exceeded only by that of Byzantine, Cairo, Baghdad, and Damascus of that time.
European historiography usually dismisses Mongols as crude barbarians. However, before they appeared in Europe, they borrowed a good deal from their civilized Chinese and Muslim neighbours in their administrative, tax, and military systems. The Ottoman Empire was accepted as a member of the European system only when it was thought useful to contain Austria and Russia. Typically, it was treated as 'the sick man of Europe' to be amputated from its European possessions. A civilizational superiority that allowed Mongols and Ottomans to sustain their huge empires is seldom acknowledged in the West. Only recently did the awareness of EU interests in the Persian Gulf and the desire to have a finger in the Middle East provoke debates about Turkey's 'merits' to join the EU.
(5) Central Europe (Poland, Czech Republic, Slovakia, and Hungary) is a predominantly Catholic but non-Germanic region. It has a history of domination by Germans, Austrians, and Russians. Together with ex-Yugoslavia, Bulgaria, and Romania these countries are not fully accepted as European nations because of the Cold War legacy. Respected culturologists in the West seriously discuss such criteria of *non-Europeanness* as the number of years spent under Leninist regimes: the more years spent under the communist rule–the less of a European character the country has.[27] Upon accession to the EU, former Soviet bloc countries were 'upgraded' from *Eastern Europe* to *Central Europe*, which shifted the epithet *Eastern* to the former Soviet republics of Ukraine, Byelorussia, and Moldavia. There is no doubt that in a few years Central Europeans will refer

to themselves as *the West*, passing *Central Europe* to Ukraine and Moldova and leaving the attributive *Eastern* with all its negative connotations exclusively for Russia. Some observers have reservations regarding the true 'European' character of the new EU entrants, as they believe that the invisible East/West division is rooted in times going far beyond the communist divide:

> The imagery of the Cold War was of Europe divided into two halves: 'their' Europe and 'ours', held in stable tension by the balance between the two alliances. In reality the political, economic, and demographic balance of Europe has been titled towards a western core region – stretching from south-eastern England through the Low Countries and the Rhine valley, and on through Burgundy and southern Germany into Northern Italy – for the past 1,000 years. 19th- and early 20th-century Eastern and South-Eastern Europe differed sharply from the industrialising states to the west, which were successfully imposing common languages and national identities on their populations. To the east of Berlin and Vienna lay peasant societies speaking a profusion of languages and dialects under imperial rule, with German the prevailing language of towns and commerce. Optimists among the elites of those countries emerging from socialist rule were speaking in 1989–90 of 're-joining the West': implying that their states had been comparable to those of Western Europe in political and economic development before they were subordinated to Soviet rule. Hungary, Poland, the Baltic states had been part of Western Christendom, but they had only experienced the edges of the 'Great Transformation' which swept across their Western neighbours before they were overtaken by war and subjugated by Soviet control.[28]

There are analysts who deny any cultural premises to the EU:

> What individual nation-states of Europe hold in common is the existence of symbols, rituals, collective representations and political myths.[29]

> The wealth, the trading power, and the yet untapped potential of the Commission are essentially what make the whole thing work. For all their differences the countries are united in one over-riding ambition: that the rich though they are, there is plenty of opportunity for growing richer still. This is sometimes known as the European ideal.[30]

The contemporary European project has neither historical precedent nor cultural premises. Europe cannot be defined in religious or linguocultural terms (Christian, Jewish, Muslim; Romance, Germanic, Slavic). In the list of historical influences that form 'the unique European civilization' one can usually find Greek philosophy, Roman law, Christianity, the Enlightenment, the Scientific Revolution, the triumph of Reason, imperialism, technological progress, tolerance, *savoir-vivre*, individualism, liberal economics, parliamentary democracy, and human rights.[31] This conception of history is uncritically selective and chauvinistic.[32] What makes this list exclusively European and applicable to whole of Europe is rarely addressed. It perpetuates the myths of imperial elite formation and turns the history of Europe into 'a genealogy of progress'[33] or the 'Plato to NATO'[34] conception of the European civilization.

Membership in the EU and NATO has become the decisive criterion for passing a nation as a part of the European civilization. Non-members like Belarus or Serbia are 'definitely' non-European in sprit. Yet this criterion is political and it characterizes the EU as a power rather than civilizational project. Definitions of *Europeanness* through notions other than the EU and NATO are unable to produce any tangible cultural or historic references that would not be at odds with historical facts or common sense. For example, Laitin asserts that the common cultural base of Europe is based on the fact that most Europeans speak one, two, or three languages (regional, national, and English). He calls this '*2±1 cultural configuration*' or '*2±1 language configuration.*' It is not clear what makes this 'configuration' European as it can easily suit any other continent.[35] The only uncontested definition of Europe that is not disappointing to anyone is in terms of physical geography: the Western part of Eurasia separated from Asia by the Ural Mountains, the Ural River, Caspian Sea, the Caucasus, Black Sea, the Bosphorus, the Sea of Marmara, and the Aegean Sea. However, even this definition is arbitrary. It can function without disappointments only when it is not prescribed any cultural or political meaning. For example, Georgia may take offence if it is classified as an Asian country, which it is.

Nevertheless the EU often evokes culture 'as a rhetorical blanket, a repository of European distinctions, a colourful decoration, hiding some purist and essentialist assumptions about the nature of European culture and idealistic notions that culture is some sort of an absolute good. And yet, all international turbulences have confirmed culture as a field of tensions and conflict, a realm of rivalry, heterogeneity more than harmony, hegemony more than equality, monopolistic pressures more than diversity.'[36] As the definitions of cultural Europe are dominated by the discourses produced with the top-down elitist approach by bureaucrats and marketing professionals in north-western Europe, they inevitably contradict the experiences of ordinary citizens and the region's periphery. Tensions occur among the implied first-, second-, or third-rate European nations that respond to the propagandistic criteria in different ways. Attitudes in the wealthy core display prejudices against huge populations with a socialist past, with Muslim or Orthodox heritage or speaking in Slavic languages.

The deep historical and cultural divisions among EU members represent one of the most serious problems of the EU legitimacy. Due to the lack of tangible cultural criteria the EU's cultural management offers pseudo-cultural definition of Europe through excellence and benevolence. As a result, 'European culture' is equated with 'Western Civilization' as opposed to 'African barbarism' or 'Oriental despotism.' This type of identity is largely negative as it is defined against non-European competitors and third-country aliens. Praising an exclusive European character and virtue pays lip service to Europe. The implied superiority of European culture (Christian civilization or 'White Continentalism'[37]) and the great patrimony of European ideas exacerbate tensions between EU insiders and outsiders. Despite the turbulence in transatlantic political relations and outcries against an intrusive 'Hollywood culture' from Europe, a large part of the Oriental and Black anti-Western rhetoric rejects with resentment and anger the entire Western culture as immoral, making no distinction between the USA and the EU.[38]

The concept of 'the West' as well was invented purely for political reasons. The discourse of a 'Western civilization' was launched with the purpose to improve the image of post-WW2 Germany, and to justify the Marshall Plan's spending on West Germany and its integration into the Euro-Atlantic institutional mainstream of NATO.[39] Even though the West is even more difficult to define in cultural terms than Europe, attempts to do so occur from time to time: 'The various countries lumped together under the rubric of "the West" conventionally celebrate certain features that differentiate them from the rest of the world: democracy, rational government, scientific and technological inventiveness, individualism, and certain ethical and cultural commitments.'[40]

The concepts of 'the West' and of 'the rest' are further defined and redefined depending on changing circumstances. Inspired by the earlier work of Russett, Huntington offers his own map of world civilizations making adjustments for the time factor (Map 4.3). Like Russett, he keeps Papua New Guinea in the domain of the 'Western civilization,' but he extends the West to encompass more recent NATO adherents: 'semi-developed Latins' from Spain and Portugal and Eastern European countries.[41] 'Communists' with their culture are now defeated and their lands become 'Orthodox.'

Increased attention to Middle Eastern oil causes the emergence of the 'Islamic civilization' out from Russett's broader category 'Afro-Asians.' Notably, growing concerns about the rise of Chinese power upgrade China to a 'Sinic civilization' from the unclassified status in the earlier Russett's work. All in all, Huntington divides the world into nine geocultural areas and attributes international conflicts to cultural misunderstandings rather than to the strivings for domination and the competition for resources.

The ideas of Japanese Ambassador Yoshiji Nogami illustrate the transient and phantasmagorical nature of the concept of the 'Western civilization' better than anything else. In one of his speeches Nogami characterized Japan as a 'truly Western' society, which shared the values and ideals of the West. Even though Japan was not a formal member of the EU, it belonged to the EU 'emotionally and spiritually.' In answer to the question why Japan was obstructing Russian participation in Asia-Pacific cooperation fora, Nogami replied that Russia was a Western power, which simply extended itself to Asian soil without a sense of belonging there. In contrast to Japan, 'Muscovites' hearts' were not in Asia, and therefore Asia-Pacific was not their business.[42] Asia-Pacific was indeed Japan's business despite the 'truly Western character' of the Japanese society.

A number of observers believe that not only does cultural diversity in Europe represent a significant obstacle to integration and undermines the political project, but that it makes the EU a meaningless enterprise. According to them the EU has a haphazard historical character and operates through fragmented and partial arrangements. It pursues fairly bad policies as their evaluation is based only on market results, which separate people instead of uniting them:

> The European Communities were steps to a federation that might have to operate indefinitely in intermediate zones. It was federal minimalism confined to certain economic areas. The creators of the Community were surprisingly ignorant of, and indifferent to, historical precedent. The system corresponds to no previous constitutional form.[43]

> The history of the formation of an 'ever-closer union' has followed a consistent pattern: the real or apparent logic of mutual economic advantage not sufficing to account for the complexity of its formal arrangements, there has been invoked a sort of ontological ethic of political community; projected backward, the latter is then adduced to account for the gains made thus far and to justify further unificatory efforts. It is hard to resist recalling George Santayana's definition of fanaticism: redoubling your efforts when you have forgotten your aims.[44]

Indeed, if the definition of culture is not confined to fine arts and music but spills into issues of economic life, government, and sovereignty, unbalanced standardization targeting only economic aspects is fraught with conflicts not only among economic agents, but also in relationships among economic and non-economic spheres of life. To leave aside the concept of citizenship, it is clear that the lack of 'fellow feeling' among Europeans is undermining even the formation of the single market through the unfavourable conditions for labour mobility and the formation of consumer market set for Eastern Europe. The rhetoric of 'unity within diversity' can hardly hope to solve the substantive problems involved, and a championing of regional interests over those of nation-states may lead to fragmentation rather than integration.[45]

4.2.2 Regional Identity in the Southern Cone

The civilizational history of Latin America is shorter and less confusing, as it does not need exploration going beyond 1500 AD into the pre-Columbian epoch. The core of MERCOSUR—Argentina, Uruguay, and Southern Brazil—is relatively homogeneous. It is represented by societies formed on the basis of late European migration, which can be classified as a single type of civilization different from Afro-American and Indo-American cultural realms in the rest of Latin America. Yet, MERCOSUR is far from being a culturally uniform region. It can be analyzed through contrasting rather than common features: Hispanic MERCOSUR and Lusophone MERCOSUR (Spanish-speaking countries versus Brazil), indigenous cultural base and European base (Paraguay versus Uruguay), and transplanted societies of Europe against autonomous identity self-construction (Argentina and Uruguay versus Brazil and Paraguay). Brazilian Northeast and Venezuela have African heritage. MERCOSUR cannot claim the status of a cultural community primarily because of the linguistic barrier that separates Brazil and Hispanic countries.

Thus, a Hispano-American community, which excluded Brazil, was emphasized at the beginning of the nineteenth century rather than the Ibero-American unity. Hispanic and Brazilian literary processes and cultures were often approached as separate phenomena.[46] For a long time in Spanish America the term 'Literature of the Southern Cone' included Peru but excluded Brazil. Comparative studies of national literatures did not have serious consequences for literary research in South America before 1983 when Uruguayan critic Ángel Rama suggested the parallel study of Hispanic and Brazilian literatures.[47] Since then the comparative studies of national literatures in MERCOSUR have produced evidence of common social traits, problems, discourses, and interesting observations about interactions between Brazil and Hispanic countries.[48]

In addition to the zones of Luso-Hispanic contact and linguistic contamination (Uruguayan-Brazilian, Paraguayan-Brazilian, and Argentinean-Brazilian), a number of extra-linguistic features distinguish MERCOSUR from other cultural zones inside and outside of Latin America. MERCOSUR stands apart by the fact that the traditional axes of orientation of cultural movements North→South and West→East are reversed: South→North and East→West. These were the directions of expansion of civilization both in pre-Columbian and post-Columbian times: migrations of Tupi-Guaraníes to the north, and settlements of Europeans from the coast to inner lands. A number of MERCOSUR cultural traits appear to be results of geographic settlements on the Atlantic coast and in the basins of the Río de la Plata, the Amazon, and other great rivers. These are fluvial, mobile, nomadic, and coastal characteristics. Most of the MERCOSUR cultural peculiarities are marked historically by consequences of conquests, colonization, and immigrant waves.

The Indigenous Component

Indigenous groups and pre-Columbian civilizations had a limited influence on the formation of present-day culture on the MERCOSUR territory. Common to the whole area, the Arawakan people inhabited all of the MERCOSUR area as they used to be the most widely disseminated Amerindian group that settled from Venezuela up to Florida, the Caribbean and Central America, and down to Colombia, Peru, Brazil, Chile, Bolivia, and Argentina. However, these people began to disappear by the end of the sixteenth century. The other group, the Tupi people, spread at least across Brazil, Argentina, Paraguay, Bolivia, Peru, and French Guiana. In pre-Columbian times Tupi-Guaraníes were the groups that dominated in the MERCOSUR region and were the core people of the zone. They had a large capacity for expansion, and they remain present in contemporary MERCOSUR. Their successors form the Paraguayan nation.

Like other primitive cultures, pre-Columbian Indians left epics marked by a strong identification with nature and pantheism. Sadly, in the Southern Cone their heritage is less known than Classical literature. As for the production of post-Columbian indigenous cultures in MERCOSUR, it was very much affected by the interference of Creole and metropolises' cultures, and in common perception is marginalized to local crafts. With the exception of Paraguay, indigenous people have had a negligible effect on the identity of MERCOSUR. Thus the indigenous population of Uruguay was totally exterminated. Argentina has always pursued a racist immigration policy, encouraging European immigration and keeping borders closed for Amerindians, Asians, and Africans. The ethnic and cultural existence of Indians in Argentina was not recognized before 1994. They are 1% of population divided among 25 living languages. The indigenous population in Brazil was patronized in legal and official terms but segregated and exterminated in practical terms. In 1990 it represented 0.17% of the Brazilian population with approximately 195 surviving languages. The Indian identity has been systematically erased in both Brazil and Argentina.

However, the indigenous culture survived in Paraguay. Guaraní, one of the Tupi-Guaraní languages, became the national language of Paraguay. It is spoken by half of the country's total population making Paraguay the only truly bilingual country in South America. Besides Paraguay, Paraguayan Guaraní and some other Guaraní languages are also present in Brazil and Argentina. In addition to Guaraní languages, a few Brazilians speak Tupi and other Tupi-Guaraní languages as well as non-Tupi-Guaraní Tupi languages.[49] The activities of Jesuits with their distinguished organizing and indoctrinating capacity exercised on Tupi-Guaraníes were a strong unifying factor for the Southern Cone. Jesuits appreciated local arts, handicrafts, and the Indian literary heritage; they respected and stimulated the creativity of Indians. Jesuits monopolized education in the colonies and encouraged Indians to adopt the common language Guaraní (*lingua geral*). It underwent mayor expansion in Brazil until the second half of the eighteenth century when Portuguese replaced it. According to sociologist Gilberto Freyre, Guaraní became 'one of the strongest elements of Brazilian unity.'[50] In 2006 Guaraní received formal recognition as one of the three MERCOSUR's languages.[51]

The Conquest
The colonization from the sixteenth to the nineteenth century was a 'second birth' of Latin America that caused a complete geopolitical and ethno-cultural recomposition of the continent. Political and historical changes converted the region into a periphery of Europe, and caused social transformations through miscegenation and racial shocks. Not only did these transformations concern Spain, Portugal, and Latin America,

but they also reflected the whole history of westernization of the planet, irrefutably related to colonialism. Colonizers built cities in the centres of settlement of indigenous people. The cities displaced original communities culturally and physically and imposed a new social reality. The reaction of the indigenous people was ambiguous. On the one hand they shared an inferiority complex that drove them towards the acceptance of the colonizers' culture and assimilation. On the other hand, assimilation as a process had limits posed by race, property, and social opportunities. These limits provoked resistance and struggle against the colonizers.

Asunción emerged as the generating centre of colonization that expanded down towards the Argentinean coast. The relationship between Spaniards and the Portuguese on the Iberian Peninsula was characterized by competition and rivalry that later evolved into alienation between Argentina and Brazil. In Paraguay, the dangerous presence of the Portuguese compelled the Spanish Crown to organize Asunción as a defence base against the Portuguese. On the other side, the settlement was confronted by warlike indigenous centres in the Chaco valley, the Pampas, and Patagonia. Ultimately, Indian centres fell under the onslaught of the colonizers.

The principal unifying factor of the Conquest period was the cohesive strength of the colonial regimes of Madrid and Lisbon. They imposed institutions, customs, and their languages, Spanish and Portuguese. The histories of the countries that make up MERCOSUR-4 have strong interconnections. One of the factors that brought the Hispanic sector of the Southern Cone together in MERCOSUR was the common history of governance in the Viceroyalty of the Río de la Plata of Argentina, Uruguay and Paraguay. Historically, the sense of national sentiment in these three countries evolved from identification with Spain, local settlements, South America, and Latin America, and was not restrained by territorial, political, and citizenship belonging to a specific Río de la Plata province.

The early colonization period left evidence of one of the oldest visions of regional integration by Ruy Díaz de Guzmán, the first *mestizo* historiographer of Paraguay (1558 or 1560–1629), who wanted to create communication routes to connect Upper Peru with el Río de la Plata, Tucumán, Paraguay, and the Atlantic coast of Brazil. In 1974 de Gandía prophetically wrote about Díaz de Guzmán that his geopolitical vision could not have been wiser. It is exactly what Paraguay, Bolivia, Brazil and Argentina with their enormous common efforts are doing today: building railways and roads that unite these nations and allow trade from the Atlantic and the Río de la Plata to penetrate into Paraguay, Chaco, and Bolivia... He would have needed to bring more people, to invent more money, to found more towns. But Díaz de Guzmán was poor; he had neither means nor opportunities. Likewise today these are not enough to undertake and accomplish the project that has not yet been started after four centuries. Díaz de Guzmán had to give everything for this idea, but he also had to abandon this superhuman work that no one has ever decided to continue after him. Only time with the slow penetration of civilisation one day will possibly be able to make his dream come true.[52]

'The Second Conquest'
'The Second Conquest' that brings together the histories of the Southern Cone countries has to deal with population movements from cities to *selvas* and *pampas*. This was the conquest of jungles in Brazil and deserts in Argentina and Uruguay. Both *pampas* and *selvas* were rough areas, and their exploration was comparable to settling in the Wild West in North America. This epoch of the Southern Cone preserved many anecdotes, stories of heroism, and exaggerated ambitions. The conflict between civilization and barbarism was the topic that dominated in the Southern Cone. Fanaticism, intolerance, violence, and the ideology of bad blood were characteristic practically of the whole Latin America of this period. 'The Second Conquest' is responsible for the recurrence of *gaucho* values, ruralism, *machismo*, rigidity, individualism, serenity, and creativity due to the difficult conditions of fighting and exploration of unsettled lands.

This period was accompanied by an important re-definition and enforcement of borders on political and cultural maps. The impulse was first given by the conquest and colonization, then by independence wars, and finally by civil wars. Brazil, Argentina, and Paraguay defined their borders. Uruguay emerged as a separate buffer state on the territory claimed by Brazil and Argentina. The theme of borders came along as Spain and Portugal were constantly readjusting their agreements in legal battles and intrigues involving the papacy. However, the *bandeirantes* (mine and *selva* explorers in Brazil) remained unaware of the theoretical obstacles posed by the European deals. They simply settled further west, south, and north expanding the Brazilian territory. The severity of their lives matched the reality of *gauchos*. *Gaucho/gaúcho* became one of the central types of national identification of Argentina and Uruguay, and of local identity in the Brazilian state of Rio Grande do Sul. This type has a perfectly matching equivalent in the rest of Brazil called *sertanejo*. During the 'Second Conquest' *Civilización Gaucha* [Gaucho Civilization] replaced the earlier *Civilización Guaranítica* [Guaraní Civilization].

The construction of nation states in the nineteenth century contributed to the affirmation of national identities. Importantly, the borders emphasized the position of the nations in relation to each other. Colonial invaders were no longer a threat. However, the independence of Brazil and Argentina from the Iberian monarchies did not change the sentiment of inherited antagonism of the colonial period. Neighbours who shared a recently acquired liberty became enemies. The urgency to construct symbols of the newborn identity for the new people required a series of negations and affirmations that characterized the nineteenth century. First of all this was a clear negation of *Madre Iberia* [Mother Iberia] and a fascination with something new in the search for other models that represented progress. In particular, *Francia civilizada* [Civilized France] became a new cultural benchmark. French neoclassicism had a profound influence on the MERCOSUR zone immediately after the manifestation of the first constitutions and theatres. However, though non-Iberian Europe affected littoral cities, the inlands remained practically untouched by these influences.

The Twentieth Century
In the beginning of the twentieth century *modernismo* [modernism] was characteristic of both Hispanic countries of MERCOSUR and Brazil. This diverse and complicated cultural movement appeared between the nineteenth and twentieth centuries in the Spanish-language zone. It found its repercussions in the decade of the 1920s in Brazil in the process known as *vanguardias*. Common influences were coming to the Southern Cone from external centres such as London, Paris, New York, Madrid, Barcelona, Miami, and Rome. They drew a number of schemes revealing similarities and were brought by media, symposia, the life of people in exile, and cultural work of embassies. This cultural movement was characterized by a cosmopolitan view of the world, selective, polarized and sometimes idealized presentation of reality, and the emphasis on the conflict between an individual and the bourgeois society.

One of the major trends in the MERCOSUR literatures of the twentieth century is the lack of personality and individuality among characters and communities:

> A Brazilian does not have a character because he does not possess neither proper civilisation, nor traditional consciousness.
>
> The Uruguayan writer suspects that his capital lacks literary tradition and novel verisimilitude, the conditions credible for a literary adventure.
>
> The Cosmopolitan resident of Buenos Aires lives here as though in a hotel.[53]

Such perceptions of an individual and the society differentiate MERCOSUR from other countries of Latin America with old civilizations such as Mexico, Peru, Bolivia, Ecuador, and Guatemala. Intellectual nomadism, lack of personality, search for identity of the new nations, individualism, and tension between constructivism and deconstructivism are characteristic features of the Southern Cone's modernism.

Following the 1920s the MERCOSUR countries lived through technological innovations, an immigration boom, the disruption of WW2, and the new neocolonial credo of the Western world that viewed the region as a land of opportunity and a supply base of natural resources. The topics that preoccupied the minds of MERCOSUR intellectuals later in the century were uneasiness with their northern neighbour (the USA), a division between sympathies to communism and resistance to it, fights with Bolshevik-inspired *guerrilla* movements, and opposition to dictatorships that installed themselves in every Southern Cone country without exception. The brutality of the 'dirty war' with *guerrillas* sent many Southern Cone intellectuals into exile. The crisis in the relations between intellectuals and the people was embodied in the new discourse of populism. Another central topic of the period was poverty. It compelled more people to leave the Southern Cone than all the dictatorships taken together. Along with poverty, there were other common themes: disenchantment, repression, and the search for the sense of proper life within the national identity that was blurred and contradictory.

The second half of the century was marked by economic hardships, political and moral crises, the cycle of populist dictatorships, the 'dirty war' with *guerrilleros*, the repression of state, and the subsequent return to democracy. It produced MERCOSUR's own postmodernism, which is characterized by strong persistence of nostalgia for the past and the sense of marginalization; scepticism about government; the criticism of poverty, corruption, and bad administration; the frequency of topics of exile, immigration, and repatriation; the emphasis on contrasts and asymmetries (centre/periphery, affluence/poverty, beauty/ugliness); recurrence of critical and sceptical attitudes; social inequality; large gaps between intellectuals and the working class; environmental protests; populist discourses; liking for kitsch; and a strong presence of magical realism.

4.3 INTER-STATE RELATIONS IN THE SOUTHERN CONE PRIOR TO MERCOSUR

The major division within MERCOSUR between Brazil and the Spanish-language countries is a consequence of events in Iberian history of the twelfth century, when seniorial cantonalism and linguistic nationalism transformed the Dukedom of Portugal into a separate kingdom and fixed the distinction between *Hispania castellana* and *Hispania lusitana*. Only partially were the two kingdoms of Spain and Portugal reunited by the Union of Felipe II in 1580–1640. Circumstances that kept Portugal apart from Spain could have been overcome, as Portugal would be unable to sustain itself as a separate nation. Without the backing of England it would now be a region of Spain like Catalonia. In this respect, integration between Brazil and Argentina in the late twentieth century represents an adjustment of a somewhat artificial and externally sustained division in medieval Europe. This division made Spaniards and the Portuguese competitors in 'the Indian empire' on the dividing line of the Treaty of Tordesillas (1494).[54] The zone of the Río de la Plata, the Paraná, and the Uruguay rivers became a field of disputes and political confrontation of the two Iberian crowns and their successor states, the Brazilian Empire and the Argentinean Confederation, for the period from the sixteenth to the nineteenth century.

The foundation of Nova Colônia do Sacramento by the Portuguese in front of Buenos Aires and the dispute over control of the territory of modern Uruguay (*Banda Oriental* or *Província Cisplatina*) caused the formation of the Spanish Viceroyalty of the Río de la Plata in 1776. Whereas *rioplatenses* wanted to prevent the expansion of Brazil in the river basin (because this area offered access to the rich resources of the interior), Brazil sought to obstruct the consolidation of Argentina through the decomposition of the Viceroyalty and the acquisition of Uruguay. It was particularly important to secure the autonomy of Paraguay from Argentina, as this would have allowed Brazil to exploit waterways for access to inland provinces. The rivalry between the two countries was based not only on the strategic goal of preventing each other's expansion, but also on power asymmetries. Brazil was formed earlier than the Argentinean state. In addition, Brazil inherited from the Portuguese Empire all its institutions practically intact.[55] The organization of Brazil as a monarchy and empire constituted one of the principal factors of tension and insecurity of the fragmented republican regimes of Spanish America.

Even though in many cases the Iberian Crowns and their successors remained military and diplomatic adversaries, none of the three wars in the Southern Cone (the War of the Triple Alliance, the Pacific War, and the Chaco War) was between Brazil and Argentina. On the contrary, the Triple Alliance War against Paraguay indicated the first convergence of Brazilian and Argentinean interests in the nineteenth century. The war was preceded by intense conflicts in the area of the Río de la Plata, but its end changed the dimension of bilateral relations because Brazilian power declined and Argentinean power increased due to its alliance with Britain. Before the 1930s Brazil significantly lagged behind Argentina as a naval power. Bolivia and Paraguay were very dependent on the Argentinean navy and access to the port of Buenos Aires.

After the proclamation of the Brazilian Republic in 1889, Brazil started rapprochement with the USA and Brazilian-Argentinean relations began to reflect US–British rivalry, as Argentina still allied with England.[56] Brazilian–Argentinean competition for regional hegemonic influence on the small nations of the region (Uruguay, Paraguay, and Bolivia) resulted in the formation of two axes of power: Buenos Aires–La Paz–Lima and Rio de Janeiro–Asunción–Santiago de Chile. In contrast to contemporary integration schemes based on the Atlantic and Pacific countries (MERCOSUR and CAN), this old map of alliances was unnatural from the point of view of physical and economic geography.[57]

In the twentieth century stakes on alliances with external powers (Argentina's on Britain and Brazil's on Germany and the USA) were linked to the Brazilian–Argentinean competition for regional hegemony. In spite of manifestations of this competition, border conflicts between the two protagonists of MERCOSUR were not significant and neither were the memories of these conflicts. Trade exchange between the two countries remained miniscule. According to Argentinean President Sáenz Peña (1910–1914) everything united Brazil and Argentina, and nothing separated them.[58] Yet the dynamic of political and economic relations offered little to support this statement. Strategic considerations restricted advances in the improvement of infrastructure, except in the energy sector. The cold detachment of the two countries did not contribute to the growth of mutual confidence while preoccupations about security impeded the growth of interdependence and maintained economic self-sufficiency inherited from the colonial and early postcolonial history. For a long time the two countries had heated emotional relations only on 'soccer fields.'[59]

Because of internal political dynamics and different strategies in relations with other powers, the priority of the two countries in foreign policy regarding each other fluctuated, at times becoming a topic of secondary importance. Nevertheless Brazil and what today is Argentina have had important roles in the political and commercial agenda of each other since the time of the conquest. The long common border, even though not densely populated, cultural affinity, and complementarity of climates and resources have always been a factor conducive to all types of exchanges and communication; and the first cross-border trade was registered as early as in the beginning of seventeenth century. Already in the late colonial period, the decision to crown princess Carlota Joaquina de Bourbon (the Spanish princess and the Portuguese queen) in the Río de la Plata appeared as a strategic idea to create a political union between Argentina and Brazil.[60]

Thus the rapprochement between the countries has been steady and constant, though not without regressions. The first exchange of visits between the two heads of states took place under Rocas and Campos Salles in 1899 and 1900. These goodwill visits indicated a clear intention to establish special relations between the two countries, even though tensions remained at that time. More than simply tensions, between 1906 and 1910 the two countries were anticipating a military conflict and were buying weapons from the USA and Britain. In 1907 Rocas re-visited Argentina and in 1912 Rocas and Campos Salles exchanged visits again, but this time in the capacity of ambassadors. They managed to terminate the circle of conflicts, and in 1915 the ABC Treaty offering a mechanism for peaceful resolution of conflicts and a preferential trade regime was signed among Argentina, Brazil, and Chile, but it was not ratified by the national parliaments.[61]

In the early 1930s after Brazil bought military ships from the USA, the tensions between Brazil and Argentina resumed. Nevertheless, between 1933 and 1935 the two countries signed a series of 21 agreements.[62] One of them was on the compatibility of geography and history textbooks to avoid the dissemination of antagonistic views in the educational systems. Another agreement resulted in the construction of the first bi-national bridge between *Paso de los Libres* and *Uruguaiana* that was inaugurated by Presidents Perón and Dutra in 1947. In 1941 Argentina and Brazil reaffirmed the goals of the ABC Treaty and agreed on an FTA, but they did not implement this agreement after Brazil entered WW2.[63] The war alienated the two countries as Brazil was on the side of the Coalition while Argentina maintained neutrality.

The postwar Argentinean leader Juan Domingo Perón was quite integration-minded. He signed a treaty on a customs union with Chile in 1946 just six months later after taking up the presidency.[64] He repeatedly suggested the reanimation of the old idea of the ABC strategic alliance with the inclusion of provisions on commercial and economic matters. In 1953 he said: 'Alone none of the three countries has economic potency. Together, their economic capacity is extraordinary. For 2000 there are two alternatives: to be united or to be dominated.'[65] In February 1953 he and his Chilean counterpart Ibañez del Campo signed a memorandum of commitment to a future treaty on economic union.[66] This new treaty was intended to represent the first multilateral strategic alliance in the region. Brazilian President Getúlio Vargas was supposed to join it at the summit planned in March 1953 in Santiago, but he was arrested and committed suicide.[67] Perón was soon removed from power by a military rebellion. Thus the memorandum resulted only in a bilateral Chilean–Argentinean treaty on economic union signed and put into force in July 1953.[68]

Even though the agreement on a large-scale strategic partnership failed due to domestic turmoil in Brazil, the governments of the region continued cooperation. In 1946 Argentina and Uruguay agreed on the first binational project in the Basin of the Río de la Plata.[69] The agreement allowed the use of waters in equal proportions and prioritised navigation over electricity production. In 1956 Paraguay and Brazil signed a preliminary agreement on the construction of power plant *Itaipu.*[70] In 1958 Paraguay and Argentina agreed on proposals to improve navigation on the Paraná and to build hydroelectric plant *Yaciretá* below *Itaipu.*[71] In 1960 Argentina, Brazil, and Uruguay signed a mutual declaration that allowed free navigation on the Uruguay River and recognized the right of Brazil to build electric plants anywhere on its territory.[72] In 1961 Argentina and Uruguay settled their water disputes.[73] One of their agreements reflected the convergence of common interests in fixing the exterior limit of the Río de la Plata. In the meantime Brazil began cooperation with Uruguay in the mutual exploitation of border lake Merín.[74]

In 1960 Argentina and Brazil became founders of LAFTA. The 1961 Declarations of Uruguaiana by Presidents Arturo Frondizi and Jânio Quadros appeared as another important landmark of bilateral cooperation in different spheres ranging from commercial and technological cooperation to diplomatic consultations on regional and global issues and free movement of people.[75] The declarations instituted a regular mechanism for consultations on external policy that was maintained by the subsequent military governments. In 1967 Brazilian President Castelo Branco proposed the creation of a sectoral customs union with Argentina. In 1968 bi-national Argentinean–Uruguayan hydroelectric plant *Salto Grande* was approved.[76] In 1969 Argentina, Brazil, Paraguay, Uruguay, and Bolivia signed a treaty that institutionalized their cooperation in the Paraná basin.[77] The 1973 Treaty of the Río de la Plata finally established the Río de la Plata as a river and not as a gulf, bay, or estuary as Britain, the EC and the USA insisted.[78] The Treaty caused protests of the mentioned parties as the waters lost their international status that entailed free navigation. However, this agreement helped to restrict participation of third parties in the internal affairs of the *rioplatenses*.

The 1970s were marked by conflicts over the construction of hydroelectric plants that threatened navigation and environmental balances. In 1973 the Treaty of *Itaipu* between Brazil and Paraguay caused a conflict with Argentina.[79] Several months later Argentina signed a treaty with Paraguay on the *Yaciretá* plant.[80] The two countries intended to build another power plant *Corpus* between *Yaciretá* and *Itaipu*. Argentina was concerned about the safety of the *Itaipu* dam located just 17 km away from its frontier. The dam promised to lower the level of water in the Paraná, spoiling prospects for *Corpus* and complicating navigation.

Itaipu allied Paraguay with Brazil. Through the construction of roads and railways Brazil linked the Río de la Plata Basin (the Brazilian inlands, Bolivia, Paraguay, and Argentinean provinces Misiones and Entre Rios) to the Brazilian Atlantic ports of Santos, Paranaguá, and Rio Grande. This significantly reduced the commercial and geopolitical importance of the port of Buenos Aires and subsumed Paraguay, Uruguay, and Bolivia under Brazilian influence. Besides, there occurred coups in Bolivia (1971), Uruguay (1973), and Chile (1973). Brazil offered support to all of them, which reduced the scope for Argentinean strategic manoeuvres and left the country isolated.

In one of his trips to Brasília Argentinean President Alejandro Lanusse referred to the Brazilian approach to water resources as 'Brazilian imperialism.' Soon Argentina restricted Brazilian imports, which was not received well in Brazil given its chronic deficits in trade with Argentina. However, the aggravation of the US–Brazilian contradictions and the threat of a military conflict between Argentina and Chile over the Channel of Beagle stimulated a rapprochement between the military governments of Videla and Figueiredo. They managed to solve the *Itaipu* dilemma through a number of agreements that regulated the use of the rivers. In 1979 the Trilateral Agreement on *Corpus* and *Itaipu* ended the major river conflict and the last border dispute.[81] Brazil accepted a smaller number of turbines and Argentina agreed on a lower level of water for the *Corpus* project.

The Agreement on *Corpus* and *Itaipu* favourably changed the political climate between the two countries. The following year (1980) President Figueiredo travelled to Buenos Aires where a number of important agreements were signed.[82] These agreements covered nuclear cooperation, double taxation along the Paraná River, joint production of military planes and rockets, and the interconnection of national electrical systems. The two countries negotiated a number of commercial deals and economic cooperation measures, completed an agreement in the automotive sector, and announced the construction of a gas pipeline bringing Argentinean gas to southern Brazil. The agreements established a bi-national working group of representatives of foreign ministries and ministries of economy that met every three months in order to identify obstacles to bilateral trade. However, having soon reached the conclusion that Argentina and Brazil were not ready for economic integration, the group terminated its work.

It became clear that Brazil was not hostile towards Argentina as it refrained from any inimical participation either in the 1978 Argentinean border conflicts with Chile or during the 1982 War over *the Malvinas*.[83] On the contrary, the Brazilian military government took a constructive part in the negotiations with Britain to solve the crisis. Rather than taking advantage of the conflict replacing Argentina as a major meat and cereals exporter, Brazil allowed Argentina to use Brazilian ports to bypass the embargo imposed by Britain and its allies. In its turn the Argentinean government expressed serious interest in the development of political and economic relations with Brazil in 1983 when it ordered the first study on feasibility and conditions of greater cooperation and established a small working group in charge of improving relations with Brazil. In 1984 the Argentinean and Brazilian ministers discussed the idea of economic integration.[84]

The democratically elected governments proclaimed the first serious intention of integration in the Declaration of Iguazú and the Political Declaration on Nuclear Policy.[85] Both were signed in 1985 on the occasion of inauguration of the cross-border bridge between Puerto Iguazú and Foz do Iguaçu. The Declaration of Iguazú began economic, commercial, transport, communication, scientific, technological, energy, and nuclear integration. It established a Senior Level Joint Commission for Cooperation and Bilateral Integration, presided over by the two ministers of foreign affairs and consisting of official experts and private business representatives. In 1986 the two parties signed the Act for Argentinean-Brazilian Integration that started PICE.[86] In addition to the Act, ten sectoral agreements, one agreement on nuclear incidents and radiological emergencies, and one on aeronautic cooperation were signed. Twelve other agreements were signed later during the period 1986 to 1990. All in all PICE resulted in the implementation of 24 agreements.

The sectoral integration promoted by PICE addressed commercial and industrial cooperation. It reflected interest in planning and consolidating industrial development and laid emphasis on the achievement of balanced sectoral trade to attenuate the fears of businesses about possible losses. One of the important consequences of PICE was that the traditional competing axis Brazil-Chile and Argentina-Peru disappeared. The small countries Uruguay, Paraguay, and Bolivia received commercial advantages simultaneously from the two parties and lost the necessity of search for 'balanced pendulum politics.'[87] The results of PICE agreements converted Brazil and Argentina into the largest suppliers and buyers of each other's goods. Each of them exceeded the share of the USA in their foreign trade in 1987 and 1988.[88]

In 1988 in Buenos Aires, Brazil and Argentina signed the Treaty of Integration, Cooperation, and Development that was ratified by their congresses in 1989.[89] This Treaty aimed at the formation of a common market within 10 years. It clearly formulated the objective of gradually establishing a common economic area 'based on reciprocity and equilibrium of advantages.' The document envisaged two stages. The first dealt with the 'elimination of tariff and non-tariff obstacles to trade in goods and services during the ten year period' in order to pass to the second stage of 'harmonisation of other policies necessary for the common market.' The Act of Buenos Aires of 6 July 1990 shortened the deadline for the common market to 1995.[90] On 1 August 1990 the bilateral Treaty of Buenos Aires was joined by Uruguay and on 21 August 1990 by Paraguay.[91]

In November 1990, Argentina and Brazil signed ACE 14 within the framework of LAIA.[92] This Agreement formally closed the period of sectoral integration and opened the stage of progressive, linear and automatic tariff reduction. In essence it provided the instrumental base of the Treaty of Asunción and adopted a new model of integration that became crucial for the formation of MERCOSUR.[93] The progress of the bilateral Brazilian–Argentinean cooperation in ACE 14 and the accession of Uruguay and Paraguay to the Treaty of Buenos Aires required the revision of the Treaty of Buenos Aires. This revision gave birth to the Treaty of Asunción among the four countries, which established MERCOSUR in March 1991.[94]

Three points of the pre-MERCOSUR cooperation are worthy of reiteration. First of all, from a historic perspective MERCOSUR is not a random phenomenon but an event that has roots and antecedents in the Latin American past. In contrast to the European process that started from scratch after WW2, MERCOSUR is a process of historic continuity, and is a product of efforts of previous governments rather than just a result of democratization in the mid-1980s. It came out from the agreements between Alfonsín and Sanrey in the 1980s, but these agreements were possible only because of the earlier compromises among the military administrations, which settled water and border disputes and promoted political rapprochement.

Secondly, the survey reveals the following issues dominating the agenda of inter-state relations in the Southern Cone in the 1960s, 1970s, and 1980s: the countries were busy with the construction of the first cross-border bridges, connecting their few cross-border roads, and resolving territorial disputes in non-populated areas and conflicts over the use of border waters. At the same time Western European countries concentrated their efforts on the consolidation of the common market and were tackling issues of trade, investment, competition rules, and supranational institutions, some of which are still unresolved in MERCOSUR. This difference in the topics of intra-regional relations reflect huge variations between MERCOSUR and Western European countries along the physical, geographic, demographic, historic, and economic characteristics.

Lastly, contemporary commercial alliances in South America replicate the map of population distribution across the continent. South American population is dispersed across three major areas. One stretches from São Luís and Fortaleza in the North to Córdoba and Buenos Aires in the South and corresponds to MERCOSUR. The second, along the coast from Caracas to Lima and La Paz, corresponds to CAN (Venezuela was CAN's full member from 1973 to 2006). The third is central Chile, and Chile forms neither part of CAN nor MERCOSUR. For MERCOSUR this means that its Lusophone versus Hipsanophone division has not been stronger in challenging intra-regional cohesion than the factor of geographic neighbourhood in inducing various forms of cooperation. This also suggests that MERCOSUR has as a distinct sub-regional geographic identity, which may not be easily dissolved into other projects of Latin American unity.

4.4 CASE STUDY: LINGUISTIC POLICIES

Many studies have claimed that regional integration affects self-perception and self-identification of individuals, population groups, and countries. The evaluation of regional blocs' influence on cultural transformations and cognitive perception of identities and loyalties is neither productive nor easy as it requires analysis of huge data collected systematically over a long period of time. The conclusions of such research risk being highly uncertain. However, the effects of cultural integration may be identified through the study of specific policies implemented at the regional level. This section analyses linguistic policies. In terms of culture and identity as aspects of politics, notions like language, religion, and race have affected separatist and unification claims at national levels and thus have relevance for integration at the supranational level. However, language as the custodian of culture is the most important cultural phenomenon because neither religion nor race restricts interpersonal communication and interaction as much as the necessity of having translators and interpreters. The changes described below have so far affected a small fraction of people: employees and contractors of the European institutions and some schoolchildren in Brazil, Argentina, and Uruguay. However, communication is an important part of the integration process, and language is one of the key instruments of identity formation.

Both the EU and MERCOSUR are multilingual regions where linguistic diversity is an obstacle to integration. Both restrict multilingualism as they recognize as official languages only the national languages of the member states. Sub-national languages, languages of immigrant groups, and national languages with little communication value like Luxembourgish and Guaraní do not receive a full formal recognition. In the EU, this discriminatory approach disappoints certain groups like Catalans. Their language of

11 million speakers across three member states (Spain, France, and Italy) has a status inferior to that of 11 official languages spoken by fewer people, including Maltese with just 300,000 speakers.

In both regions, monolingualism, as the alternative to multilingualism, is unrealistic. In MERCOSUR Portuguese is the language of just one member state, while Spanish is the language of only one-quarter of the bloc's population. Portuguese as the main language of the union would not appeal to Hispanic countries, particularly given MERCOSUR's aspirations for greater influence across Latin America. In the EU the calls for Anglophonic monolingualism are common, but so is the resistance against English. English was not an official language in the original EC countries; it is strongly associated with US power and interference; in addition, Britain is systematically an opponent to many Continental initiatives, and is now going to leave the union. In both MERCOSUR and the EU one single language would contradict the principle of a pluralist community. It would unfairly benefit their native speakers to the disadvantage of other citizens. The solution of the linguistic dilemma is in linguistic plurality (bilingualism in MERCOSUR and multilingualism in the EU). However, multilingualism exhausts the list of similarities between the two blocs' approaches towards regional language policy. The unions affect linguistic preferences on their territories in significantly different ways. These differences shed more light on the character of their cultural integration than the proclaimed adherence to linguistic plurality.

The EU recognizes 24 official languages.[95] This has never implied ideal multilingualism, even in the publication of official documents, as at various times institutions were allowed to ignore the official status of Irish Gaelic and Maltese. *De facto* there are four working languages: English, French, German (whose application is very limited), and Spanish (used only in the meetings with officials from Latin America). Ministerial and diplomatic meetings are usually interpreted into three languages, meetings between officials of states and institutions are held in two languages, expert meetings use one language. EU citizens are free to use any of the 24 languages together with Catalan, Basque, Galician, Welsh, and Scottish Gaelic in their correspondence with the EU. However, they usually use English, as do consultants and tenderers.

Before the mid-1970s French was the predominant language of the European institutions. The institutions were set up in French-speaking Brussels, Luxembourg, and Strasbourg. French was official in the three founding states of the EC and a familiar language in the three others.

English was introduced in the EC only after the incorporation of Britain and Ireland in 1973. This coincided with the rise of English in the economy, technology, science, and international communication. Globalization, which favoured English, and the accession of countries where English was the first or the preferred second language improved its status vis-à-vis French. Table 4.3 illustrates the gradual expansion of English within the EC institutions.

The predominance of French in communications in the EU until the mid-1990s was extraordinary, as no other language could compete with English as the language of international communication at that time. Today English is almost the only language used in external communications. It has surpassed French in written and oral forms of communication within the European institutions. As for German, it has marginal relevance. The European Central Bank is located in Germany but it operates in English even though Britain is not its member. Thus instead of official linguistic pluralism, which is the unrealistic ideal of the EU, there is hegemony of English in EU institutions. The passive submission of European institutions to English contributes to the strengthening of English as a second language in Europe and causes the decline of other second languages. By all means English is not a neutral language, as it certainly benefits the maintenance of closer ties between Europeans and the Anglo-American *laissez-faire* capitalism.[96]

In Latin America, of the two languages—Spanish and Portuguese—Spanish has always enjoyed more prestige. If Spanish was present in the most developed areas of Brazil such as Rio de Janeiro, São Paulo, and Rio Grande do Sul in textbooks and literature, the penetration of Portuguese

Table 4.3 Languages used in primary texts of the European Commission, 1986–1999

Year	French, %	English, %	German, %	Other languages, %
1986	58	26	11	5
1989	49	30	9	12
1991	48	35	6	11
1996	39	45	5	12
1997	40	45	5	9
1998	37	48	5	10
1999	35	52	5	8

Truchot, 2003. p 104

into Hispanic America did not occur.[97] Portuguese was considered unworthy to learn. Only the rise of Brazilian economic power made Portuguese an important language along Brazil's borders. In Argentina national identity was strongly associated with European cultures and European immigration that was assimilated through a state-imposed monolingualism based on Spanish. More Italians than Spaniards came to Argentina, and the former had to be assimilated into Spanish. Any references to Portuguese in Argentina were simply irrelevant, especially before the 1950s when Argentinean economy and power prevailed over Brazil.

As in Argentina, the Uruguayan governmental policy had always tried to homogenize its population through the enforcement of Spanish. Uruguay was constituted as a union between two regions with different linguistic traditions. The make-up of the central, western, and southern strips was strongly influenced by European immigrants and had a composition similar to that of Buenos Aires. The north of Uruguay was populated by Portuguese peasants who remained in Uruguay after the border with Brazil was defined. They preserved what is called *brazilero, portunhol, fronteiriço, riverense,* or *misturado,* a variety of Portuguese distinct from the language spoken in Brazil. In addition to 'the Portuguese dialects of Uruguay,' Brazilian Portuguese has become relevant for Uruguay as a factor reflecting Brazilian economic influence. Uruguay always viewed the presence of Portuguese as a threat to Uruguayan unity and excluded it from the system of public education.

The language situation in Paraguay is characterized by fragile Spanish/ Guaraní bilingualism. Guaraní is the language of the majority of the population. However, it is more disadvantaged in formal spheres. Measures are being implemented to improve its position vis-à-vis Spanish. Foreign language teaching remains limited in this rural country as Paraguay has few contacts with non-Spanish speaking foreigners. The presence of Portuguese 'in full and aggressive expansion in the extensive border area with Brazil' was considered a threat to Paraguay's cultural and linguistic identity, and an obstacle to the development of its educational and training system.[98]

The situation in Brazil was similar to that in Argentina and Uruguay in the sense of enforcing a common identity through one language, Portuguese. In the early days Brazil lived under external threats of European invaders (Dutch, Spanish, French). Later, it needed to assimilate massive European, Japanese, and African immigration. Brazil's participation in WW2 against the Nazis intensified its assimilation policy towards huge Italian and German minorities. The postwar period was characterized by a special partnership with the USA that gave English the status of the only mandatory foreign language in the educational system. This trend reflected a distancing from Hispanic America.

Thus Spanish and Portuguese were irrelevant as second languages in the MERCOSUR region. Moreover, Brazil's neighbours saw Portuguese as a threat to their linguistic identities based on Spanish monolingualism or Spanish/Guaraní bilingualism. Even when Spanish and Portuguese were not viewed as threats, they were not treated as languages to learn properly due to their similarity and mutual comprehensibility. MERCOSUR brought a change in this state of affairs. As early as 1992 it agreed on a plan to facilitate and develop the teaching of Spanish in Brazil and of Portuguese in the Spanish-speaking countries at all education levels.[99] This intergovernmental decision was a significant breakthrough of the alienating policies of the past.

As time went by, laws 11.161/2005 in Brazil and 26.468/2008 in Argentina were introduced to oblige all secondary schools to offer classes in Spanish and Portuguese as foreign languages.[100] Even though the universal teaching of Spanish and Portuguese has not been achieved due to practical reasons (lack of qualified teachers and funding), the number of university programmes for teachers of Spanish and Portuguese has substantially increased, and so have the enrolments to these programmes. Thus in Brazil there were only 18 universities offering a specialization in Spanish in 1970 and 30 universities in 1990. Their number increased to 324 in 2008 and was estimated 348 for 2009.[101]

The agreed language teaching policy does not affect the educational sphere alone but has more serious implications. In MERCOSUR there are concerns that Spanish and Portuguese undermine English as the preferred second language. This debate goes beyond the educational system into the topic of geopolitical strategy and the choice between Latin Americanism and Pan-Americanism. Concerns were also expressed in Europe in 2000 when MERCOSUR ministers of education reinforced the programme of teaching of Spanish and Portuguese in schools. France, Britain, and Italy protested against this measure because it implied a potential reduction in the teaching of their languages.[102]

Throughout history the fate of languages has been linked to power relationships. The EU and MERCOSUR have transformed power relations in the regions that diminished the relevance of French and increased the role of Portuguese. European integration has contributed to the hegemonic expansion of English as a facilitator of intra-regional communication. This happened involuntarily and despite resistance to this process.[103] MERCOSUR is promoting Portuguese and Spanish as second languages intentionally. The growth of Brazilian power would have strengthened Portuguese in South America anyway, but the simultaneous decision of the three Spanish-speaking countries to teach Portuguese in schools would hardly be possible without MERCOSUR. The union has set an interesting precedent with two regional languages. If developed further, the regional policy can lead to the formation of a bilingual regional identity with Spanish and Portuguese being not foreign languages for the citizens, but languages of 'wider communication,' 'participation,' and 'integration,' as some observers already refer to them.[104]

There are substantial differences in the scope and results of linguistic policies in the two regions. The level of ethnic diversity of the EU restricts the scope of linguistic policies to the institutional domain only, while the MERCOSUR's policy is a conscious decision to strengthen cultural community and is meant to affect citizens. The EU is not allowed to tell the member states what to teach in schools, while this type of intervention from regional institutions is occurring in MERCOSUR. Any European measure targeting indiscriminate multilingualism is destined to fail for obvious reasons, and EU institutions are compelled to discriminate other languages in favour of English, French, and German. In MERCOSUR, even though the decision to include Spanish and Portuguese in the national curricula has not dramatically changed the existing pattern of foreign language teaching yet, the number of university programmes for Spanish and Portuguese teachers has substantially increased, and so have the enrolments to these programmes. If MERCOSUR's policy sustains, it will have consequences for the construction of a bilingual regional identity based on Spanish and Portuguese.

4.5 Cultural Work of Regional Institutions

As clearly seen, MERCOSUR's relative linguistic homogeneity has been favourable for the policies attempting linguistic integration. So does MERCOSUR's relative cultural homogeneity give the bloc a wider area for manoeuvres in cultural integration. The ongoing experiment in Europe is more developed in economic matters. Inspired by the desire to achieve postwar reconciliation and ensure peace, the initiators of European integration defined their mission chiefly in economic terms, starting with such practices as trade, and coal and steel production. European institutions gradually ensured the free movement of goods, services, capital, and labour. Foreign policy, monetary and, to some extent, social elements were added to this complex construction. However, the cultural dimension of the EU has remained modest and guarded. Despite frequent rhetorical invocations of a common European cultural heritage and common cultural traditions, the perception of culture remains framed mainly in terms of national culture, seen as a pillar of the national state and as a source of national identity.

The concept of the EU citizenship has so far been limited to that of producer and consumer. Only after 1985 did there appear policies emphasizing the symbolic and cultural dimensions of citizenship through education and Euro-symbols. Proper culture and education were not incorporated into the competences of the EU activity before the 1992 Maastricht Treaty.[105] Article 128 of the Maastricht Treaty acknowledged culture as a common concern. According to Paragraph 1 of this Article 'the Community shall contribute to the flowering of the culture of Member States, while respecting their regional diversity and at the same time bringing their cultural heritage to the fore.' 'Apart from this being, in the words of one commentator, a nice example of the EC baroque legislative language, the lay reader is left wondering what these words could mean in practice.'[106]

Article 151 of the Amsterdam Treaty contains two restrictive clauses for cultural integration: the requirement of the unanimity of ministerial vote in decision-making in the cultural sphere and the exclusion of harmonization of national cultural systems.[107] Thus, in contrast to other social dimensions, culture is excluded from regional integration *de jure*. Indirectly though, the European Commission has been influencing culture through regulations coming from other spheres that affect cultural industries and cultural goods. At the same time, Paragraph 4 of Article 151, stipulating that the EU will consider the cultural implications of all its legislation, has remained a dead letter.

The EU's commitment to cultural development has so far been rhetorical while cultural projects and programmes have been symbolic. Actions and programmes undertaken by the EU to make citizens learn more about each other and their respective cultures facilitate local events even when they include participants from three or four member states. Cultural operators complain that the Commission's cultural budgets are miniscule, the EU-sponsored projects lack transparent selection procedures, have too many administrative complications, and that *eurocrats* are insensitive to cultural cooperation.[108] The EU budget for the enhancement of multilingualism, for instance, had only 2.5 million per year available, and it buried the provisions of the Socrates Programme.

As in the EU, the economic agenda dominated in MERCOSUR. The founding Treaty of MERCOSUR was signed in 1991 in the period when neoliberalism was a dominant economic ideology all over the world and particularly in Latin America. The Treaty focused exclusively on economic themes and did not have a single provision on culture. However, in contrast to the EC, MERCOSUR became involved in the spheres of culture, education, and research since its early days through specialized meetings, which later evolved into more elaborated institutional forms, such as regular ministerial meetings and permanent working groups. Thus already in 1992 MERCOSUR ministers of education defined strategies for their sector and approved a three-year plan that became the main document for MERCOSUR's educational, cultural, and linguistic integration. This document treated integration in education as a prerequisite for economic and political integration. It set programmes for the development of citizen awareness of integration, programmes for the harmonization of educational systems through the coordination of academic, information, legal and administrative systems, and programmes for training professionals able to contribute to integration at various educational and research levels.

This plan included the recommendation of the teaching of Spanish in Brazil and of Portuguese in the Spanish-speaking countries within the respective national education systems. Among the accompanying protocols there were those that prescribed the recognition of educational qualifications and revalidation of diplomas. It also included measures to facilitate communication and circulation of professionals in the field; however, priority was given to the circulation of cultural goods and services and the integration of cultural industries among the MERCOSUR countries, Chile and Bolivia. Also in 1992, there began regular meetings for science and technology.[109] The first meeting formulated priorities for cooperation in scientific research. (The institutions in Brussels were not involved with European scientific networks before the 1980s.) Meetings of the ministers of culture became regular in 1995. The Memorandum of Understanding issued in their first specialized meeting stated that 'the common heritage of Latin American nations and especially of MERCOSUR is a powerful factor for rapprochement capable of facilitating political and economic integration.'[110]

In 1995 a protocol about recognition of secondary and higher education qualifications was signed. Agreements on secondary and higher education and on training staff for universities came out in 1996 along with a protocol on cultural integration in MERCOSUR that adopted norms regarding customs treatment of cultural objects and defined cultural stamp of MERCOSUR to facilitate the movement of cultural objects within the region.[111] This protocol became crucial for the intensification of cultural exchanges. Subsequently, a series of agreements among the MERCOSUR countries were achieved: on cooperation among institutions and cultural agents (historic archives, libraries, museums, and other institutions responsible for the preservation of historic and cultural heritage), on the promotion of joint programmes and projects, on production and co-production of cultural events, on training human resources, on implementing cultural and historic research, and on cultural promotion in third countries.

By 1997 MERCOSUR recognized the achievement of compatibility and equivalence of educational systems except in higher education. The new strategic plan for educational development from 2001 to 2005 established additional normative and operational benchmarks for educational integration at all levels: primary, secondary, secondary technical, and tertiary. It created information and communication systems in education, introduced the common curricula for the teaching of history and geography, spelled out the requirements for a greater dissemination of the teaching of Spanish and Portuguese, described the mechanism of recognition of university degrees (analogous agreement took decades to achieve in the EU), and agreed on the free movement of students seeking university education within MERCOSUR.

At present MERCOSUR supervises or supports common actions in the following areas: funding and administration of scholarships; adult education; evaluation of educational quality and educational reform; educational television; communication and information (*Ibermedia*); linguistic policy; regulation in cultural industries[112]; organization and promotion of cultural events (festivals, seminars, courses, concerts, exhibitions) and of professional, technical, artistic and cultural exchanges; preservation of cultural and historic heritage and support to indigenous groups; publications; encouragement of cultural tourism; scientific and research cooperation; inventory and database creation; and the creation of archive and library networks and their support. Of the mentioned activities several programmes are particularly visible because of their emblematic value. These are the programmes targeting the preservation of Jesuit[113] and Guaraní heritage,[114] which is a common historic property of MERCOSUR-4. MERCOSUR patronizes the operation of the MERCOSUR Centre for Musical Documentation in Montevideo[115] and the Houses of Culture of MERCOSUR in the national capitals.[116]

4.6 CONCLUSION

The exercises to identify elements of the common civilizational base of the EU bring about such notions as Western Christianity, the support of the neo-imperialist geopolitical agenda of the USA and NATO, and the accompanying rhetoric about the commitment of all truly European nations to liberal democracy, human rights, and the market economy. In addition, the profile of Western Europe, a sub-region of the EU, is associated with the history of domination over colonial empires, and the image of the area as an avant-garde in philosophy, arts, science, technology, and fashion. Discourses on *the European identity* often serve the goal to legitimize the authority of European institutions. However, *the European identity* hardly exists, and notions like institutional loyalty among EU employees or a sentiment of solidarity among some citizens are more appropriate to discuss instead. As *Europeanness* clearly has more of a political than cultural meaning, it is defined in pseudo-cultural terms. 'EU culture' does exist, but it is a bureaucratic culture, remote and inaccessible to people outside bureaucratic circles.

Compared to Europe, MERCOSUR is an area with solid cultural premises manifested by key affinities of language, religion, government systems, and by common historic experiences. The history of *Guaranies*, the Iberian cultural substratum (two Ibero-Romance languages Spanish and Portuguese, Roman Catholicism, similar political, administrative and legal systems), immigrant experience, and hardships from imperialism and neocolonialism constitute the basis of regional identity and solidarity in MERCOSUR. An important advantage of MERCOSUR over the EU is that its citizens can freely communicate across national borders without translators, interpreters, or years spent acquiring a foreign language.

MERCOSUR also distinguishes itself from the rest of Latin America by a weaker impact of the original cultures (in contrast to Mexico, Peru, and Guatemala) and the later beginning of colonization (if compared to Mexico and the Caribbean). As MERCOSUR is a region of fairly recent immigration, nowhere else in Latin America are national identities as fragile as in Brazil, Argentina, and Uruguay. The history of European immigration, a shorter period of autonomous development, and a less prominent pre-Colombian record than elsewhere in Latin America explain

MERCOSUR's strong orientation towards Western Europe and great susceptibility to influences coming from this part of the world. Whereas MERCOSUR is better consolidated by cultural and linguistic affinities, greater interaction and interdependence is a stronger cohesive force in the EU. To a large extent EU legitimacy has rested on the union's capacity to generate wealth for its members, and if the EU fails to deliver economically, its prospects will not be optimistic. MERCOSUR is in possession of cultural affinities that generate popular support to integration and stimulate converging visions on matters of foreign policy. Achievement of consensus on political interests is currently failing in the implementation of the CFSP in the EU for a number of reasons. Many of them can be attributed to matters of cultural diversity.

The agreement on the programme targeting the achievement of Spanish-Portuguese bilingualism is a good illustration of MERCOSUR's efforts in cultural integration. Strengthening the cultural community of MERCOSUR is a realistic goal given the historic and cultural affinities of the five countries, and the similarity of their languages, institutions, and social practices inherited from Spain and Portugal. Measures of cultural integration in MERCOSUR were implemented even in the late 1990s, at a time when nationalistic tensions were hard to overcome because of economic recession, heated trade conflicts, competitive devaluations, and express differences in the geopolitical orientation of Brazil and Argentina. The progress of integration under conditions of economic disruption caused by the Argentinean financial crisis of 2002 showed that at least for Brazil the logic of neighbourhood solidarity at times superseded pragmatic calculations of the costs and benefits of integration.

In contrast to the EU where cultural policy formally remains a business of the member states, MERCOSUR started cultural work almost since its beginning, even though its founding documents did not mention culture as a domain of integration even once. The cultural work of MERCOSUR and measures of cultural integration are facilitated by the relative cultural homogeneity among its member states and the growing understanding of the necessity to support economic and political integration by ideological and cultural work. However, integration initiatives should not be over-reliant on cultural affinity, as regionalization is subject to a variety of predictable and unpredictable factors of economics, domestic politics, and geopolitics. These factors do not allow accurate projections of the union's cultural affinities on the future of the process. Notwithstanding, cultural and cognitive aspects of integration should not recede into the background of MERCOSUR studies.

NOTES

1. Malamud, Andrés and Schmitter, Philippe C. 2011. The experience of European integration and the potential for integration in South America. In *New Regionalism and the European Union: Dialogues, comparisons and new research directions*, edited by Alex Warleigh-Lack, Nick Robinson and Ben Rosamond, pp 135–157. Routledge, London. p 143.
2. Idem, p 148.
3. Haas, Ernst Bernard. 1967. The uniting of Europe and the 'uniting of Latin America.' Journal of Common Market Studies, 5/4, pp 315–343. p 333.
4. Malamud, Andrés. 2010. Latin American Regionalism and EU Studies. *Journal of European Integration*, 32:6, pp 637–657. p 654.
5. Ermácora, Ramón. 2000. *El Mercosur de la Gente*. Ediciones del INCASUR, BsAs. p 12.
6. Speech in Washington, 30.4.1952.
7. Holmes, Douglas R. 2000. Surrogate Discourses of Power: The European Union and the Problem of Society. In *An Anthropology of the European Union: Building, Imagining and Experiencing the New Europe*, edited by Irène Bellier and Thomas M. Wilson, pp 93–115. Berg, Oxford. For anthropological commentaries on definitions and uses of culture concept see: Cohen, Anthony P. 1982. Belonging: the experience of culture. In *Belonging: Identity and Social Organisation in British Rural Cultures*, edited by Anthony P. Cohen, pp 1–18. Manchester University Press, Manchester. Wright, Susan. 1998. The Politicization of 'Culture.' *Anthropology Today*, 14:1, pp 7–15.
8. Neveu, Catherine. 1997. Anthropologie de la citoyenneté. In *Anthropologie du politique*, edited by Marc Abélès and Henri Pierre Jeudy, pp 85–88. Armand Colin, Paris.
9. Schnapper, Dominique. 1997. The European Debate on Citizenship. *Dædalus*, 126:3, pp 199–222. The MIT Press, Cambridge.
10. Smith, Anthony D. 1992. National Identity and the Idea of European Unity. *International Affairs*, 68:1, pp 55–76.
11. The studies of public opinion confirm that citizens' perception of MERCOSUR was largely positive even in critical moments for inter-state relations. In 1994 the polls of *el Centro de Estudios Unión para la Nueva Mayoría* revealed that 47% of Argentineans supported the Treaty of Asunción while 9% were against it. The friendly attitude towards MERCOSUR prevailed regardless of ideological beliefs. In 1996 after the emergence of highly politicized trade disputes in the automobile industry, 39% of respondents thought that MERCOSUR was going to consolidate and 24% thought that it was going to weaken. In 1997 the perceptions of

MERCOSUR were still positive with 38% of respondents having a favourable impression and 23% negative. In spite of widely cultivated fears of 'Brazil-dependency', Argentineans trusted Brazil more than they trusted the USA: 54% of respondents gave priority to MERCOSUR and only 13% to the USA. In 1998, 75% of the interviewed believed that a war between Argentina and Brazil was impossible. Of the 7% of people who thought that the war was possible, most had no education beyond primary level. Thus MERCOUR had the constant support of Argentineans. Relations with Brazil were important for the Argentinean public opinion even in the moments when official Buenos Aires adopted highly negative stances towards Brazil (Fraga, Rosendo. 2000. Uma visão política do Mercosul. In *Mercosul: entre a realidade e a utopia*, edited by Jorge Campbell, pp 271–236. Relume Dumará, Rio de Janeiro).
12. Even though common markets presuppose the free movement of labour, in practice cultural, social, linguistic, economic, and bureaucratic barriers create obstacles. The owners of capital are able to shift their resources more quickly and effectively than the workforce. Therefore integration creates more favourable regimes for capitalists at the expense of other groups and can potentially damage the intra-national and intra-regional social balance. Integration favours stronger and bigger economies and the interests of capital among production sectors and internationally, and it hurts small countries and workforce engaged in import-competing sectors.
13. Aron, Raymond. 1962. *Paix et guerre entre les nations*. Calmann-Lévy, Paris. p 125.
14. Wendt, Alexander. 1992. Anarchy is what states make of it: Social construction of power politics. *International Organization*, 42:2, pp 391–425.
15. See various contributions to the volume García, Soledad (editor). 1993. *European Identity and the Search for Legitimacy*. Pinter Publishers, London.
16. Yoder, John Howard. 1994. *World Order Visions Since Early Modern Europe*. Unpublished.
17. Bellier, Irène. 2000. The European Union, Identity Politics and the Logic of Interests' Representation. In *An Anthropology of the European Union: Building, Imagining and Experiencing the New Europe*, edited by Irène Bellier and Thomas M. Wilson, pp 53–73. Berg, Oxford.
18. BBC, 8.4.2004, Translating is EU's new boom industry, http://news.bbc.co.uk/2/hi/europe/3604069.stm, 1.11.2017.
19. Gómez Mera, Laura. 2005. Explaining Mercosur's Survival: Strategic Sources of Argentine-Brazilian Convergence. Journal of Latin American Studies, 37, pp 109–140.

20. Only recently did the two pairs of countries set up permanent mechanisms for bilateral cooperation. In 1986, Spain and Portugal did this within the framework of the EC while Brazil and Argentina agreed on PICE. In 1991, Spain and Portugal initiated the Ibero-American Community of Nations while Brazil and Argentina launched MERCOSUR. The complexity of Spanish–Portuguese historical relations is discussed in: Jakovlev, P'otr. 2004. Portugalija i Ispanija: novaja paradigma otnoshenij. *Latinskaja Amerika*, 6, pp 4–17. Institute of Latin America of the Russian Academy, Moskva.

21. Grimson, Alejandro. 2002. *El otro lado del río: periodistas, nación y Mercosur en la frontera*. EUDEBA, BsAs.

22. Molle, Willem. 2001. *The Economics of European Integration: Theory, Practice, Policy*. Ashgate Publishing, Aldershot. p 43.

23. Sampson, Anthony. 1968. *The new Europeans: a guide to the workings, institutions and character of contemporary Western Europe*. Hodder & Stoughton, London. p 26.

24. Smith, Gordon. 1983. *Politics in Western Europe: A Comparative Analysis*. Heinemann Educational, London. p 244.

25. McNeill emphasizes ecological and technological aspects of European history. McNeill, William H. 1979. Patterns of European History. In *Europe as a Cultural Area*, edited by Jean Cuisenier, pp 7–94. Mouton, 's-Gravenhage.

26. Russett, Bruce Martin. 1975. International Regions and the International System: A Study in Political Ecology. Greenwood Press, Westport. pp 26–27 and 72–73.

27. Fuchs, Dieter and Klingemann, Hans-Dieter. 2002. Eastward Enlargement of the European Union and the Identity of Europe. In *The Enlarged European Union: Diversity and Adaptation*, edited by Peter Mair and Jan Zielonka, pp 19–54. Frank Cass, London.

28. Wallace, William. 1995. *Regionalism in Europe: Model or Exception?* In *Regionalism in World Politics*, edited by Louise Fawcett and Andrew Hurrell, pp 201–227. Oxford University Press, Oxford.

29. Shore, Cris and Black, Annabel. 1994. Citizens' Europe and the Construction of European Identity. In *The Anthropology of Europe: Identity and Boundaries in Conflict*, edited by Victoria A. Goddard, Josep R. Llobera and Cris Shore, pp 275–298. Berg, Oxford. p 291.

30. Toner, Michael. 1988. *Bluff Your Way in the EEC*. Ravette Publishing, Horsham. p 10.

31. See: Schlesinger, Philip. 1994. Europeanness: A New Cultural Battlefield? In *Nationalism*, edited by John Hutchinson and Anthony D. Smith, pp 316–325. Oxford University Press, Oxford. de Clercq, Willy. 1993. *Reflection on Information and Communication Policy of the European*

Community. The European Commission, Brussels. Nederveen Pieterse, Jan P. 1994. Unpacking the West: How European is Europe? In *Racism, Modernity and Identity: On the Western Front*, edited by Ali Rattansi and Sallie Westwood, pp 129–149. Polity Press, Cambridge. Wistrich, Ernest. 1991. *After 1992: The United States of Europe*. Routledge, Oxford.
32. Shore and Black, 1994. Shore, Chris. 2001. *European Union and the Politics of Culture*. Paper 43, The Bruges Group, London.
33. Eric Wolf as cited in Shore, 2001.
34. Elie McBride as cited in Shore, 2001.
35. Laitin, David D. 2002. Culture and National Identity: 'The East' and European Integration. In *The Enlarged European Union: Diversity and Adaptation*, edited by Peter Mair and Jan Zielonka, pp 55–80. Frank Cass, London.
36. Galtung, Johan. 2002. *Rethinking Conflict: A Cultural Approach*. Working paper, Council of Europe, Strasbourg.
37. The Guardian, 23.1.1989, Community Whitewash, Alibhai, Yasmin.
38. European Cultural Foundation. 2005. *Europe as a Cultural Project*. Amsterdam. p 16.
39. Jackson, Patrick T. 2006. *Civilizing the Enemy: German Reconstruction and the Invention of the West*. University of Michigan Press, Ann Arbor.
40. Herzfeld, Michael. 1993. *The Social Production of Indifference: Exploring the Symbolic Roots of Western Bureaucracy*, The University of Chicago Press, Chicago. p 2.
41. Huntington, Samuel P. 1997. *The Clash of Civilizations and the Remaking of World Order*. Touchstone, New York.
42. Talk in Glasgow on 9 November 2005.
43. Duchêne, François. 1994. *Jean Monnet: The First Statesman of Interdependence*. Norton, New York.
44. Judt, Tony. 1996. *A Grand Illusion? An Essay of Europe*. Hill and Wang, New York.
45. Shore and Black, 1994. p 296.
46. Rama, Ángel. 1985. Algunas sugerencias de trabajo para una aventura intelectual de integración. In *La literatura latinoamericana como proceso*, edited by Ana Pizarro, pp 85–97. Centro Editor de América Latina, BsAs.
47. Boldori de Baldussi, Rosa. 2002. *La identidad cultural del Mercosur*. Ciudad Argentina, BsAs.
48. Idem, p 19.
49. The Tupi family of languages among other groups includes the Tupi-Guaraní group. The Tupi-Guaraní group is further divided into several sub-groups, two of which are Tupi and Guaraní.
50. Henríquez Ureña, Pedro. 1949. *Las corrientes literarias en la América Hispánica*. FCE, México. p 37.

51. Decisión 35/2006, 'Incorporación del guaraní como idioma del MERCOSUR', 15.12.2006.
52. de Gandía, Enrique. 1974. Introducción. In *La Argentina*, by Ruy Díaz de Guzmán, pp 11–25. Librería Huemul, BsAs. p 19.
53. Different authors are cited as in Boldori de Baldussi, 2002.
54. Tratado de Tordesillas, 7.6.1494.
55. In 1808, the Portuguese court and government apparatus fled to Brazil from Napoleon's invasion of Portugal, making Rio de Janeiro the capital of the Portuguese Empire until Brazilian independence was proclaimed in 1822.
56. Vizentini, Paulo G. F. 1999. El MERCOSUR en el contexto de la estrategia brasileña de reinserción internacional. In *Procesos de integración en América Latina: Perspectivas y experiencias latinoamericanas y europeas*, edited by Raymond Buve and Marianne Wiesebron, pp 155–170. Universidad Iberoamericana, México.
57. Campbell, Jorge, Rozemberg, Ricardo, and Svarzman, Gustavo. 2000. Argentina e Brasil na década de 1980: entre a cornija e a integração. In *Mercosul: entre a realidade e a utopia*, edited by Jorge Campbell, pp 31–98. Relume Dumará, Rio de Janeiro.
58. Attributed to Sáenz Peña's written or oral communication to Barão do Rio Branco.
59. The Economist. 1996. *A Survey of MERCOSUR. Remapping South America*. pp S1-S32. *The Economist*, 12–18.10.1996, London. p S4.
60. Fraga, 2000.
61. Pacto de No Agresión, Consulta y Arbitraje, 25.5.1915.
62. Convenio para la prevención y represión del Contrabando, 10.10.1933; Convenio para reglamentar la Navegación Aérea, 10.10.1933; Tratado de Navegación y Comercio, 10.10.1933; Convenio de Intercambio Intelectual, 10.10.1933; Acuerdo para el Canje de Publicaciones, 10.10.1933; Convenio de Intercambio Artístico, 10.10.1933; Convenio para la revisión de los textos de enseñanza de la Historia y Geografía, 10.10.1933; Convenio sobre exposiciones de muestras y ventas de productos nacionales, 10.10.1933; Protocolo adicional al Tratado de Comercio y Navegación, 10.10.1933; Convenio para el fomento del Turismo, 10.10.1933; Tratado de Extradición, 10.10.1933; Notas reversales respecto a la construcción de un Puente Internacional sobre el Río Uruguay, 15.6.1934; Acuerdo por notas reversales sobre coordinación y cooperación en materia de Defensa Sanitaria Vegetal, 1.2.1935; Protocolo para la construcción de un Puente Internacional sobre el Río Uruguay en la zona entre Paso de los Libres y Uruguayana, 24.5.1935; Protocolo adicional al Tratado de Extradición del 10.10.1933, 24.5.1935; Convenio sobre luchas civiles, 24.5.1935; Convenio para el fomento del Intercambio de Profesores y Estudiantes, 24.5.1935; Tratado de Comercio y

Navegación, 29.5.1935; Acuerdo por notas reversales referente al art. VI del Tratado de Comercio y Navegación de la misma fecha, 29.5.1935; Convenio para facilitar la visita recíproca de técnicos fitosanitarios, 29.5.1935; Acuerdo por notas reversales acerca de la expansión del consumo de yerba mate que se llevará a cabo por la Comisión Mixta, a crearse en Buenos Aires, 29.5.1935; Acuerdo por notas reversales informando que de acuerdo a las leyes de ambos países, existen disposiciones legales que obligan a establecer la prohibición de adicionar a los productos alimenticios, sustancias nocivas a la salud, 29.5.1935.

63. Tratado para promover un Régimen de Libre Intercambio Comercial, 21.11.1941.
64. Convenio sobre unión aduanera y cooperación económica y financiera, 13.12.1946.
65. Abadie-Aicardi, Oscar. 1999. *Fundamentos históricos y políticos del Mercosur*. Melibea Ediciones, Montevideo. p 61.
66. Acta suscripta por los excelentísimos presidentes de Argentina y Chile, 21.2.1953.
67. Ermácora, 2000. p 18.
68. Tratado de unión económica argentino-chileno, 8.7.1953.
69. Convenio entre la República Oriental del Uruguay y la República Argentina para el aprovechamiento de los rápidos del Río Uruguay en la zona de Salto Grande, 30.12.1946.
70. Convenio de cooperación para el estudio del aprovechamiento de la energía hidráulica de los ríos Acaray y Monday, 20.1.1956.
71. Convenio para el estudio del aprovechamiento de la energía hidráulica de los saltos del Apipé, 23.1.1958.
72. Declaración conjunta, 23.9.1960.
73. Declaración conjunta sobre el límite exterior del Río de la Plata, 30.1.1961; Tratado de límites en el Río Uruguay, 7.4.1961.
74. Acordo para a Criação de uma Comissão Mista para o Aproveitamento da Lagoa Mirim, 26.4.1963; Ajuste Complementar ao Acordo sobre a Criação da Comissão Mista para o Aproveitamento da Lagoa Mirim, 5.8.1965.
75. Declaración Conjunta, 21.4.1961; Declaración Económica, 21.4.1961; Declaración sobre Intercambio Cultural, 21.4.1961; Convenio de Amistad, 21.4.1961.
76. Acuerdo por notas reversales a efectos de concretar los propósitos tendientes a la puesta en servicio de la obra de Salto Grande antes del invierno de 1979, 8.7.1968.
77. Tratado de La Cuenca del Plata, 23.4.1963.
78. Tratado del Río de la Plata y su Frente Marítimo, 19.11.1973; Acta de la Confraternidad Rioplatense, 19.11.1973; Acuerdo complementario del Tratado del Río de la Plata relativo a los canales de acceso a los puertos y libertad de sobrevuelo, 19.11.1973.

79. Tratado para o Aproveitamento Hidroelétrico dos Recursos Hídricos do Rio Paraná, Pertencentes em Condomínio aos Dois Países, Desde e Inclusive o Salto Grande de Sete Quedas ou Salto de Guairá, até a Foz do Rio Iguaçu, 26.04.1973.
80. Tratado de Yaciretá, 3.12.1973.
81. Acuerdo sobre aprovechamiento hidroeléctrico de Corpus e Itaipú, 19.10.1979.
82. Fourteen different documents were signed on 17 May 1980: **Notas** reversales relativas a la creación de una Comisión Mixta para la construcción de un Puente sobre el Río Iguazú, **Convenio** para evitar la Doble Imposición y prevenir la Evasión Fiscal con respecto a los impuestos sobre la renta, **Notas** reversales sobre interconexión del Sistema Eléctrico argentino con el Sistema Eléctrico brasileño, **Memorándum** de Entendimiento relativo a Consultas sobre asuntos de interés común, **Protocolo** de Cooperación Industrial entre la Comisión Nacional de Energía Atómica de Argentina y Empresas Nucleares Brasileiras S.A., **Convenio** de Cooperación entre la Comisión Nacional de Energía Atómica de Argentina y Empresas Nucleares Brasileiras S.A., **Convenio** de Cooperación entre la Comisión Nacional de Energía Atómica de Argentina y la Comisión Nacional de Energía Nuclear del Brasil, **Acuerdo** por notas reversales sobre importación de materiales y elementos destinados a la construcción o mejoras de los edificios afectados exclusivamente a Misiones Diplomáticas de la Argentina en territorio brasileño y viceversa, **Acuerdo** sobre Sanidad Animal en áreas de frontera, **Nota** reversal poniendo en vigor el Convenio de Cooperación entre la Comisión Nacional de Energía Atómica de Argentina y la Comisión Nacional de Energía Nuclear del Brasil y el Protocolo de Cooperación Industrial entre la Comisión Nacional de Energía Atómica de Argentina y Empresas Nucleares Brasileiras S.A., **Tratado** para el aprovechamiento de los Recursos Hídricos compartidos de los tramos limítrofes del Río Uruguay y de su afluente el Río Peperí-Guazú, **Acuerdo** de cooperación para el desarrollo y la aplicación de los usos pacíficos de la Energía Nuclear, **Acuerdo** de Cooperación Científica y Tecnológica, and **Declaración** Conjunta.
83. Relations with Chile were developing more slowly. The last agreement that settled remaining border disputes was achieved only in 1998, 20 years after the analogous agreement with Brazil.
84. Gardini, Gian Luca. 2005. Two Critical Passages on the Road to Mercosur. *Cambridge Review of International Affairs*, 18:3, pp 405–420. p 411.
85. Declaración de Iguazú, 30.11.1985; Declaración política sobre política nuclear, 30.11.1985.
86. Acta para la Integración Argentino-Brasileña, 29.7.1986.

87. Moniz Bandeira, Luiz Alberto. 2003. Brasil, Argentina e Estados Unidos – Conflicto e Integração na América do Sul (Da Triple Aliança ao Mercosul 1870-2003). Editora Revan, Rio de Janeiro.
88. Campbell et al, 2000. pp 76–77.
89. Tratado de Integración, Cooperación y Desarrollo, 29.11.1988.
90. Acta de Buenos Aires, 6.7.1990.
91. The participation of Paraguay in the trilateral process became possible after the overthrow of Stroessner in 1989.
92. Acuerdo de Complementación Económica 14 entre la República Argentina y la República Federativa del Brasil, 20.12.1990.
93. Campbell et al, 2000.
94. Tratado para la Constitución de un Mercado Común entre la República Argentina, la República Federativa del Brasil, la República del Paraguay y la República Oriental del Uruguay, 26.3.1991.
95. On linguistic preferences in the EU institutions see Truchot, Claude. 2003. Languages and supranationality in Europe: The linguistic influence of the European Union. In *Languages in a Globalising World*, edited by Jacques Maurais and Michael Morris, pp 99–110. Cambridge University Press, Cambridge.
96. Idem.
97. On history of foreign language teaching in the MERCOSUR countries see Hamel, Reiner Enrique. 2003. Regional blocs as a barrier against English hegemony? The language policy of Mercosur in South America. In *Languages in a Globalising World*, edited by Jacques Maurais and Michael Morris, pp 111–142. Cambridge University Press, Cambridge.
98. Corvalán, Graziella. 1997. Políticas lingüísticas e integración en el Paraguay. In *Ñane ñe' e. Paraguay bilingüe. Políticas lingüísticas y educación bilingüe*, edited by Bartomeu Meliá, pp 38–47. Fundación en Alianza, Asunción.
99. Decisão 07/1992, 'Plano trienal para o setor educação no contexto do MERCOSUL', 27.06.1992.
100. 11.161 of 5.8.2005 (Brazil) & 26.468 of 17.12.2008 (Argentina).
101. Martínez-Cachero Laseca, Álvaro. 2008. *O ensino do espanhol no sistema educativo brasileiro*. Thesaurus, Brasília. pp 98–99.
102. Hamel, 2003. p 130.
103. In order to sustain French, the European Commission and France sponsor courses of French for *eurocrats* and organize various events promoting French across the EU, but these measures are hardly able to change language preferences in the European institutions. See *Financial Times*, 18.03.2004, Paris backs plan to uphold status of French language in the EU.
104. Barrios, Graciela. 1999. Minorías lingüísticas e integración regional: La región fronteriza uruguayo-brasileña. In *Políticas lingüísticas para América Latina*, pp 85–92. Universidad de Buenos Aires, BsAs.

105. Treaty on European Union, 7.2.1992.
106. Quoted as in Shore and Black, 1994. p 284.
107. Treaty of Amsterdam Amending the Treaty on European Union, the Treaties Establishing the European Communities and Certain Related Acts, 2.10.1997.
108. EFAH. 2004. *Report on the Programme Culture 2000.* EFAH, Brussels.
109. Reunión Especializada de Ciencia y Tecnología del Mercosur.
110. Memorandum de Entendimiento de la Primera Reunión Especializada de Cultura, 15.3.1995.
111. Tratamento Aduaneiro para a Circulação, nos Países do Mercosul, de Bens Integrantes de Projetos Culturais Aprovados pelos Órgãos Competentes, 31.10.1996.
112. See contributions to the volume Álvarez, Gabriel (editor). 2003. *Indústrias Culturais no Mercosul.* IBRI, Brasília. The studies in this book emphasize the economic importance of cultural industries for production, consumption, employment, and trade. In MERCOSUR cultural industries are a powerful tool of mutual learning of people about each other as these industries involve the production and circulation of cultural goods and services (Loza Aguerrebere, Ruben. 2003. Industiras culturales en el Uruguay, una aproximación. In *Indústrias Culturais...*, pp 365–393. p 365). Cross-border circulation of cultural goods and services in the region is high due to the language factor. Unfortunately, cultural production does not occur in the realm of cultural heritage or artistic creativity but in the cultural industry endowed with the capacity to mass-produce cultural products and disseminate them. Cultural industries have a strong homogenizing effect, and their mass products are marked by standardization and homogenization. Their domination strangles autonomous local artistic practices and imposes steady sets of expectations, conventions, genres and themes (Smiers, Joost. 2003. *Arts under pressure: promoting cultural diversity in the age of globalization.* Zed Books, London).
113. Acta 1/97 de la Cuarta Reunión de Ministros de Cultura, 7.6.1997.
114. Acta 2/95 de la Segunda Reunión Especializada de Cultura, 2.8.1995.
115. Acta 1/98 de la Sexta Reunión de Ministros de Cultura, 18.7.1998.
116. Acta 2/97 de la Quinta Reunión de Ministros de Cultura, 1.12.1997.

CHAPTER 5

External Factors and Geostrategic Considerations

Even though MERCOSUR and the EU differ significantly along many economic, political, cultural, and institutional criteria, the external dimension of their integration allows us to identify a number of similar motivations for their formation and development. The external dimension is indispensable for the study of regionalism as MERCOSUR and the EU are not autonomous processes exempt from external influences, but integral elements of the international system. They are shaped by this system and, at the same time, they exercise their own influence on the system. Neorealism provides the theoretical grounds for the comparison of this chapter because it is the approach that is primarily concerned with external factors of regionalism.[1]

MERCOSUR and the EU operate in conditions in which international politics and economics are characterized by a highly unequal distribution of resources and power in favour of the USA. The USA uses its power and resources to influence internal and external affairs of weaker states. Neglect of international agreements and commitments and the increasingly aggressive and unpredictable behaviour of the hegemon meet international resistance. Neorealism explains integration by convergence in foreign policy due to commonalities of interest, and these are not hard to find among weaker countries. Most of them share socio-economic concerns and the need to overcome vulnerability.[2] Promoted by foreign policy, integration is undertaken to improve their position in the global environment while consolidating regime control and enhancing state capabilities. Thus regionalism is driven by the search for stability and equilibrium in international relations.

© The Author(s) 2019
M. Mukhametdinov, *MERCOSUR and the European Union*,
https://doi.org/10.1007/978-3-319-76825-0_5

However, as this chapter argues, regionalism as a response to US hegemony in Europe and South America is not exactly the same. In comparative terms, the process in MERCOSUR has been more of a geoeconomic nature, and in the EU, of geopolitical. As relations with the USA constitute a special topic in any international agenda and because the US retains the ability to influence MERCOSUR and EU politics, the historic comparison of USA–MERCOSUR and USA–EU relations constitutes the basis of this chapter: Sections 5.1 and 5.2 portray regional integration in the two blocs as the processes deeply influenced by their interactions with the USA. Section 5.3 analyses the MERCOSUR–EU partnership, which offers further evidence in support of the neorealist hypothesis about integration being either a measure of adaptation to a strong hegemony or a measure of resistance against a contracting hegemony (See Subsection 1.3.4). Conclusion 5.4 highlights the differences in the agendas of USA–MERCOSUR and USA–EU relations. The different nature of the problems the two regions have in their relations with the superpower has predetermined some of the individual features in the character and outcomes of their integration.

5.1 The EU and the USA: 'Natural Allies,' Unequal Partnership, and Diverging Interests

The neorealist argument is particularly valid for the earlier stages of European integration, as during the Cold War era Western European integration was totally dominated by the ideological and security agenda of the USA:

> One of the central myths is that of Western Europe as a 'civilian power', pursuing economic objectives. The central reality was that Western European integration was rooted in a wider security framework, and constructed in large part around the security dilemmas which faced France, the Low Countries, and divided Germany.[3]

> The image of Western European regional integration in the 1960s and 1970s as a construct entire of itself, providing a model for others to follow, is an illusion. Western Europe was a sub-region within a wider Atlantic region: an Atlantic security community, committed to shared 'Western' values, within which the political, economic, and cultural influence of the USA on Western Europe was immense.[4]

Concerns about dynamic postwar Soviet development; socialism expanding to Eastern Europe, Asia, and Cuba; and intensifying activities of the domestic left movements consolidated the bonds between the USA and European ruling elites. The USA orchestrated European integration to strengthen the anticommunist coalition and financed it through the Marshall Plan. The institution of NATO and the Council for Mutual Economic Assistance in 1949, of the Warsaw Pact Organisation in 1955, and of the EC in 1957 signalled the formation of two rival blocs, 'Western' and 'Communist.' Rather than anything else, the EC was a US instrument of the Cold War against the USSR.

Outside the context of the East–West confrontation Western European countries had little common ground for integration. For West Germany, alignment with the USA meant an irrevocable breakup with the German Democratic Republic and territories of German prewar influence. French society was torn between the partnership with Germany against the emerging Anglo–American leadership and the search for allies among the USA and other European countries to resist the strengthening of Germany that caused France to participate in three wars between 1870 and 1945. Britain had priorities in the English-speaking world. It was losing colonies and experiencing an unwelcoming attitude of Continental Europeans who viewed the kingdom as an outsider promoting the US agenda on the Continent. Fears of communism and active US prompting caused the European actors to admit Britain and consolidate the transatlantic cooperation in the uneasy *Trans-La Manche* union.

As time went by, the EU and the USA became 'natural partners.' Their interests converge when it comes to relations with peripheral countries. With the collapse of communism, the EU and the USA saw a unique opportunity for the enforcement of openness and deregulation of peripheral and socialist economies. The USA locked Mexico in NAFTA, and the EU incorporated Central European countries. The objective was to accelerate the reconstruction of the global economy under the political and military control of developed countries through the political and economic subordination of the poorer countries, their disarmament and vertical proliferation of NATO military technology. Europeans see the USA as their main partner in the maintenance of the world order that they benefit from. The USA encourages the spread of international rules favourable to the rich countries and punishes those countries that break these rules. The USA also provides a security framework within which the EU can rely on energy supplies from the Persian Gulf.[5] In its turn, Europe offers support to the legitimization of US international initiatives.

However, the weight of the EU and the USA in international politics is not identical in spite of the fact that the EU population and economy exceed those of the USA. Europe is also the largest trading entity and the largest source of official development aid, comprising more than half of the assistance from the Development Assistance Committee in 2012—50.7%—followed by the USA (24.3%) and Japan (8.4%).[6] However, EU military capability is estimated in the range of 10% to 30% of the US armed forces. For a centre of power comparable with the USA, the EU lacks political unity. Without the unity of a single political nation, its foreign policy enterprise is being pulled in different directions. Even the main promoters of the European 'power' project, France and Belgium, have no objectives to build a United States of Europe super-state in the image of the USA, and do not accept the idea of a central government. There remain contradictions among the EU Franco-German core, Atlanticist pro-US countries (like Britain), and Central Europe. The political disunity of Europe accounts for a number of failing policies in the external sphere and inadequate responses to the crises in Yugoslavia, Iraq, Lebanon, Libya, and Syria, the inability to help to solve North-African, Sub-Saharan, and Middle Eastern problems, miniscule influence in Asia, and dubious results of policies in relation to Russia and Latin America.

As the USA has fewer incentives to work with international organizations and is often reluctant to follow its own rules and procedures, Europeans show an interest in subjecting the USA to the norms of international regimes. However, securing legal frameworks is typically a position of weaker parties. European declarations of adherence to multipolarity are other signs of weakness comparable to Russia and France's affirmations of the superpower status that they lost.[7] Europe will not become a power comparable to the USA soon as it has few means for military development and is not ready for a close political union. The new bipolar system will not emerge out of the predominance of the USA and the EU as the EU remains in a subordinated position and is disintegrating (Brexit).

Nevertheless, transatlantic relations are changing and the EU is becoming more articulate in the affirmation of its own preferences. The end of the Cold War diminished the strategic relevance of transatlantic security and revealed contradictions between the EU and the USA. Dynamic implementation of the SEA, the introduction of a common currency, and the adoption of the Treaty of Maastricht stimulated European ambitions to re-establish influence in the region and the world that they lost to the USA and USSR as a result of two big wars in the twentieth century.[8] To achieve prewar control over the whole continent, Western European countries incorporated Central Europe into their political and economic system. These developments have caused the USA to perceive the EU as a rival.

Re-establishment of Western European control over Central Europe found resistance from the USA, Atlanticist circles, and Eastern Europeans themselves. The latter wanted to secure the presence of the USA in order to counterbalance the German and Russian dispute over influence on the region. In principle, Washington's and Brussels' positions on Eastern enlargement seemed to coincide: both parties were using rhetoric about enlargement having an ultimate historic and geocultural meaning in being a virtue of 'return to Europe' for the 'victims of communism.' However, their strategic understandings were different. While the European establishment wanted to strengthen their control over the new entrants, Americans hoped to raise influence on Europe through an enlarged NATO and the ability to affect European politics through manipulations with the new members.

Europeans are concerned by the USA's hegemonic tendencies and pressures on Eastern Europe. With the disappearance of the USSR as a restraining factor, the USA became more single-handed in pursuing its pragmatic interests, at times causing damage to Europe. Showing unease with American unipolarity, Europeans say that there is a need to evolve towards a more balanced multipolar world. In practice this rhetoric obscures their desire to achieve a ruling status in the administration of the world system that would be equivalent to that of the USA.[9] This is why the EU long-term strategy is to organize a political union with armed forces. The EU has already achieved equipollence with the USA in economic terms. The common market and the euro allow the EU to manage commercial and investment relations with the USA as an equal. Neither of the parties is imposing grandiose transatlantic free trade projects like the FTAA and EUROSUR on each other, as most of their trade is already duty free. A similar level of economic development allows the USA and the EU to avoid irresolvable arguments as those in the WTO, the FTAA, and EUROSUR with their third-world negotiators. Even though arguments over bananas, genetically modified organisms, hormone-treated beef, and agricultural subsidies have shaken the transatlantic alliance for years, they remain outside more pressing agendas.

More serious US disappointments came with the euro, which undermined the dollar's status and made it more difficult for the USA to finance its current account deficits. Large amounts of trade are sensitive to the dollar–euro exchange rates and are a potential source of conflict due to temptations of competitive devaluations. An increasing European presence in the WTO (as a single negotiator on trade in goods), the IMF (France and Germany are discussing the possibility of merging their quotas), and the G-7 is making it harder for the USA to get its way. EU–US cooperation on security has faded. The USA disengaged from Europe, reducing its military presence by three times over the 1990s.[10] US interventions to Yugoslavia, Afghanistan, and Iraq intensified the work over the CFSP, integrated the Western European Union (a defence organization) into the EU overall structure, and stimulated the initiative for the creation of a rapid reaction force of 60,000 warriors.

So far Europeans have no intention to bypass NATO, but they are organizing their own military assets. The CFSP also has an eastern dimension as Russia and Iran have opted against their subordinated status. Washington worries that the CFSP can make Europeans less dependent on the USA and that the Policy can be used against US interests. For their part, Europeans are uncomfortable with the US missile interception system. This system is making the USA a safer and more secure country and is weakening US commitments to Europe. Besides, it causes Russia to develop its own system, partially neutralizing the British and French nuclear arsenal. Russian missiles are unlikely to reach the USA anyway, but the fact that Russia has retargeted many of them at NATO destinations in Europe brings uneasiness to the EU. A solution in the form of a joint US-EU system is not feasible. It would be an expensive project dominated by the USA, and it would be fraught with worrying reactions from China, Russia, and Iran. Divergences in extra-continental affairs are apparent as well, especially regarding the Persian Gulf and the Middle East. Intensifying antagonisms between the USA and the Islamic world further divide Europeans and Americans. The USA does not intend to re-evaluate its objectives in the Middle East, while European support of these objectives exposes a more vulnerable Europe to dangers of terrorism and Islamic radicalism.

Even though internal considerations drive the primary goals of the EU, many Europeans believe that through the union they can resist external threats. Integration efforts are largely motivated by the intention to achieve internal cohesion and to increase power on the global scene. This point may be illustrated by the fact that the countries that have benefited from the EU most as political powers are most committed to the integration. Thus Germany and France are international actors. However, without a strong union they could only play secondary roles on the international arena. In contrast to them, the countries that adhered to the EU mainly for economic reasons have remained on the margins of certain phases of integration.[11]

Thus Britain, Sweden, and Denmark did not adopt the euro and resisted further supranationalization of the union. However, resistance to US unilateralism is increasing among these countries too. Even the British think that their national interests are better served by a European foreign policy with a common defence component. A traditional ally of the USA, Britain initiated *the European Security and Defence Policy*. In July 2011 German, French, and Polish governments spoke of the need of a European military headquarters because they felt they could no longer rely on NATO. This time, however, Britain objected to what they said was a costly and unnecessary duplication of NATO.

Today the priorities of European integration lie precisely in the spheres where the EU lags behind the USA: political cohesion (attempts to introduce a European constitution), military power (the development of the CFSP), regional policy, consolidation of political power in financial institutions, and the salvation of the monetary union. Through economic and military development the EU is striving for greater equality in transatlantic relations. Europeans understand that greater internal consolidation of the union increases its external impact. They also encourage regionalism in some other parts of the world (Latin America, Southern Africa) as a means to constrain unstable American hegemony and establish more reliable security relations among the regions. Among other factors, the condition of European integration will depend on events in the USA.

5.2 MERCOSUR Changes Emphases

Undoubtedly, Latin America has suffered more from the pressures and consequences of the US hegemony than Europe. According to John Coatsworth, former Director of the Harvard Centre for Latin American Studies and current Provost of Columbia University: 'Between 1898 and 1994, the US government succeeded in overthrowing, or inducing friends to overthrow, no fewer than 41 Latin American governments (a dozen of them freely elected). That's one every 28 months.'[12] Another source says that in Latin America and the Caribbean during just the first 50 years of the twentieth century alone, the USA used over 50 armed interventions to secure its domination.[13] Coups in the 1960s all over Latin America (Brazil, Argentina, Peru, Bolivia, Ecuador) occurred not just as consequences of domestic turmoils, but also as manifestations of international controversies sharpened by the conflict between the USA and revolutionary Cuba. All the more, for the US ruling stratum Latin America comes out as a mirror reflecting internal threats to US security and prosperity.[14]

Nevertheless, regionalism in the Southern Cone and the rest of Latin America is usually discussed within the prism of economic rather than political and security relations. For Brazil and Argentina the USA is an invincible and somewhat distant power. For the USA, whose foreign policy towards Latin America varies according to sub-regions, the Southern Cone has a lower degree of priority than Mexico, Central America, and the Caribbean as vital areas for national security due to their geographic proximity, Venezuela as the largest supplier of oil, and Colombia as an alarming source of drug trafficking. The lower priority accorded to MERCOSUR has been favourable for its development: 'We have a little more luck than Mexico does. What we are not so far from God and not so close to the USA helps our lives a lot.'[15] However, MERCOSUR and other Latin American markets are extremely important for the USA, as Latin America is the principal consumer of US exports. Thus Mexico is importing more US products than Germany, France, and Italy taken together, Brazil more than China, the Dominican Republic more than India and Indonesia, Chile and Argentina each more than Russia, and Costa Rica more than whole of Eastern Europe.[16]

Over many years in the twentieth century regional and sub-regional integration in Latin America was taking place on the background of economic liberalization promoted by Washington that culminated in the FTAA initiative in the 1990s. Economic openness pursued by liberal regimes in Latin America achieved inflows of goods and investments from the industrialized countries that weakened national industrial and banking industries. Optimism about foreign investment disappeared as soon as foreigners captured the most profitable and strategically important industries in the process of privatization, which led to outflows of capital and a sharp increase in domestic prices. All over Latin America there were concerns that liberalization of trade with the USA through the FTAA would further weaken Latin American production bases and contribute to the growth of unemployment and social instability. Considering inequalities in competitiveness, there were risks of the preferential scheme with the USA causing a significant increase in the share of North American exports in Latin American imports and increase in the negative trade balance of Latin America. In relation to services, investment, intellectual property rights, and technology sectors, the FTAA threatened to significantly constrain Latin American economies by means of regulation and to convert them to exporters of primary products with declining incomes and growing unemployment.

Even though governments usually understood this, powerful export-oriented groups remained pro-FTAA and were able to demand and achieve the facilitation of their cross-border business activities regardless of everybody's dissatisfaction with US protectionism. The FTAA threatened to dissolve all Latin American groupings, and in case of MERCOSUR this could have easily happened through the demolition of its CET. MERCOSUR and other blocs in Latin America faced a real choice whether to adapt to the US economic system and disappear, or to resist being absorbed by the Northern hegemony. Even Brazil was ambiguous about the FTAA.[17] The larger but less consolidated sector was against it. Overall, the Brazilian government was anti-FTAA, but it remained cautious, as it understood that Brazil had limitations. Therefore all of the following scenarios were discussed as realistic for MERCOSUR: absorption of MERCOSUR by the FTAA, MERCOSUR entering the FTAA as a consolidated group with a CET and common currency, and the FTAA without Brazil.

The financial crises and oil wars have diverted the attention of the US diplomacy away from Latin America. However, the USA retains objectives to maintain economic and financial dependence of Latin America using IMF agreements and direct governance. It is imposing administrators to enforce liberalization policies and to adjust Latin American legislation to US external policy.[18] Plans to regain control over Latin America remain real through trade agreements, the Organization of American States and the efforts to keep the region demilitarized while securing the presence of US troops in adjacent areas. Neither can the USA bury entirely the idea of the FTAA or some other type of economic leadership in Latin America. Latin America is the only mega-region that gives surpluses to US trade in contrast to Europe and Asia with which US trade is in deficit. In addition, the ideas about the necessity to prioritize cooperation with the USA and Europe over MERCOSUR and Latin America remain fairly strong in both protagonists of MERCOSUR, more so in Argentina than Brazil.

Observers have ascribed many difficulties of MERCOSUR integration to fragile social and economic bases and to external vulnerability of the participant countries.[19] In contrast to the EU, which has a co-ruling status in the international stratification of power, Brazil, in Juagaribe's view, belongs to the intermediate level between dependency and resistance.[20]

Even though average incomes in Brazil are 8–10 times higher than in the poorest countries, they are as much lower than in the richest countries. Brazil has high-tech industries and a relatively stable democratic regime (attributes of industrialized countries), but its industrial system is not competitive enough. Brazil suffers chronic balance of payment deficits, and remains dependent on the financial system controlled by the USA. The Brazilian *Landless Peasant Movement* and urban crime rates are highly disconcerting. They are traits of instability of dependent countries. Bernal-Meza observed that there was a certain contradiction between Brazilian foreign policy that kept a distance from Washington and an economic ideology that was based on neoliberalism, economic openness, and deregulation, the principles exercised by Mexico, Chile, Argentina, and the USA itself.[21] Another eloquent evidence of Brazil's semi-dependency is its ambivalent position in relation to MERCOSUR and the FTAA in the 1990s.

On the one hand, Brazil strongly supported MERCOSUR and wanted it to incorporate additional countries (Chile, Bolivia, Peru, and Venezuela, if not all South American countries). On the other hand, Brazil was involved in the FTAA process. All through the 1990s it was not clear whether Brazil would overcome its reliance on the international financial system and whether MERCOSUR would expand in South America and resist the absorption by the FTAA. The ambiguity of Brazil's status in the international system is long-standing. According to Pinheiro Guimarães, there are two streams of Brazilian development thinking that dominated each particular government since 1822.[22] One emphasized the necessity of industrialization, the development of internal market, regional integration, scientific and technological progress, diversification of external relations, and the reduction of vulnerability and dependence in relations with the 'great powers.' The second stream of thought suggested that the best way for the country to fit into the international economy was through comparative advantage in production that privileged foreign capital and promoted the view of Brazil playing a secondary role because of its civilizational deficiency.

The position of Argentina in the world power stratification system is less ambiguous. Its size, economic status, and foreign policy strategy classify it as a dependent country. However, Argentina used to be a more powerful nation when it entered the twentieth century as one of the 10 leading economies.[23] Brazil, on the contrary, remained economically depressed until its industrialization policy and immigration boom helped it to overtake the southern neighbour in terms of political influence in the 1950s.[24] Argentina lost its status of an advanced nation with the loss of advantages in the production of agricultural goods. Its forced industrialization was perceived a mistake, so Argentineans dismantled their industries hoping to bring back times of prosperity when Argentina was a great agrarian nation.[25]

Changes in the balance of power between Argentina and Brazil revolved the paradigm of their relationships with the USA. Historically, Brazil maintained better relations with the USA while more powerful Argentina tried to resist US hegemony. The growth of Brazilian industry was provided by protectionist policies under Vargas and Kubitschek. However, Argentineans believed that the rise of Brazil was a success story based on its special partnership with the USA. As Argentina prospered on the border of the nineteenth and twentieth centuries with its semi-colonial status in relation to Britain, it seemed to make sense to ally with the USA after the USA replaced Britain as the major world power. The decline of their country caused Argentineans to see their former confrontation with the USA as self-defeating.[26] Brazil, on the contrary, was adopting a more independent position regarding the regional and international undertakings of Washington. The USA met the growth of Brazilian power and attempts of Latin American integration with reluctance, and Argentina under Menem tried to use this for its own advantage.

In addition to political and economic decadence, several historic factors affected the vulnerability of Argentina. Whereas Brazil's participation in WW2 improved its international image, Argentina's neutrality and silent support of Nazism gave it a lot of disadvantages. The Argentinean military regime of the 1970s and early 1980s was more violent and closed. It was marked by hyperinflation, high foreign debt, border conflicts with Chile, and, more importantly, the *Malvinas* war against Britain with disastrous political and embargo consequences. Thus the weaknesses of Argentina and its bad reputation influenced Menem's decision to present the nation as a normal postcolonial country: peaceful, unarmed, friendly to foreign interests, militarily cooperative, submissive, and respectful of 'great powers' superiority and ideology.

In Menem's understanding, the recognition of Argentina's inferiority and unconditional alignment with the USA was the most beneficial strategy for foreign and economic policies. This strategy was based on the principles of 'peripheral realism' elaborated by Carlos Escudé. According to Escudé, peripheral realism was 'the ideal type of foreign policy,' one that served best 'the narrow interests of citizens of peripheral states' as they could only fight for international power at a great cost to their people.[27] Though peripheral, this ideology was not realist. The orientation towards the USA was to the detriment of relations with Brazil and neglected the fact that Brazil was Argentina's major economic partner and the biggest consumer of Argentinean exports, while Argentina's commercial exchange with the USA was in deficit.[28] Escudé himself recognized that Argentina was not particularly important for the USA because of the competitive character of the two economies and Argentina's geographic isolation.[29]

The brightest poetic expression of peripheral realism belongs to Argentinean Foreign Minister Guido di Tella: 'We want to belong to the Western Club. I want to have a cordial relationship with the United States and do not want a platonic love. We want carnal love with the United States. We do because we know we can benefit from it.'[30] Peripheral realism was grounded in the belief that Latin Americans represented 'an inferior branch of the human species,'[31] and Argentina's policy under Menem did everything to win the acceptance of the 'great powers.' Starting from the election period, Menem promised to dollarize the Argentinean economy and restrict imports of textiles from Brazil, China, and Pakistan. This caused tensions between Brazil and Argentina during the formation of MERCOSUR. Chancellor Luiz Felipe Lampréia characterized Menem's electoral promise as 'a stupid joke of a bad character.' He said that over 35 years of his diplomatic work never had he experienced such 'arrogant behaviour' towards Brazil even from the USA. The gravity of the conflict was so strong that the Brazilian government pronounced Menem's visit to Brazil undesirable.

Thus it was Israel where Menem paid his first official visit in the capacity of president. During *Desert Storm* in 1990 he was the only Latin American leader to have sent troops to the Persian Gulf.[32] Immediately upon taking office, Menem accepted the US conditions on the restructuring of the Argentinean debt and adopted peso–dollar parity. Following that, he dropped the project of production of ballistic missile Condor II, ratified the Treaty of Tlatelolco, which prohibited nuclear arms in Latin America, declared Argentina a 'European' nation in Latin America, left the Non-Aligned Movement, requested memberships in NAFTA, NATO, and the OECD, adhered to the NPT, supported the US interventions to Haiti, Kosovo, and Colombia, welcomed the FTAA and so on.[33] If in 1990 Argentina voted with the USA in the UNGA in 12.5% of cases, in 1994 it did in 68% of cases; in 1994–1995, when Argentina was a non-permanent member of the UNSC, the Argentinean and US votes coincided in 98.5% of cases.[34] Argentina's most embarrassing votes were against the UNGA's resolution condemning the US embargo of Cuba, and for the support of US resolutions on human rights violations in Cuba. With the only goal to please official Washington, Menem went as far as breaking diplomatic relations with Cuba on two occasions.

Under Menem Argentina sent 15,000 troops to international operations in Croatia, Haiti, Angola, Mozambique, Guatemala, West Sahara, Kuwait, Lebanon, Slovenia, and Cyprus. In 1999 Buenos Aires was the eighth biggest contributor of troops for international peacekeeping operations and represented 45% of the total Latin American contribution.[35] By placing the Argentinean military on the US payroll Menem sought to achieve two goals: to win sympathies of the USA through the provision of human resources to the US 'international police force' and to ease domestic unemployment. Confronting unemployment was less realistic through Menem's 'open skies' programme, which replaced Argentinean airlines on domestic routes by US airlines.

The abandonment of its historical posture of non-interference in the internal matters of other countries, sending troops to the Gulf, support to US operations on drug traffic control in the region and an active role in the criticism of the governments of Cuba and Haiti isolated Menem in Latin America. However, he earned Bush Senior's recognition as 'the world leader of privatisation'; and Clinton repeatedly confirmed that 'bilateral relationships were excellent and they would continue improving.'[36] These dubious accomplishments were hardly worth the costs incurred by Argentina: it was deprived of such attributes of sovereignty as foreign policy and monetary policy (through the Convertibility Law). Subordination to the economic and political interests of the USA throughout Menem's years practically converted Argentina to an entity like Panama and Puerto Rico.

Brazil's contemporary history was not as extreme as that of Argentina. Its military regimes were less brutal and more efficient, and Brazil had nothing like the *Malvinas* war episode. The traditional campaign to internationalize the Amazon region and the memories of resentments between republican regimes in Spanish America and the Brazilian Empire prevented the full impact of 'cooperative' policy with the USA, even though Brazil still had the objective to present itself as a 'mainstream' and non-confrontational country. Brazil was able to challenge the USA when it refused to host US military bases and disapproved of the Colombia Plan, supported the International Criminal Court,[37] condemned the NATO operation in Kosovo, continued space and nuclear submarine programmes, and proposed its own candidacy for a permanent seat in the UNSC.[38] Argentina opposed Brazil's membership in the UNSC, which became the most damaging blow to bilateral relations. Discouraged by Argentinean demarches, Brazil took certain diplomatic initiatives with Mexico, which reflected decreased Brazilian interest in MERCOSUR.

The described differences and fluctuations in economic ideology and foreign policy orientation and changes in the international environment make it clear that MERCOSUR did not have uniform attitudes and goals. However, the years of its formation came on the full bloom of neoliberalism in Latin America when the regions' ruling strata blindly accepted reforms of the *Washington Consensus*. The Treaty of MERCOSUR was preceded by the EU Treaty of Maastricht. The construction of 'Fortress Europe' after Maastricht went along with the re-orientation of Eastern Europe towards the West. Eastern Europe was widely publicized as a martyr of communism, and both the USA and the EU declared their 'moral commitments' to help Eastern Europeans. The consolidation of the EU market and enlargement caused fears that the EU protectionist barriers and the 'moral obligations' of the 'free world' to the 'victims of communism' would leave Latin America without attention from the West given such advantages of Eastern Europe as proximity to the EU and better technological, social, and industrial bases.

Latin American countries had advantages in the presence of an entrepreneurial elite, banking community, and the overall capitalist system that made the absorption of foreign capital easier. However, their status of former European colonies was ambiguous as the extension of Lomé Conventions to Latin America meant privileged access to the European market through semi-peripheral Spain and Portugal, which implied alienation from the dynamic centres in Europe.[39] Thus policy-makers and opinion-formers were afraid of the tendencies that drove the Western World away from Latin America and seemed to exclude the region from the dynamic economic life. These fears affected the open strategy chosen for MERCOSUR, which intended to promote both intra-regional and external liberalization.

Besides these fears, real commercial flows illustrate well why MERCOSUR was not perceived as a development project and was considered a 'second-best' strategy compared to multilateralism: in 1991 only 11% of Brazilian and 16% of Argentinean exports went to MERCOSUR (SM). Respectively 29% and 33% went to the EU, and 24% and 13% to the would-be NAFTA (SM). As a welfare-generation project MERCOSUR was even less important, as trade made up a small fraction of production, and welfare effects of intra-regional liberalization promised to be negligible. Therefore MERCOSUR was considered simply as an addition to the multilateral policy of economic openness. The original aspirations of Brazil and Argentina were to use MERCOSUR to facilitate their access to the global market and to improve their relations with the 'great powers.' MERCOSUR was designed as a training ground for recently closed economies and a publicity tool to show South Americans' readiness for insertion into the international economic structures dictated by the industrialized countries.[40]

In the beginning, the new territorial reorganization of the region promoted by MERCOSUR was in line with the reforms that targeted achievement of economies of scale through firm and market enlargement. Orthodox theoreticians of trade, conservative politicians, powerful countries, and international organizations such as the WTO welcomed MERCOSUR as a step towards the achievement of complete integration of the participating states into the global economy that would not hurt interests of the developed countries. In reality, through MERCOSUR North Americans expected to open up the Brazilian market. The Treaty of Asunción was 'an additional instrument' to compel liberalization of the Brazilian economy 'without disagreements with the great lines of the Washington Consensus.'[41] According to a 1993 quotation of US special trade representative Mickey Kantor, 'Regional trading arrangements can prepare developing nations for admittance to the global trading system. They can complement global trading and lubricate negotiations.'[42]

At the political level, the record of the MERCOSUR members was spoiled by military dictatorships. The West held military regimes responsible for all the evils of the world: economic stagnation, inflation, corruption, human rights violations, and confrontation with the 'great powers.' The mere commercial liberalization within MERCOSUR did not seem sufficient to earn favourable disposition of the West, which anticipated political changes as well. In this, Argentina took the initiative in its hands. Political coordination of MERCOSUR was not a jointly planned action, but became a series of eccentric measures suggested by Buenos Aires.[43] These measures targeted disarmament and 'democratization' and coincided with the major US objectives in the region: reduction of the region's defence capability and the establishment of transparent regimes.

Thus the two MERCOSUR democracy clauses were a success of the US strategy.[44] They allowed suspension or expulsion of a MERCOSUR-4 or MERCOSUR-6 member state that violated democratic norms. The two documents did not specify what constituted these democratic norms and represented a deviation from the principle of traditional non-interference in domestic affairs. The clauses posed delicate questions in terms of their interpretation and practical implementation in the future.[45] In the ideal military perspective, Washington saw the Southern Cone's armed forces reduced, and their functions limited to drug trafficking control and police. Argentina presented disarmament as a reasonable policy for MERCOSUR. Disarmament would prevent an arms race (Brazil/ Argentina), military adventurism (*the Malvinas*), and border conflicts (Argentina/Chile). There would be no threat in the region after the disarmament of Argentina, Brazil, and Chile with the USA being a far-away, 'non-aggressive,' and military invincible power anyway.

The Argentinean initiatives puzzled Brazil but were tolerated and sometimes accepted. Relations with Brazil had two parallel goals for Argentina. The first was to involve Brazil in US geostrategic objectives. The second was to open up Brazil's market without losing the prospect of integration into the US market. Aligning military and foreign policy with the USA, while keeping Brazilian suspicions low and the Brazilian market open, was a delicate issue for Argentina. But these seemingly contradictory objectives were achieved as Brazilian and Argentinean elites shared their views. For example, President Collor de Mello suspended the Parallel Nuclear Programme to demonstrate that Brazil was not going to have any type of nuclear production. This Brazilian ideological counterpart of Menem did not jeopardize national sovereignty like Menem did in his country, but he pursued economic policies that undermined the Brazilian economy and threw it into recession. Fortunately for Brazil, the subsequent governments (Franco, Cardoso, Lula, and Dilma) were less prone to neoliberalism.

In the meantime strategists in the US Treasury and the Departments of State and Defence understood that strengthening cooperation between Brazil and Argentina in politics, economics, technology, and weapons would reduce their dependence on the USA and create a centre of power capable of challenging US political, economic, military, and ideological influence. In addition, US exporters experienced losses as a result of changes in the commercial traffic caused by MERCOSUR intra-regional trade liberalization. Because of the substitution of the US imports by imports from MERCOSUR, the estimation of losses of the US exporters to Brazil alone made US$624.1 million in single year 1996 (See Subsection 2.4.1). Further, in 1995 MERCOSUR introduced the CET that raised Argentinean tariffs to the level of Brazilian ones contrary to the expectations of Washington and the WTO, who anticipated the reduction of Brazilian tariffs to the level of those in Argentina. The MERCOSUR CET together with the subsequent announcement of the EU-MERCOSUR strategic partnership EUROSUR caused official Washington to express annoyance through a series of events starting in 1996. As soon as it became evident that Brazil was not rushing to jump into the US-led FTAA, the US administration launched an unscrupulous diplomatic and media campaign to discredit Brazil and MERCOSUR.

All of a sudden, after eight years since the last official visit, the US Secretary of State travelled to Latin America calling at Brazil, Argentina, and Chile among other places. There appeared a report of *the Commission on America's National Interests*, which listed among 'the vital national interests'—'conditions that are strictly necessary to safeguard and enhance the well-being of Americans in a free and secure nation'—the necessity to 'prevent the emergence of a hostile major power on U.S. borders or in control of the seas.'[46] It was clear that in the context of the US 'own Western Hemisphere' it was neither Canada ('America's longtime ally and greatest trading partner'), nor Mexico ('best friend').[47] Following this report, in October 1996, a 'leakage' of a WB internal report on MERCOSUR was organized. Alexander Yeats, chief economist of the WB Division for International Trade, characterized MERCOSUR as a 'perversion of regionalism.' He accused MERCOSUR of trade diversion, protectionism, and abuse of competition rules. The conclusions of his report were published in the *Wall Street Journal* and *Financial Times*.[48]

Both articles referred to MERCOSUR as a 'zone of artificial growth where inefficient industries prospered behind external barriers' concluding that 'to protect markets from external competition MERCOSUR perpetuated industrial inefficiency and did not give local producers incentives to achieve international competitiveness.' The two publications provoked diplomatic scandals with energetic responses from the Brazilian, Argentinean, and Uruguayan Foreign Ministries, the Argentinean Ministry of Trade and Industry, the Paraguayan presidency and the UN Conference on Trade and Development. Numerous protests compelled the bank to apologize in an official communiqué and individual responses. The bank stated that Yeats's views had not been discussed among the economists of the bank and did not express the official view of the institution, and that the notorious working document was not meant for publication.

In 1997 US State Secretary Madeleine Albright declared MERCOSUR 'harmful' to US interests and demanded 'high priority' attitude from the Senate to 'the early addition' of Chile to NAFTA in her official statement before the US Senate Foreign Relations Committee. Brazilian Senator and Former President José Sarney reacted to this statement by accusing the USA of the destabilization of MERCOSUR and the encouragement of an arms race and military disequilibria in the Southern Cone through arms supplies to Chile and the offer of NATO partnership and access to modern weapons to Argentina. Even though Sarney's reaction caused the removal of the epithet 'harmful' in relation to MERCOSUR from the text of the official statement, Albright requested apologies from the Brazilian government. Brazilian President Henrique Cardoso suggested that she did not worry about the words of a Brazilian senator, as the Brazilian government never demanded apologies from the US executive for the words of US senators. In his public address in *O Globo* Cardoso alluded to Argentina: 'We, Brazilians, do not have this sick preoccupation with what the USA thinks and does. We do not want to have carnal relations with anybody.'[49] This reaction did not remain unnoticed and the US Senate asked Albright what the problem of her diplomacy with Brazil was. The State Secretary bluntly excused herself by saying: 'We must continue shaping the global economic system that works for America.'[50]

Another example of arrogant nationalism is found in Ambassador Charlene Barshefsky's statements. In the debate with senators she said that the absence of the *fast track* created a vacuum of leadership that led towards 'agglomeration of other countries by other trading partners in our own hemisphere as a means of building their own little unit or system of rules and obligations.'[51] The Brazilian ambassador reminded her that MERCOSUR was not 'a little unit or system.' Yet she insisted that the lack of the *fast track* authority was detrimental to US prosperity and leadership, mentioning MERCOSUR as a bloc that had expanded its prerogatives in South America.[52] She did not refer to MERCOSUR as 'a little unit' any more, but she indicated that it had a 'clear strategic objective regarding commercial expansion and a stronger position in world affairs.' She recognized that her policy had the objective 'to support US prosperity, US jobs and health of US companies.' There was nothing bad if it were to the detriment of Latin Americans as the perception of Latin America was generally negative: dependent, weak, inferior, incapable, inefficient, and corrupt.

Cardoso's sentence 'The FTAA is an option but our destiny is MERCOSUR' at a 2001 MERCOSUR summit was commented on in a *New York Times* article that explicitly said that MERCOSUR opposed the USA.[53] Henry Kissinger cited this article:

> Especially in Brazil, there are leaders attracted by the prospect of a politically united Latin America confronting the United States and NAFTA.[54]
>
> All this has makings of a potential contest between Brazil and the United States over the future of the Southern Cone of the Western Hemisphere.[55]

Kissinger referred to MERCOSUR as a 'challenge to US policy' and an 'irritation caused by Brazil.'[56] Fred Bergsten, director of the Washington-based Institute for International Economics, saw in MERCOSUR a clear danger to the FTAA.

According to Bill Clinton whether MERCOSUR liked it or not, 'global economic integration was on a "fast track".'[57] Even though he said that the US government did not have any objections to MERCOSUR, since his second term in 1996 the US administration heavily attacked Brazil for expanding cooperation with the EU, Latin American, and Asian countries.[58] Statements of US officials clearly indicated that the US objectives were to get Chile into NAFTA and to prevent the consolidation of MERCOSUR. The *fast track* process was activated specially for this purpose. Such an approach to Brazil in the late 1990s did not undergo significant changes under Clinton's successor Bush Junior. For example, the conclusion of the CSN agreement resulted in a prompt publication of *'Brazilian Leader's Tippling Becomes National Concern'* in the *New York Times* in which a US journalist diagnosed Lula with alcoholism.[59] This article caused indignation in Brazil because at home Lula had no reputation as a drunkard.

The promise of MERCOSUR's non-confrontation, political, economic, and military alignment with the leaders of the world was unfulfilled as became clear after 1996. The disarmament of the region did not reduce risks of conflicts, but facilitated US intervention in Peru and Colombia. The 'great powers' further increased their military capability, continued arbitrary exercise of power and received more influence on the peripheral countries. Nuclear nations refused to disarm according to Article 6 of the NPT. As time passed, MERCOSUR learnt that the prescriptions of Western economists were not worth following. The neoliberal strategy weakened MERCOSUR production bases, and changed its trade balance from US$27.64-milliard surplus in 1990 to 13.59-milliard deficit in 1998, causing greater dependence of the region on compensations from the IMF. The US increased protectionist measures and intensified demands for trade liberalization despite MERCOSUR's growing trade deficits.[60] Financial centres consistently refused to impose legal controls over volatile capital flows.[61] The 'great powers' were unable to overcome attitudinal stances of arrogance in relation to MERCOSUR.[62]

Argentina remained enchanted by neoliberalism a little longer than Brazil. Yet the search for 'carnal love' with the USA resulted in no gains. The US imposed sanctions on Argentinean exports and sold military planes to Chile. Britain refused to negotiate sovereignty over *The Malvinas*. NAFTA, NATO, the OECD, and APEC refused to accept Argentina. The disastrous collapse of the dollar–peso parity resulted in horrible consequences for economic growth, poverty rates, distribution of income, and social conditions. The USA and international institutions placed all the responsibility for the shock on Argentina, even though Argentineans did everything prescribed by the *Washington Consensus*.

Evidently, the analyses of the neoliberal governments (Collor and Menem) were mistaken by believing that the more you offered to the USA, the more you would get in return.[63] The neoliberal social and economic model failed without achieving any social integration, peaceful politics, or improvements in education, health, and employment. The Argentinean crisis compelled Argentina to re-evaluate its geopolitical and economic strategies and to give increasing priority to relations with Brazil. After the crisis Argentinean rhetoric about 'carnal relations' changed. Foreign minister Carlos Ruckauf started to talk about polygamous relations: 'I do not see why we cannot be polygamous at least in the foreign and economic policy. No country can have only one relation.'[64] If 1996 became a turning point when MERCOSUR started a transformation from a hegemon-friendly to counter-hegemonic project, the Argentinean crisis of 2001 reinforced this trend as it helped Argentina to shake off its neoliberal government. The presidential elections of 2003 brought Argentina closer to Brazil.

The 'return' of Argentina to MERCOSUR was symbolized by the re-establishment of diplomatic relations between Argentina and Cuba and Argentina's official invitation to Cuba to join MERCOSUR. New Argentinean President Néstor Kirchner and his Brazilian counterpart Lula referred to MERCOSUR as a top foreign policy priority. According to them MERCOSUR had to become an area of convergence in industry and agriculture with a common infrastructure and integrated science and technology policies. They also pronounced the ideas about the creation of a regional development bank and a parliament, whose deputies would be elected by direct vote, and about the introduction of a body for the emission of a common currency. Lula made it clear that he wanted to consolidate MERCOSUR into a 'community-like' model.

The trend reverse to the FTAA was clearly exemplified by the introduction of the bloc's motto '*Our North is the South.*' The decision of 2006 to begin the process of admission of Venezuela occurred largely on neorealist accounts and symbolized a renunciation of MERCOSUR's dependency status and reaffirmation of its own identity and development policy. In July 2012 Venezuela formally entered MERCOSUR, and Hugo Chávez with his notoriously anti-American views became one of the bloc's leaders. Such a switch in MERCOSUR's objectives and foreign policy orientation was facilitated by frustrated experiences of liberal reforms that led this region to: economic regress; aggravation of poverty; sharpened inequality; increased corruption, crime, and debt; and greater external vulnerability. This common experience consolidated and deepened MERCOSUR and boosted agreements on SAFTA, CSN and UNASUR. Latin Americans rejected neoliberalism as the reconstruction of the old empires whose planners reserved for the region the role of disarmed, dependent, and currency-less modern colonies administered by native technocratic proconsuls. Brazil, Venezuela, and MERCOSUR won in resisting the satellization of Latin America.

In the absence of MERCOSUR, the FTAA could have absorbed South America by 2005, perpetuating its dependency status, but this did not happen because MERCOSUR gave their countries a greater bargaining power. This power helps them in the acquisition of international competitiveness and implementation of national development programmes. Brazil, Argentina, and Venezuela need MERCOSUR as alone none of them can promote changes in favour of Latin America. Only united can they influence decisions on such threats to continental stability as Central American and Colombian crises and external debt, and on such issues as arms race, protectionism in industrialized countries, instability of commodities prices, and development of technological capability.

5.3 MERCOSUR AND THE EU: DUALISM OF THE RELATIONSHIP

The character of MERCOSUR–EU relations fits well into the concept of hierarchical relations within the international system. The essence of these relations is two-fold. On the one hand, the two blocs have a relatively strong orientation towards each other because of their political, economic, and cultural interests. The partial convergence of interests is conditioned by their intermediary position in the international stratification of power, relatively similar goals and problems of integration, and historic, cultural, and economic bonds. The US neoliberal concept of globalization represented a threat of dissolution in a global FTA for both of them. For MERCOSUR this threat was greater as it did not consolidate itself as a monetary union. Therefore the two blocs have been interested in each other as challengers to US power.

In respect to counterhegemony, MERCOSUR–EU relations reveal a number of similarities in approaches to global and regional problems. MERCOSUR and EU policy-makers emphasize regionalism and multipolarity for the sake of a more equitable international system. They say that they believe in regional integration as a positive, fair, and less unbalanced trend that responds to global interests better than exacerbating contradictions between developed and underdeveloped countries. At least at the rhetorical level, both MERCOSUR and the EU advocate a more 'human' face of interdependence that respects interests of weaker parties. The EU–MERCOSUR cooperation was a strategic asset for MERCOSUR in the FTAA and WTO negotiations. For the EU, EUROSUR was helpful in the accomplishment of certain goals in the WTO.

EU policy aims at reinforcing those regional blocs that the EU does not perceive as competitors: MERCOSUR, ASEAN, CAN, SADC, and CACM. MERCOSUR occupies a more important place in the list of EU foreign policy prerogatives than the mere criteria of geographic distance from Western Europe would suggest. It is the EU's preferred strategic partner due to the size of its economy and stronger integration ambition. Whereas the USA treated MERCOSUR as a trade deviation enforcing Brazilian power and wanted to remove it by absorption into the FTAA, Europeans were concerned that MERCOSUR was not institutionalized enough not to be absorbed by the FTAA. The EU provides direct technical and financial assistance to MERCOSUR institutions and administers aid programmes to support MERCOSUR civil society and implementation of the regional market.

Aside from elements of strategic, theoretical, and rhetorical character, there is a hard-core economic basis reinforcing mutual interest in bi-regional cooperation. In spite of greater proximity to the USA, MERCOSUR-4 countries' economic relations have always been oriented more towards Europe. EU investments, import and export participation in MERCOSUR-4 exceed those of the USA in contrast to other areas of Latin America. Interest in economic cooperation based on already existing relations drove MERCOSUR and European leaders to declare the intention of creating the EUROSUR FTA in 1995. This was an unprecedented agreement between the two customs unions. While the scale of the project was surprising, it was not something entirely unexpected, as the FTAA plans had already been announced. In a situation when the two blocs were compelled to confront the US hegemony, EUROSUR was perceived as a project of geostrategic and global relevance that increased the influence of Brazil and the EU in international politics.[65] The idea about rapprochement between the EU and MERCOSUR received support from both parties, but opinions varied on how and how soon EUROSUR was to be implemented. In addition to disagreements between the regional executives, successful bi-regional cooperation required solutions of significant differences in national approaches within each of the blocs.[66]

On the other hand, EU–MERCOSUR relations cannot be a partnership of equals in conditions when MERCOSUR economy represents less than a quarter of the EU economy, 23%.[67] In essence, there is no difference in the way the EU and the USA want to keep South American economies open while keeping their own markets protected against agricultural goods originating from MERCOSUR. The USA and the EU do not heed any expectations of Latin Americans regarding agricultural market liberalization and debt relief. In no particular way were US interests in the FTAA different from EU interests in EUROSUR. The strongest stimuli for the EUROSUR negotiations were 'the fears to lose the game to NAFTA'[68] and the intention to *Mexicanise* Brazil and Argentina before the USA could do so. Both the EU and the USA enjoy enormous surpluses in trade with MERCOSUR, and they do everything possible not to lose their advantage. In case of the EU, 'fledging MERCOSUR's common market was the focus of the European interest' as the EU intended 'to consolidate its position in the MERCOSUR market and safeguard it against outside competition.'[69] The FTAA negotiations collapsed in 2005 after MERCOSUR-4 and Venezuela rejected the USA's final proposal at the Summit of the Americas. The EUROSUR process continued, but with periods of suspension and reactivation.

The necessity to confront US interests in the region has resulted in a more cooperative European policy towards MERCOSUR. The EU's narrower choice of instruments for coercion has compelled Europeans to play the card of Latin America's desire for autonomy, something the USA has long been unable to accept in principle. EU–US competition has allowed South Americans to extract certain benefits as the EU chose to support MERCOSUR not only theoretically as an example of integration, but also through active policy measures targeting consolidation of its institutions. However, if it were not for the USA, Europe would not want to see a stronger ally in MERCOSUR. Relations between the EU and MERCOSUR resemble those of the USA with the EU. Both are not partnerships of equals. Support from the stronger actor is conditional and fades along with the louder manifestation of the weaker party's diverging stances. The paradigm of MERCOSUR's relations with the USA and EU illustrates that developing countries may benefit from a multipolar system, as greater equilibrium and dispersion of power secured through multiple alliances reduces the effects of political and economic pressures from the hegemon.

5.4 Conclusion

Contemporary regionalism can be analysed as an attempt to counterbalance US hegemony to achieve a more equitable system of international relations. MERCOSUR and EU countries have important reasons to embrace integration and bring together available resources in order to strengthen their political and economic standing within the international system and vis-à-vis the hegemonic structures. Many integration developments (such as introduction of the euro, the CFSP, Eastern enlargement, and signing of the Constitutional Treaty in the EU; SAFTA, UNASUR, accession of Venezuela and MERCOSUR's extra-regional agreements) confirm the view of the analysts explaining interest in regionalism through the relative decline of US power on the one hand and by growing US unilateralism on the other.

Despite a continuously changing international environment and the adjustment of concepts of regionalism, the external perspective reveals the underlying logic of integration: through the unions, the states strive for greater influence in international affairs. Weaker countries resort to regionalism to increase their leverage in dealings with the hegemonic structures. Integration is a measure to strengthen their national economies and improve negotiating capacity in order to pursue converging foreign policy objectives more effectively. By increasing political power (through political alignment) and economic power (through economic liberalization and development policy) vis-à-vis the USA, the EU and MERCOSUR are praised for their contribution to a more stable international system through facilitation of a more balanced distribution of power at the global level, even though their social effects at the regional level are asymmetrical.

However, regionalism does not always challenge the hegemon. Sometimes it is expedient to hegemonic interests; when so, it may receive sympathies and support of the hegemonic structures. Thus regionalism is explained either through the subordination to the interests of a strong hegemon or through the inability of a declining hegemon to resist counterhegemony. The historical development of MERCOSUR and the EU confirms this hypothesis. The USA supported or encouraged these instances of regionalism when they served the US wider geopolitical and economic agenda or specific objectives. After losing control over the dynamics in MERCOSUR and the EU, the US counteracted the two blocs and obstructed regional integration by playing on the tendencies of their members to compete among themselves rather than to cooperate with each other. Today the development of MERCOSUR and the EU occurs contrary to US aspirations, and the two blocs meet resistance of the hegemonic structures.

The histories of MERCOSUR and the EU may be divided into three phases that characterize the evolution of the international system, changing objectives of integration, and changing attitudes of the superpower. These phases confirm the neorealist assumption of integration being either a process of adjustment to a powerful hegemon or a measure of resistance against a weakening hegemon. The phases also confirm the hypothesis about the two blocs' transformation from hegemonic to counterhegemonic projects. This transformation reflects the changes in integration objectives that appeared along with the evolution of the international system and the decline of the superpower.

Table 5.1 shows the goals and strategies of integration have changed several times since the ECSC and PICE. Initially, France, Germany, Italy, and Brazil and Argentina were seeking ways to overcome existing antagonisms in regional relations for the sake of peaceful coexistence. The end of WW2 gave a strong impetus to European integration making postwar settlement the main motivation for integration efforts. Expanded cooperation between Brazil and Argentina meant to overcome the legacy of military dictatorships by presenting a new pleasanter face of the countries to the

Table 5.1 The evolution of geostrategic perceptions of the EU and MERCOSUR

Period	Common regional problems	Strategic goals of integration	Measures undertaken	Reaction of the US
The EU				
1. Post-WW2	Destruction of WW2	Handling WW2 consequences, overcoming antagonisms between France and Germany	Sectoral integration in militarily strategic sectors	Indifference
2. Cold War	Fears of communism among the elites	Contention of the Eastern Bloc	Economic integration	Energetic support
3. Post-Cold War	Difficulties in exploiting the Gulf's oil, unpredictability of the US unilateralism, terrorism threats	Consolidation of Western Europe's role in international arena	CFSP, euro, extra-territorial commercial agreements, enlargement	Resistance
MERCOSUR				
1. PICE (1986–1991)	Instability of transition from the military regimes to civilian governments	Elimination of ambivalences inherited from the military governments for the sake of good neighbourhood relations	Sectoral integration in economically strategic industries	Indifference
2. The 1990s	Exclusion from international economic life	Better insertion into the global economy	Intra-regional economic liberalization, acceptance of FTAA	Encouragement
3. The 2000s and the 2010s	External vulnerability and dependency	Achievement of autonomy in domestic and foreign affairs	Resistance to FTAA, CSN-UNASUR, economic alliances with South Africa, India and Mexico, admission of Venezuela	Resistance

world. Soon both the processes gained economic and geostrategic relevance that made them interesting to the USA: the EC was strengthening US allies in the Cold War against communism, and MERCOSUR was viewed as a process of adaptation to the global economic order promoted by the USA.

'The US nourished united Europe since infancy and promoted the region to the condition when it became second to the US in terms of power.'[70] MERCOSUR did not have such a luxury. It started to integrate not because of the fears of the past, but because of the fears of the future and the necessity to survive in the turbulence of globalization. During the 1990s MERCOSUR was considered a project of consolidation of diplomatic and commercial relations of Brazil and Argentina for a better insertion into the globalizing economy. From the second half of that decade MERCOSUR started to display aspirations for leadership in South America, becoming an essential topic in any discussions of Latin American affairs that affected governments' decisions on international economic policy.[71] The USA has been the major external player in European integration both as a promoter of integration and as a factor against which European countries were compelled to integrate. The role of the USA in the MERCOSUR process has been evident as well, but it has been more negative as the USA perceived Brazil as a dissident in its hemispheric agenda (comparable to France in the transatlantic context) even before MERCOSUR was set up.

At present, the nature of the unions' relations with the USA is characterized by increasing competition, even though both remain dependent on the USA: the EU in foreign policy and security, and MERCOSUR in financial and economic terms. In spite of the shared pro-hegemony/counter-hegemony pattern, the nature of external forces in the development of the two unions has been different. It has been more geoeconomic in MERCOSUR and more geopolitical in Europe. Consequently, these forces have affected the undertaken measures of integration and its quality. For South America, MERCOSUR is primarily a means to leverage economic power. Economic deficiencies in Brazil's position vis-à-vis the USA are well illustrated by the energetic efforts of the Brazilian diplomacy to enlarge MERCOSUR and consolidate SAFTA and UNASUR. The external economic dimension of South American integration is so important that with all the differences in national production structures and tensions arising from them (See Section 3.3), the MERCOSUR CET survived the 1999 and 2001 crises.

The aspects of political and military confrontation between MERCOSUR and the USA cannot be disregarded as the accession of Venezuela and US interventions to Colombia and Peru demonstrate. The mentioned interventions caused a lot of frustration across South America. In its turn, the USA is suspicious about the resumption of the Brazilian nuclear military programme. Accusations of this were expressed when Brazil barred a UN inspection of its power plant in 2004.[72] Despite such episodes, MERCOSUR's proper institutions have no whatsoever jurisdiction over security and defence areas. In contrast to the EU, this aspect of integration in MERCOSUR is still lacking.

Without a doubt, the European single market is one of the key achievements of European integration. However, during its consolidation stage, it was not a goal on its own but a means to increase collective power of the NATO countries in relation to the Soviet bloc. Only later did European integration gain incentives to ascertain the capability of building economic power able to rival the USA.[73] The achievement of equipollence with the USA in commercial terms through the common market and the euro proved that unity was strength and a way to preserve autonomy, while separation meant unimportance. Acknowledging this should help the acceptance of sacrifices needed for integration in other spheres. Recent integration initiatives of the EU cover precisely the areas where the EU is weaker than the USA: political cohesion and armed forces.

Strategic goals of integration in MERCOSUR and the EU have been different. While the EU is seeking equipollence with the USA, the MERCOSUR countries hope to reduce dependence on the 'great powers' and achieve greater autonomy in decision-making on internal and external affairs. These varying perceptions are conditioned by the difference in the blocs' absolute power and their different weights on the regional and international scales. MERCOSUR is a regional actor whose narrower interests, dependence, and underdevelopment do not allow a comparison with the EU's role of a global player. As the EU and the USA retain common interests in relation to developing countries, South Americans have more compelling reasons for integration as a measure to protect sovereignty and capability of their states.

Correspondingly, the EU and MERCOSUR have different strengths of preoccupation with the US power. Europeans are less perplexed by the international leadership of the USA because the EU has more converging interests and more power leverage. In Latin America, aspirations for a more equitable international order are much stronger because the region is more vulnerable and dependent. South Americans have compelling reasons for integration as a measure to protect their states.[74] As consequence, their counter-hegemonic tendencies are stronger and their relations with the USA are more antagonistic. On 2 July 2013, for example, the plane of Bolivian President Evo Morales was grounded in Vienna after Spain, France, Portugal, and Italy abruptly blocked their airspace following the instructions from the USA who hoped to find Edward Snowden on board. This incident made it clear that cosier European countries would not protect such enemies of the USA as Julian Assange and Edward Snowden, both of whom sought and were granted asylum in South America.

However, dependence and external vulnerability have been making integration in MERCOSUR a difficult process. Not only do externalities favour integration (US support of the EC, the fear of communism among European elites during the Cold War, the support of MERCOSUR institutions by the EU). More often they obstruct regionalism (conditionality of Argentina, Britain, and Eastern European countries on the USA). In some instances, externalities may have an ambivalent influence on integration (EUROSUR as affirmation of MERCOSUR's identity and a measure with asymmetric effects on MERCOSUR members sharpening intra-bloc controversies). Weaknesses certainly reduce chances of success, and dependence with external vulnerability have been making integration in MERCOSUR a more difficult process.

The character of external forces does not allow realistic quantification of the effects of the associated notions and ideas to determine which of the two regions has had stronger geostrategic incentives for integration. Besides, the geopolitical scene is fluid compared to more persistent trends of geography, history, and culture: the visions of European unity and Latin American solidarity among statesmen and philosophers already existed 200 years ago, before the US emerged as a global power. Over the last 100 years Argentina's relations with the USA changed from confrontation to submission twice while the physical neighbourhood of Brazil remained a constant that called for cooperation efforts at least since the 1915 ABC Treaty.[75]

Also, the external perspective alone cannot explain why different states respond to identical international dilemmas and opportunities in different ways (for example, why Uruguay is in MERCOSUR and Chile is out and why the EU border is not moving beyond the Polish-Belarusian frontier). Different responses of some similar countries are outcomes of unique political interpretations and varying perceptions of political and economic gains. In cases when integrating countries have a different ideology and conflicting history, they adopt different strategies for managing their international relations. Sooner or later the divergences narrow the scope and possibilities of integration. Therefore, sustainable integration projects need converging ideologies, similar visions of the world, and similar interpretations of international roles. External circumstances and threats, real or imaginable, such as globalization, terrorism, 'Yankee imperialism,' or 'red plague' alone are unable to cause neighbouring countries to integrate unless these countries are similar enough culturally, ideologically, and economically to have converging interests and understandings of the existing problems.

This does not mean that perceptions of geostrategic interests among integrating countries must be identical. On the contrary, there have occurred a number of persistent disagreements within the unions (like those among France, Germany, and Britain and between Brazil and Argentina on the degree of alignment of their interests with the USA). However, no matter how strong these disagreements were, interest in expanded cooperation together with cultural affinities or political solidarity compelled the necessity to preserve the unions and come up with compromising solutions. If so, the external dimension of MERCOSUR and EU integration may run secondary to internal factors. Externalities do matter as catalysts or inhibitors of integration, but the determinants of the process are more likely to be rooted within than outside the regions.

Notes

1. For neorealist interpretations of the US international role see: Gills, Barry K. 1993. *Low Intensity Democracy: Political Power in the New World Order*, edited by Barry Gills, Joel Rocamora, and Richard Wilson. Pluto Press with the Transnational Institute, London. Jaguaribe, Helio. 2003. General Introduction. In *The European Union, Mercosul and the New World Order*, edited by Helio Jaguaribe and Álvaro de Vasconcelos, pp 1–25. Frank Cass, London. Mukhametdinov, Mikhail. 2005. Neravnomernoje raspredelenije vlasti i resursov kak osnovnaja prichina nestabil'nosti mezhdunarodnoj sistemy. *Mir Peremen*, 1, pp 118–127. Institute of International Politics and Economics of the Russian Academy, Moskva.
2. Braveboy-Wagner, Jacqueline Anne. 2003. 'Conclusion.' In *The Foreign Policies of the Global South: Rethinking Conceptual Frameworks*, edited by Jacqueline Anne Braveboy-Wagner, 183–188. Lynne Rienner, Boulder.

3. Wallace, William. 1995. *Regionalism in Europe: Model or Exception?* In *Regionalism in World Politics*, edited by Louise Fawcett and Andrew Hurrell, pp 201–227. Oxford University Press, Oxford. p 208.
4. Idem, p 211.
5. Bertram, Christoph. 2003. Multilateralism, Regionalism, and the Prospect for International Order: A View from Germany and Europe. In *The European Union, Mercosul and the New World Order*, edited by Helio Jaguaribe and Álvaro de Vasconcelos, pp 53–61. Frank Cass, London. p 54.
6. OECD, http://www.oecd.org/dac/stats/aidtopoorcountriesslipsfurther-asgovernmentstightenbudgets.htm, 1.10.2014.
7. Melandri, Pierre and Vaïsse, Justin. 2001. L'empire du milieu. Odile Jacob, Paris.
8. This thinking was particularly prevalent in the writings of Jean Monnet, the founding father of the EC.
9. Pinheiro Guimarães, Samuel. 2003(a). The International and Political Roles of Mercosul. In *The European Union, Mercosul and the New World Order*, edited by Helio Jaguaribe and Álvaro de Vasconcelos, pp 92–123. Frank Cass, London.
10. Grant, Charles. 2003. Europe, Mercosul and Transatlantic Relations: A British Perspective. In *The European Union, Mercosul and the New World Order*, edited by Helio Jaguaribe and Álvaro de Vasconcelos, pp 41–52. Frank Cass, London. p 42.
11. de Vasconcelos, Álvaro. 2003. The European Union and the New Multilateralism. In *The European Union, Mercosul and the New World Order*, edited by Helio Jaguaribe and Álvaro de Vasconcelos, pp 26–40. Frank Cass, London. p 27.
12. Coatsworth, John H. 2006. Degrees of Latitude: Can US, Latin America Find Common Ground? *The Boston Globe*, 15.1.2006.
13. Oliva Campos, Carlos and Prevost, Gary. 2002. Preface. In *Neoliberalism and Neopanamericanism: The View from Latin America*, edited by Gary Prevost and Carlos Oliva Campos, pp ix-x. Palgrave Macmillan, New York.
14. In contrast to the postwar era, the USA is no longer a country that is in possession of a common culture. Racial polarization, effects of excessive immigration, increased social and economic stratification, distrust of authority and dissolution of common values make certain observes to conclude that the US national project is unravelling (Ayerbe, Luis Fernando. 2002. Culture and National Interest in the United States: Conservative Perceptions of Latin America. In *Neoliberalism and Neopanamericanism: The View from Latin America*, edited by Gary Prevost and Carlos Oliva Campos, pp 29–45. Palgrave Macmillan, New York. p 31). Although not considered a hostile agent, Latin America looms up as explicit reference to

what may represent the road to decadence for the USA (Idem, p 36). According to Lawrence Harrison, director of the USAID missions in Latin America, in Latin America 'traditional Iberian values and attitudes impede progress toward political pluralism, social justice, and economic dynamism' (Harrison, Lawrence E. 1992. *Who Prospers? How Cultural Values Shape Economic and Political Success.* Basic Books, New York. p 2). In his view not only do Latin American cultures represent the mirror that reflects the image of decadence threatening the USA, but also they are responsible for the erosion of US traditional values. 'The Chinese, the Japanese, and the Koreans who have migrated to the US have injected a dose of their work ethic, excellence, and merit at a time when those values appear particularly beleaguered in the broader society. In contrast, the Mexicans who migrate to the US, bring with them a regressive culture that is disconcertingly persistent' (Idem, p 223). 'That Latin America has not made its peace with democratic capitalism and the US is principally the consequence of the incompatibility of traditional Iberian culture with political pluralism and the free market, on the one hand, and the inevitable resentment of the successful by the unsuccessful, on the other' (Harrison, Lawrence E. 1997. *The Pan-American Dream: Do Latin America's Cultural Values Discourage True Partnership With the United States and Canada?* Westview Press, Boulder. p 69). Conservatives like Landes suggest that differences between wealth and poverty originate not from the international division of labour and the imperial politics of the 'great powers,' but from the options and practices adopted by the proper societies: 'If we learn anything from the history of economic development, it is that culture makes all the difference. Yet culture, in the sense of the inner values and attitudes that guide a population, frightens scholars' (Landes, David. 1998. *The Wealth and Poverty of Nations: Why Some Are So Rich and Some So Poor.* Norton, New York. p 516). 'Cynics might even say that dependency doctrines have been Latin America's most successful export. Meanwhile they are bad for effort and morale. By fostering a morbid propensity to find fault with everyone but oneself, they promote economic impotence. Even if they were true, it would be better to stow them' (Idem, p 328). Thus Latin America reformed in the image of the USA becomes a matter of strategic relevance for the USA. For Huntington, the policies of President Salinas de Gortari represent a positive example of alignment with the West in the 'clash of civilizations': 'Salinas dramatically reduced inflation, privatised large numbers of public enterprises, promoted foreign investment, reduced tariffs and subsidies, restructured the foreign debt, challenged the power of labour unions, increased productivity, and brought Mexico into the North American Free Trade Agreement with the United States and Canada. Just as Ataturk's reforms were designed to transform Turkey from a Muslim Middle Eastern country into a secular European country, Salinas's reforms were designed to change Mexico from a Latin American country into a North American country,' 'Salinas became, in effect, the Mustafa Kemal of Mexico' (Huntington, Samuel P. 1997. The Clash of Civilizations and the Remaking of World Order. Touchstone, New York. pp 150 and 149). Huntington chose to overlook that Atatürk was actually anti-imperialist.

15. Tavares, María de Conceição. 1988. Una perspectiva brasileña. In *Argentina-Brasil: El largo Camino de la Integración*, edited by Mônica Hirst, pp 13–20. Editorial Legasa, BsAs.

16. Ayerbe, 2002, p 41. Glinkin, Anatolij. 1999. Glava IX. Zona svobodnoj torgovli Amerik: trudnyj start superprojekta. In *Integratsija v Zapadnom polusharii na poroge XXI veka*, pp 178–189. Institute of Latin America of the Russian Academy, Moskva. p 189.

17. As early as in 1993, Cardoso in the capacity of the minister of foreign affairs observed: 'Privileged integration with the United States is impossible given the proper dynamism and the proper vitality of our exports to the American market. The US does not open its market for Brazil. Brazil does not have the keys to the ports of North America' (Vizentini, Paulo G. F. 2000. Mercosul: dimensões estratégicas e geoeconômicas. In *O Mercosul no limiar do século XXI*, edited by Marcos Costa Lima and Marcelo de Almeida Medeiros, pp 27–41. Cortez Editora, São Paulo. p 31–32). In 1997 Minister Jorge Campbell, Chancellor Luiz Lampreia and President Cardoso produced the following statements: 'MERCOSUR is an active promoter of the FTAA, however we propose certain measures such as the preservation of the essence of MERCOSUR, deepening sub-regional integration and the participation in the FTAA negotiations as a bloc;' 'It is important that North Americans understand the necessity of slow gradual negotiations. Brazil will not make significant concessions;' 'It will be bad if the FTAA results only in what the USA wants it to be. We want integration but without hegemony' (Cited as in Campbell, Jorge, Rozemberg, Ricardo, and Svarzman, Gustavo. 2000. O Mercosul na década de 1990: da abertura à globalização. In *Mercosul: entre a realidade e a utopia*, edited by Jorge Campbell, pp 99–180. Relume Dumará, Rio de Janeiro. p 153). In 2001 Canada imposed a ban on Brazil's beef explaining that Brazilian animals could theoretically be contaminated with 'mad cow' disease by several animals imported from Europe. Brazilians took this as a retaliation measure for the development of aircraft producer *Embraer*, which competed with Canadian *Bombardier*. Brazil's agricultural minister said that by spreading groundless rumours Canadians buried the prospects of Brazil joining the FTAA (Third World Network, 8.2.2001, Canada has buried the FTAA – charges Brazilian minister, http://www.twnside.org.sg/title/ftaa.htm, 1.10.2014).

18. Pinheiro Guimarães, Samuel. 2003(b). Reflexões sul-americanas. In *Brasil, Argentina e Estados Unidos – Conflicto e Integração na América do Sul (Da Triple Aliança ao Mercosul 1870–2003)*, edited by Luiz Alberto Moniz Bandeira, pp 9–40. Editora Revan, Rio de Janeiro.
19. Saha, Suranjit Kumar. 2000. Mercosul, competitividade e globalização. In *O Mercosul no limiar do século XXI*, edited by Marcos Costa Lima and Marcelo de Almeida Medeiros, pp 55–91. Cortez Editora, São Paulo. p 86.
20. Juagaribe proposes the following classification of countries based on their status in the international system: *Ruling countries* (the USA, the EU, and Japan). The EU has preeminent status by virtue of its economic weight. Japan was the second largest national economy. The ruling countries have achieved a high level of social development; *Resistant countries* (countries able to resist US hegemony but not to contest it). This position is typically that of China, Russia, India, Iran, and Brazil. The resistance level provides them with limited options for policy autonomy and individual development; *Dependent counties* (the rest of the world, countries that have no options of their own and are dependent on the ruling countries or, in exceptional cases, on resistant countries). They represent a variety of development levels from satisfactory to critical (Jaguaribe, Helio. 2001. Argentina y Brasil ante sus alternativas históricas. In *Argentina y Brasil en la globalización: ¿Mercosur o ALCA?*, edited by Aldo Ferrer and Helio Jaguaribe, pp 67–104. FCE, México. p 70–73).
21. Bernal-Meza, Raúl. 2000. Políticas exteriores comparadas de Argentina y Brasil hacia el Mercosur. In *O Mercosul no limiar do século XXI*, edited by Marcos Costa Lima and Marcelo de Almeida Medeiros, pp 42–52. Cortez Editora, São Paulo. p 45.
22. Pinheiro Guimarães, 2003(b).
23. In 1913 Argentina achieved a GDP per capita that by far exceeded not only that of Brazil, but also of Sweden, Spain, and Italy. A high level of prosperity made the elites and predominantly white population of Buenos Aires believe that Argentina was an overseas extension of Europe and a country significantly different from the rest of Latin America.
24. Moniz Bandeira explains the impulse towards successful industrialization of Brazil by disadvantaged position of the Brazilian coffee relative to Argentinean beef and grain. Brazilian farmers were eager to experiment with manufacturing while the Argentinean coup of 1930 enforced the conservative interests of export-oriented agrarians against the interests of the urban middle class and proletariat (Moniz Bandeira, Luiz Alberto. 2003. Brasil, Argentina e Estados Unidos – Conflicto e Integração na América do Sul (Da Triple Aliança ao Mercosul 1870–2003). Editora Revan, Rio de Janeiro. p 634). The emergence of competitors like Canada, Australia, and New Zealand further decreased the competitiveness of the Argentinean agriculture (Idem, p 637).

25. Roguelio Frigelio called deindustrialisation in the Process of National Reorganisation under general Videla 'an inverted trend of human history' (Idem, p 641).
26. This confrontation started with the refusal to accept a US free trade proposal in 1899.
27. Escudé, Carlos. 1997. *Foreign policy theory in Menem's Argentina*. University Press of Florida, Gainesville.
28. Moniz Bandeira, 2003. p 506.
29. Escudé, Carlos. 1988. *Gran Bretaña, Estados Unidos y declinación de Argentina, 1942-1949*. Editorial de Belgrano, BsAs. p 377.
30. Cited as in Rapoport, Mario. 2000. *Historia económica y social de Argentina, 1880-2000*. Ediciones Macchi, BsAs. p 957.
31. Schoultz, Lars. 1998. *Beneath the United States. A History of U.S. Policy Toward Latin America*. Harvard University Press, Cambridge. p XV.
32. When the Brazilian ambassador arrived in Baghdad in 1990 to discuss liberation of two Brazilian citizens, Menem, without giving any notice to the Brazilian government, sent two ships to participate in *Desert Storm* on the US side. This annoyed Brazil and undermined Argentina's credibility all over Latin America while the US ambassador accused Brazil of 'sitting on the fence during the conflict' (Moniz Bandeira, 2003. p 479).
33. About eccentricities of the Argentinean foreign policy of this period see: Pinheiro Guimarães. 2003(a). Moniz Bandeira, 2003. Colombo, Sandra. 2002. Argentinean Foreign Policy: Changes and Continuities in the Relationships with the United States and MERCOSUR. In *Neoliberalism and Neopanamericanism: The View from Latin America*, edited by Gary Prevost and Carlos Oliva Campos, pp 199–214. Palgrave Macmillan, New York.
34. Granillo Ocampo, Raúl. 1997. Las relaciones de la Argentina con Estados Unidos. In *Argentina y Estados Unidos: Fundamentos de una nueva alianza*, edited by Felipe de la Balze and Eduardo Rocca, pp 287–297. Asociación de Bancos de la República Argentina, BsAs.
35. Escudé, Carlos and Fontana, Andrés. 1995. *Divergencias estratégicas en el Cono Sur: Las políticas de seguridad de Argentina frente a las de Brasil y Chile*. Universidad Torcuato di Tella, BsAs. Fontana, Andrés. 1998. La seguridad internacional y la Argentina en los años 90. In *Política Exterior Argentina, 1989-1999. Historia de un Éxito*, edited by Andrés Cisneros, pp 275–341. Nuevohacer, BsAs.
36. Colombo, 2002. p 210.
37. The USA refuses to adhere to the International Penal Treaty in order to avoid accusations in past and future genocides.
38. For more details see Pinheiro Guimarães, 2003(b).

39. Guilhon Albuquerque, José Augusto. 1999. Mercosur: Democratic Stability and Economic integration in South America. In *Regional Integration and Democracy: Expanding on the European Experience*, edited by Jeffrey J. Anderson, pp 261–283. Rowman and Littlefield, Lanham. p 262.
40. de Souza, Amaury. 2003. Brazil in a Globalsing World. In *The European Union, Mercosul and the New World Order*, edited by Helio Jaguaribe and Álvaro de Vasconcelos, pp 180–204. Frank Cass, London.
41. Nogueira Batista, Paulo [an influential Brazilian diplomat]. 1993. A Política Externa de Collor: Modernização ou Retrocesso? *Política Externa*, 1:4, pp 106–135. Editora Paz e Terra, São Paulo. p 111.
42. Lawrence, Robert Z. 1996. *Regionalism, Multilateralism, and Deeper Integration*. Brookings Institution, Washington. p 3.
43. Pinheiro Guimarães, 2003(a).
44. Declaración Presidencial sobre Compromiso Democrático en el Mercosur, 25.6.1996 and Protocolo de Ushuaia sobre compromiso democrático en el Mercosur, la Republica de Bolivia y la Republica de Chile, 24.7.1998.
45. Pinheiro Guimarães, 2003(a).
46. The Commission on America's National Interests. 1996. America's National Interests.
47. The three previous quotes are from The Commission on America's National Interests. 2000. America's National Interests.
48. For details see: Glinkin, Anatolij. 1997. V poiskakh kompromissa. *Latinskaja Amerika*, 10, pp 6–13. Institute of Latin America of the Russian Academy, Moskva. Campbell et al, 2000(b).
49. O Globo, 23.08.1997.
50. For details see Moniz Bandeira, 2003. pp 507–509.
51. According to the US Constitution, the Senate and not the Executive is responsible for foreign commercial policy. This complicates the work of the Government in the preparation and negotiation of commercial agreements. Foreign parties are sceptical about offers from the Executive, as no deal reached with it is valid until approved by the Senate. The *fast track* refers to the Government's expanded competences in foreign trade policy, which may be allowed by the Senate.
52. Moniz Bandeira, 2003. p 513.
53. New York Times, 24.03.2001, South American Trade Bloc Called Mercosur Under Siege.
54. Kissinger, Henry. 2001. *Does America Need a Foreign Policy? Toward a Diplomacy for the 21st Century*. Simon & Schuster, New York. p 152.
55. Idem, p 163.
56. Moniz Bandeira, 2003. p 584.
57. Idem. p 515.

58. Vizentini, 2000. p 37.
59. *New York Times*, 9.5.2004, Brazilian Leaders' Tippling Becomes National Concern.
60. Over 1991–1997 Brazilian and Paraguayan imports were growing three times faster than exports.
61. For more details see Pinheiro Guimarães, 2003(b).
62. Every single article on MERCOSUR in *The Economist* from 1991 to 2004 had a derogatory title: 'Mercosur's malaise,' 'Some realism for Mercosur: Better a genuine free-trade area than a phoney customs union,' 'Another blow to Mercosur: A decade after it was created, South America's largest trade block is losing direction,' 'Murky Mercosur,' 'Sour Mercosur,' 'Chopping block,' 'Sweet nothings?,' 'Uruguay between two elephants: Watch it, that's us you're trampling on,' 'Brazil's 500 years of solitude: It's high time for South America's giant to shake off its inferiority complex,' 'Latin America's dying trade winds.' At the same time random titles on the EU are persistently neutral: 'The limits of Europe: Where will it all end?,' 'Looking west, looking east: What EU accession will mean,' 'The wealth effect: Joining the European Union will make the applicant countries richer, but not overnight,' 'Crisis ahead: EU countries must soon decide whether to let a split Cyprus into their club.'
63. Vizentini, 2000. pp 30–31.
64. Even during the Argentinean crisis, the idea of polygamy was not received warmly in Washington. A high-ranking official of the Department of State rebuked Ricardo Lagorio, minister-councillor of the Argentinean Embassy in Washington: 'You are looking for Brazilian patronage? You want to follow Brazil? Brazil is going to negotiate for you with the Fund? And who is going to put money for the economic programme? Brazil?' (Moniz Bandeira, 2003. p 604).
65. The European Commission emphasized, among other motivations, the interest 'in maintaining equilibrium of Latin American relations with the USA and Europe' (European Commission. 1994. *The European Community and Mercosur: An Enhanced Policy.* European Commission, Brussels).
66. The EU was divided between the supporters of EUROSUR (Germany, Italy, and Portugal) and enemies of the project (Britain and France together with Spanish, German, and Eastern European agricultural lobbies). In MERCOSUR-4, EUROSUR clashed against import-competing industrial interests of Brazil while agrarian Argentina, Uruguay, and Paraguay tended to be stronger supporters of the transatlantic FTA, even though their governments had no illusions about the EU dropping agricultural subsidies. Venezuela is against EUROSUR, and its suspension from MERCOSUR was conducive to the resumption of the bi-regional negotiations.

67. According to CIA GDP data for 2016, the EU accounts for 16.7% of the gross world product, and MERCOSUR for 3.8%. The shares of the EU in global merchandise exports and exports of commercial services are 32.7% and 42%, while the shares of MERCOSUR are 1.8% and 1.1% only. These figures combine intra- and extra-zonal trade (WTO. 2016. International Trade Statistics 2016).
68. Argentinean ambassador to the EU Diego Guelar as cited in Campbell et al, 2000. p 157.
69. Klom, Andy. 2003. Mercosur and Brazil: a European Perspective. *International Affairs*, 79:2, pp 351–368. p 355.
70. Bertram, 2003.
71. Guedes de Oliveira, Marcos Aurelio. 2005. Mercosur: Political Development and Comparative Issues with the European Union. Jean Monnet/Robert Schuman Paper Series, 5/19. p 225.
72. *The Washington Post*, 4.4.2004, Brazil Shielding Uranium Facility.
73. Strauss-Kahn, Dominique [French minister of industry]. 1996. In *Latin America – European Union. Forum 1996. Europe and Latin America: Two Ways of Integration for the 21st Century*, pp 169–172. European Commission, Brussels. p 170.
74. Gómez Mera also comes to the conclusion that economic and political factors had a marginal role in the preservation of MERCOSUR after the crises of 1999 and 2001. In fact they presented problems rather than assets. More important was the growing geostrategic role of MERCOSUR in addressing security-related problems and challenges dealing with mercantilist inter-state economic rivalry that triggered defensive incentives to act as a bloc over concerns regarding competitiveness (Gómez Mera, Laura. 2005. Explaining Mercosur's Survival: Strategic Sources of Argentine-Brazilian Convergence. *Journal of Latin American Studies*, 37, pp 109–140).
75. Pacto de No Agresión, Consulta y Arbitraje, 25.5.1915.

CHAPTER 6

Conclusion

The complex explanation of differences between the MERCOSUR and EU processes and the elaboration of a framework and criteria for comparisons of contemporary regions constitutes the main contribution of this book to the field of integration studies. The monograph calls attention to the necessity to incorporate economic geography and the evaluation of states' asymmetries of size, interest, and economic performance into the study of regions. The book redefines integration as *intentional policy harmonization* and indicates that the implementation of integration should be limited to the solution of similar problems confronted by the countries involved. Therefore, social constructivism and intergovernmentalism—as approaches emphasizing differences and similarities among the integrating states—should prevail in the study, advocacy, and criticism of regionalism. There are ten implications of the comparison of MERCOSUR with the EU undertaken in this book. Each of the following conclusions is discussed below at a greater length.

1. Integration outcomes are highly contingent on specific endogenous regional features.
2. Integration in MERCOSUR and the EU develops unevenly across various policy dimensions. The EU is more strongly consolidated politically and economically while MERCOSUR is culturally, or at least linguistically.
3. Regional integration clearly has limits, and no excessive expectations should be placed on it.

4. MERCOSUR lags behind the EU in economic consolidation due to region-specific conditions of economic and political geography resulting in low levels of economic interdependence and sharp interest divergences due to size and power asymmetries among the MERCOSUR members. If an integrated theory of regionalism is ever developed, it should incorporate the discussion of issues of regional economic geography and member states' size and power asymmetries. Smaller states have a higher propensity for regionalism than bigger states.
5. MERCOSUR and the EU are different as regions and institutions. If judged by outcomes of integration, MERCOSUR and the EU are clearly distinct processes as well. Therefore, the EU cannot serve as a model of integration for MERCOSUR, and MERCOSUR should not replicate EU institutions and procedures without adjusting them to its own needs.
6. There is a significant gap between MERCOSUR's declarations and MERCOSUR's provisions that really work. A possible explanation of this gap is the excessive exogenous influence of the EU model on MERCOSUR and MERCOSUR's inability to assimilate this external model, which serves the needs of an entirely different region.
7. MERCOSUR is losing its economic significance.
8. Even though marginalized in integration studies, culture is an important subject in the studies of regionalism.
9. The studies of regional blocs like MERCOSUR and the EU provide a fuller picture of integration if they incorporate perspectives of multiple integration and cooperation theories. An analytical framework for the comparison of various regional blocs should be based on the criteria for comparison derived from several theories. The theories that have been used to explain European integration are useful in explaining the differences in integration results between MERCOSUR and the EU.
10. Social constructivism and intergovernmentalism may prevail in the synthesis of integration theories, if integration is understood as intentional policy harmonization among the countries.

1. MERCOSUR with its various initiatives appears as an integration project significantly different from the EU. The EU is an older group dominated by richer countries; MERCOSUR is a younger process among the states of the global south that started implementation of economic liberalization programmes later. The MERCOSUR countries have a lower level of industrialization, technological development, and capital accumulation. Consequently, MERCOSUR and the EU occupy different positions in the hierarchy of international relations. External semi-dependent status, weaker national economies, and poorer social conditions make the development of MERCOSUR a difficult task. In addition, the two unions have a completely different structural composition in terms of the number of member states, their absolute and relative size and the intra-regional balance of power among them.

What became the EU was originally set up as an economic project complementing NATO in geostrategic confrontation with the Communist Bloc. The USA continues using Brussels as a channel of communication with European states. MERCOSUR's development has been motivated by the necessity to address challenges of the global mercantilist rivalry. MERCOSUR survived the turbulence of internal crises and external pressures without strong economic interdependence (as in the EU) but with cultural affinities (which the EU lacks) and stronger geostrategic incentives (which the EU is losing). Without MERCOSUR, Latin America could have submerged into the FTAA, but this has not happened. MERCOSUR has taught a lesson to other developing countries: along with the increase in the market size, integration has helped the MERCOSUR countries to improve their bargaining capabilities relative to the 'great western powers.' Thus geostrategic implications of MERCOSUR are superior to its economic results, but even these are significant if a 10-time growth in intra-regional trade between 1991 and 2012 is cited by the bloc's High Representative General.[1] However, international trade of the MERCOSUR countries makes up a much smaller fraction of total production than in Europe; and in comparative terms MERCOSUR's market results are modest.

Cultural heterogeneity of Europe makes cultural integration in the EU invisible if not impossible. In contrast to the EU, MERCOSUR is integrating culturally. Relative cultural homogeneity allows the American bloc to adopt some realistic measures of cultural integration (Sections 4.4 and 4.5). If it were not for cultural integration in MERCOSUR, MERCOSUR would be lagging behind European integration in all dimensions of inter-state relations. Not only do MERCOSUR cultural affinities encourage integration, but they also serve a perfect illustration that the MERCOSUR process is qualitatively distinct from the EU. The different nature of the two processes is particularly exemplified by the varying extent of policy harmonization in the linguistic and monetary domains. These two policy areas, language and money, represent the quintessence of the cultural and economic for the purposes of generalization about the state of economic and cultural integration in the two unions. The comparison of regional measures in linguistic and monetary policies is highly illustrative of how different original inputs result in different outputs of integration (Sections 2.5 and 4.4).

In case of the Eurozone, the relatively high extent of its economic cohesion has resulted in the introduction of the euro. In MERCOSUR, in spite of the smaller number of the countries involved in policy harmonization, the single currency is viewed as very problematic precisely because of the low level of the region's economic cohesion. In the linguistic domain, on the contrary, MERCOSUR has achieved a more advanced stage of policy harmonization in spite of its younger age. It has committed the Spanish-speaking countries to the compulsory presence of Portuguese, and Brazil—of Spanish in the curricula of all secondary schools. The linguistic diversity of the EU has not allowed for the development of any consistent linguistic policy going beyond the declaration of equal status of 24 co-official languages within the European institutions in theory and the constant violation of this declaration in practice. Europe's linguistic diversity makes an equivalent policy in the EU unthinkable.

2. Dependent on the region's unique individual features, integration in MERCOSUR progresses unevenly across specific policy domains and dimensions of social life in comparison with the EU. The variation across regional properties and integration incentives between the two blocs explains the different character and results of integration: individual inputs of regional economy, geography, and history, and different views on policy-making have produced different types of inter-state relations in the two regions. Some of the responsible factors are constant (geography), others are less stable and change in the course of history (ideology). Not only do the differences among the regional properties condition the differences in the outcomes of integration, but they also make predictable success and failures of policy harmonization in every particular policy domain in each bloc:

In the Economic Domain In MERCOSUR more than half of intergovernmental agreements on market integration are not implemented and remain dead letters because the social demand for economic integration is relatively weak. Higher economic concentration and interdependence explain the formation of the single European market and more advanced economic integration in the EU.

In Cultural Integration Relative cultural homogeneity of MERCOSUR is conducive to measures of cultural integration that are taking place despite the fact that the founding treaties of MERCOSUR were not concerned with any cultural integration or cooperation. In the EU, cultural diversity does not allow any measures of institutionalized cultural integration. With the exception of cultural industries and production, cultural policies remain the prerogative of the member states.

In Political Dimension Member states' size and power asymmetries and associated asymmetries of national interests are the factors that significantly constrain economic and political integration in MERCOSUR. The EU lacks imbalances of such scale, which is favourable to European integration in various policy domains.

In Foreign Policy Socio-economic concerns at the domestic level and economic underdevelopment relative to the global centres of power give measures of MERCOSUR integration a geoeconomic character. Integration is implemented as a measure to increase member states' leverage with the industrialized countries in economic negotiations. Parity with the USA in economic power (large market, single currency, relatively high incomes) and weakness in political and military spheres (due to political disunity and limited military capability) stimulate EU measures to catch up with the USA in political terms and add to the geopolitical identity of European integration.

Favourable conditions for integration in each specific dimension cause more tangible outcomes in this particular dimension. Table 6.1 is a graphical representation of the relative importance of the discussed social dimensions for the two regional processes. It also reflects the relative progress of integration achieved in the corresponding dimension. On the plus side it means that the dimension is relatively important and a higher level of integration has been achieved in this dimension in the respective bloc; the negative side denotes the lack of significant motivation for policy harmonization in the given dimension and consequently no progress or limited progress of integration achieved. In most instances the EU has better conditions for integration, which have resulted in more advanced integration policies in scope and in depth. As it appears, the EU is more strongly consolidated politically and economically while MERCOSUR is more strongly consolidated culturally.

Table 6.1 Relative significance of selected dimensions for integration and relative progress of integration achieved in these dimensions

	Economics (internal market)	Politics, (size, power and interest asymmetries)	Culture (cultural homogeneity)	Geoeconomic strategy	Geopolitical strategy
MERCOSUR	−	−	+	+	+/− ambiguous, depending on whether right-wing or left-wing governments are in power
EU	+	+	−	−(market integration is already achieved)	+

3. The comparison exposes limits of regionalism. Three chapters of the book are about MERCOSUR's limitations in relation to the EU (in economics, structure, geopolitics), and one about the EU's limitations in relation to MERCOSUR (in culture). For each bloc the limits vary across different social dimensions, policy domains, and specific issues. One of the aspects of regional integration is the production of single rules for the game for players with very different interests. Such rules will not work. They must change in order not to frustrate the system. Therefore, greater scrutiny is needed in assessing how much integration is needed in each particular issue area, if it is needed at all, and if any current measures are to be subdued.

4. Economic integration in Europe is a product of neofunctionalist expansions and spill-overs due to region-specific conditions of economic geography providing for high economic interdependence (small countries, small distances, and high population density resulting in high economic concentration and better developed cross-border infrastructure). Wealth and structural conditions (participation of small states and relatively balanced distribution of power among the key actors) are also favourable for European integration. These conditions are lacking in MERCOSUR. It appears a less self-sufficient, less internal and less autonomous process characterized by a lower level of involvement of socio-economic sectors.

The effects of the MERCOSUR common market are relatively unimportant. No matter what policies it implements, its inherent conditions of structure and geography will never be overcome to produce economic results on the EU scale. The effects of complete intra-regional liberalization would differ substantially in the two regions, and any expectations of MERCOSUR to perform like the EU are unrealistic.

Accordingly, the two common market regimes are also different: the MERCOSUR regional market is incomplete and deficient (Section 2.1). From the neofunctionalist view, high interdependence is important for the emergence of strong regional institutions to manage this interdependence. As MERCOSUR's interdependence is low, its institutions are less developed. An increase in interdependence will create demand for further institutionalization, especially on the part of the smaller countries. However, this increase will not be significant due to the region's structural and geographic limitations. In relation to the EU, MERCOSUR integration is constrained not only by low and asymmetric levels of interdependence, but also by macroeconomic fragility, vulnerability to external shocks and divergent national preferences. They have given 'a premium to the maintenance of flexibility, particularly on the part of Brazil. In the future these structural factors will continue to shape the context in which MERCOSUR institutions evolve. Progress towards more "dense" institutions will therefore at best be gradual and slow.'[2] Any haste in advancing economic MERCOSUR is unnecessary and harmful.

The implications of this study call integration theory to incorporate the analyses of regional economic geography and intra-bloc size asymmetries. The explanations of MERCOSUR's inability to create EU-like stronger supranational institutions are linked primarily to the size of Brazil and the bloc's relatively low propensity for intra-regional economic exchange. Variations along the inherent characteristics of economic geography, in levels of economic activity, and in bloc size, power, and interest structures can be found across any integration group. In relation to the asymmetry of size, there are blocs similar to MERCOSUR that are led by dominant powers (USA's NAFTA, Russia's CIS, India's SAARC, and South Africa's SACU), and there are blocs comprised of less unequal countries like the CACM, CAN, and the EU (at least among the bigger countries Germany, Britain, France, Italy, Spain, and Poland).

5. As appears, MERCOSUR and the EU are results of particular inimitable circumstances. They were started in different times in history, had different objectives, and incorporated countries that are not alike. Each bloc represents a unique social reality different in every possible geographic, demographic, economic, historic, cultural, and political aspect from each other and any other integrating region. Therefore, their backgrounds, settings, designs, and dynamics are individual and cannot be replicated. MERCOSUR is often expected to follow the stages of European integration at an accelerated pace because of the smaller number of members and greater practical and theoretical experience of regionalism available today than in the years of the EC formation. Such expectations are unrealistic given the significant differences between MERCOSUR and Western Europe. Identical policies do not produce identical results in different environments.

As an original phenomenon, MERCOSUR has its own way to go, and no ready-made models may be prescribed for it. There is no archetype or preferred standard of integration. This does not mean that experiences of other regional groups should not be learnt, and that elements of external models should not be evaluated and attempted in MERCOSUR. The question is not about imitation, but intellectual paternity. Originality is not based on not copying things, but on giving them a new vision and making a new version.[3] Everything in social relations is a historic product, and the whole culture is based on producing new ideas and new objects on the basis of ancestors' knowledge and experience. Thus the imitation has to be original, and no elements of the European model may be transferred to MERCOSUR blindly. Each policy has to be adapted to MERCOSUR's needs after careful consideration. MERCOSUR can also be a reference for other integration efforts and a model to learn from.

That suggestions to reform MERCOSUR in the image of European institutions and procedures are of little use is by no means bad news for MERCOSUR, as the EU-like deeper integration does not necessarily mean better or more efficient. The quality of integration depends on the nature of implemented policies and their appropriateness or inappropriateness for the specific countries. MERCOSUR is not needed for the sake of MERCOSUR, but for the improvement of the political, social, and economic environments in the countries that make it. Integration is not a goal on its own, but a means to stimulate development and improve the quality of life in the region.

6. MERCOSUR's institutional development, to some extent, has occurred contrary to the neofunctionalist logic and has been disproportionately affected by the model of European integration. The neofunctionalist forecast would predict greater spill-overs and expansion of Brazil and Argentina's cooperation with the industrialized countries because in pre-MERCOSUR years Brazil and Argentina's exchange with the USA and the EU exceeded intra-regional exchange. Moreover, between 1998 and 2004 regional interdependence significantly declined while institutional development continued. The formation of the MERCOSUR market runs contrary to a number of political and geostrategic explanations as well: political circumstances dealing with intra-bloc size asymmetry show that Brazil does not have a strong interest in the regional market, while external considerations emphasize the necessity of a sound protectionist policy against imports from the USA and the EU rather than the necessity of intra-regional liberalization. These protectionist measures could have been taken by the countries individually and did not need MERCOSUR.

At the same time, MERCOSUR institutions have done little work in altering the patterns of power and interest of the member states.[4] There is a big mismatch between far-reaching commitments of the MERCOSUR treaties and the inability of its institutions to discipline member states' policies. This gap between MERCOSUR on paper and MERCOSUR at work is explained by the historic precedence of the EU.[5] The MERCOSUR common market came largely out of the tradition of imitation of external social ideas when these ideas were at the peak of popularity in the early 1990s. In attempts to duplicate European regimes, MERCOSUR policymakers have produced tons of legislation that is not in force; and in the domain of the common market dead letters constitute half of all legislation. Many observers blame the serious implementation gap on the poor performance of bureaucrats who care little about finalizing the arrangements they produce and report about. To the contrary, politicians are keen on advancing MERCOSUR, but the project comes across natural obstacles of social character that do not depend much upon their will or caprice.

The implementation of the agreed MERCOSUR norms is delayed or forgotten because they have limited value for the region and receive little attention of the population. In Mattli's terms, MERCOSUR's supply for integration (interest on the part of national and regional bureaucracies) by far exceeds the social demand of interest groups and concerned citizens.[6] Failures of many integration initiatives are rooted in insurmountable difficulties posed by the specificity of regional economic geography, demographic settlement patterns, and member states' relative and absolute sizes (Section 2.2). Undoubtedly, the MERCOSUR process has received a lot of influence from two exogenous factors: the EU model and the US neoliberal thinking prioritizing and emphasizing market integration. Many economic initiatives adopted by MERCOSUR were inspired by the EU and were not the best policies for the South American bloc. No matter how hard they are pursued, they will not convert the bloc into a version of the EU.

As returns of the proposed common market in MERCOSUR are relatively low, it should not come as surprise that the bloc has little effective legislation regulating the regional market in the cross-border supply of services, right of establishment, and movement of capital, though it does a better job in trade in goods and movement of workers. Likewise, insufficient attention is paid to implementation of matters critical to the construction of the external dimension of the customs area. The endogenous properties of MERCOSUR reveal themselves in the progress of integration in spheres where it was not intended, anticipated, or planned (culture, education, languages): MERCOSUR has 'numerous legal acts in areas that have little relationship with the enforcement of a customs union.'[7]

For some observers, 'MERCOSUR integration is somehow paradoxical in the sense that the lack of progress in areas explicitly targeted in the Asunción Treaty as pertaining to the establishment of a common market (services and movement of factors of production) is accompanied by significant spillover into areas not initially envisaged as part of the integration process, such as education and justice. In both areas developments in MERCOSUR address issues that European integration has taken decades to tackle (or has not yet tackled).'[8] As they are endogenous regional properties rather than exogenous ideas that ultimately dictate the general course of integration, MERCOSUR's cultural integration is not really 'paradoxical,' even though the principal treaties never mentioned it and never posed the goal for the MERCOSUR members to integrate culturally.

7. Cultural integration in MERCOSUR shows that traditional explanations of regionalism that focus exclusively on commercial transactions and overlook the role of cultural affinities impoverish our understanding of integration. Apart from trade, there are other ways to integrate peoples like MERCOSUR's undertaking to provide every schoolchild in the member states with an opportunity to study the two most important languages

of the region, Spanish and Portuguese. MERCOSUR proves that less economically advantaged regions in the third world may rely on cultural affinities for sustaining political and economic cooperation in difficult times. There is no serious evidence that cultural homogeneity strongly affects regional economic institutions or that such institutions are forging regional identities. However, MERCOSUR illustrates that cultural homogeneity may be conducive to integration policies in the cultural domain.

8. Since the beginning of the century, MERCOSUR has generally been able to maintain intra-regional exports at the level of 2% of its GRP (Table 2.2). However, the global crisis has negatively affected exchange volumes among developing countries, and MERCOSUR intra-regional trade has declined both in absolute and relative terms. If the situation deteriorates and intra-regional exports come down to 1% of GRP, MERCOSUR will lose its relevance as an economic performer and will only retain its symbolic significance, as profits of the intra-regional exchange will constitute only a fraction of the 1% figure. Even the small countries Uruguay and Paraguay may not need MERCOSUR as such, because they are capable of managing their trade with Brazil and Argentina on a bilateral basis.

9. As far as theoretical debates are concerned, contemporary regional groups require complex explanations based on several integration and cooperation theories. This book illustrates the idea that for the understanding of varying outcomes of integration in different regions like MERCOSUR and the EU we need to consider a range of factors emphasized by multiple theories. Even though these theories were not developed on the basis of MERCOSUR, there appears to be no contradiction between MERCOSUR's outcomes and expectations of its performance that would be based on predictions of the discussed theories (neofunctionalism, intergovernmentalism, social constructivism, and neorealism), at least in comparison with the results of the EU. On the contrary, the varying levels of integration development between the two blocs across the specified integration dimensions have been consistent with the expectations based on these theories, at least in comparative terms.

The comparison of the two blocs urges the necessity for the development of an integrated theory of regionalism that incorporates certain themes of the four theories. The proposed analytical framework for the comparison of MERCOSUR and the EU along a number of identified criteria may be applied to the analysis of integration in other regions. The extension of application of this system to other regions will certainly cause modifications to it and will bring about new issues, themes, regional features, and criteria that may significantly affect other instances of contemporary regionalism. Comparisons of other blocs will increase and refine the pool of relevant variables, and subsequent studies will result in an improved framework explaining and predicting regionalism.

At the same time, a perfect framework and a universal theory of integration may be an unattainable goal. Attempts to create such a mega-theory will point to varying natures and degrees of intensity of cooperation within different regions and in different historic periods. As the essence of interstate cooperation changes all the time, it is unlikely that this mega-theory will ever become complete to explain every particular spatial and temporal example of regionalism. In addition, the development of a counter-theory of disintegration is highly warranted. One lesson that history teaches us is that integration and fragmentation processes go hand in hand, and are contingent on varying situational circumstances.

Many important criteria for the comparison of the two blocs proposed by this book, including member state size asymmetries and peculiarities of economic geography, lack direct references in European integration theories, because the analysts who wrote these theories wanted to explain the EU and were not preoccupied with the comparison of Western Europe with other regions. Therefore, they accepted Europe's properties as given without identifying specific regional features and qualities that served as determinants of integration. As consequence, the notions discussed in the theories did not receive the shape of measurable integration criteria that could be applied across various regions.

10. Another conclusion in relation to the whole book is about the importance of social constructivism for integration studies and the necessity to extend the use of constructivist explanations beyond cultural integration to discussions of regionalism in all integration dimensions. In constructivism integration appears naturally due to convergence of norms, values, and interests. If the essence of integration is in intentional standardization and unification of social practices, then this phenomenon should be expected only in the matters of perceived common interest and in situations where there is agreement on the effects of the proposed measures. Therefore the similarities of interests, problems, and situations are essential for integration; and social constructivism emphasizing these similarities should be placed to the fore of integration studies. Intergovernmentalism is the reverse side of this approach because it discusses differences between the countries and how these differences are overcome in the adoption of integration policies.

In this book constructivism is explicit in the analysis of cultural heterogeneity and its effects on cultural integration (in Chapter 4). However, it is implicitly present elsewhere, because it is not just homogeneity of culture that is important for integration, but homogeneity of interest. Common policy is most successful when it responds to the common interest of all the parties and addresses similar and not dissimilar problems. Therefore, integration of economically and socially co-oriented states that are similar in terms of economic development is preferable to integration schemes involving industrialized and third-world countries with sharp divergences in economic indicators.

Ideally, interdependence, which is key to the analysis of Chapter 2, should also be balanced, and it should not be of a colonial pattern when poor countries sell commodities and buy finished products. Trade deals with external partners are also easier to negotiate within the region whose members have similar production structures and are affected by the consequences of external liberalization in a similar way. It has been discussed that economic, and specifically monetary integration, needs convergence in macroeconomic performance (Section 2.5). Thus constructivism comes into conflict with liberal economics, which prescribes identical rules of behaviour for everybody regardless of the varying competition abilities.

Constructivism is implicitly present in the chapter on intra-bloc size asymmetries. It is not just similar market and production structures but also similar size and power potential among the countries that are warranted for the development of integration. Thus divergences in foreign policy approaches and expectations from MERCOSUR between Brazil and Argentina are linked to the different sizes of the two countries and also to their different geographic locations (Sections 3.3 and 5.2). Constructivists would agree that the similarity of government regimes, ideologies, perceptions of national interests, and external threats; the similar ability of the states to respond and adapt to integration; and the equity of distribution of integration benefits are all requirements of a deep and sustainable process. Overall, constructivism with its emphasis on similarities indicates that MERCOSUR's economic, political, and institutional integration is more difficult to achieve than that in the EU precisely because these are the domains where the differences among the MERCOSUR countries are bigger. As social reality does not allow occurrence of identical states whose integration would be unproblematic, flexibility and equity will remain important principles of integration policies in any regional bloc.

Social constructivism can serve as a baseline theory in the synthesis of other integration approaches. A broader application of constructivism and its application to Latin American regional integration in general and to MERCOSUR in particular is not yet a common approach. In narrow terms constructivism is confined to the domain of culture and identity politics. While every scholar is aware of common historical, cultural, linguistic, and religious base of Latin America, it is problematic to relate advances and failures of economic and political integration to these cultural phenomena. Thus Latin Americanists usually look into issues of power and trade, and as consequence, neorealist and intergovernmentalist analyses dominate the study of Latin American regional and sub-regional integration.

Enlargements of regional blocs alienate them from the expectations of a successful constructivist model by increasing differences in culture, political interests, economic ideologies, and distribution of wealth among member states. Weakening cultural bases and continued pursuit of the liberal model, which increases distributional costs of integration, present an aggravating problem for both MERCOSUR and the EU. In order to remain sustainable the unions should cultivate stronger solidarity feelings within their populations. This is only possible if fairer models of redistribution of integration gains are implemented. Transfer mechanisms should direct funds not only from richer to poor countries, but also within the countries. At the moment the poor are becoming poorer and the rich are becoming richer and more unwilling to share. This represents a difficult political problem. Growing polarization in integrating societies reduces the support for integration and may signify that the best days of regionalism are not in an observable future.

Notes

1. BBC, 12.6.2013, Cumbre del Mercosur: el comercio crece pero el bloque muestra fisuras, http://www.bbc.co.uk/mundo/ultimas_noticias/2013/07/130712_ultnot_mercosur_cumbre_vp.shtml, 1.11.2017.
2. Bouzas, Roberto and Soltz, Hernán. 2001. Institutions and regional integration: The case of MERCOSUR. In *Regional Integration in Latin America and the Caribbean: The Political Economy of Open Regionalism*, edited by Victor Bulmer-Thomas, pp 95–118. Institute of Latin American Studies, University of London, London. p 118.

3. Sanguinetti, José María [President of Uruguay]. 1996. In *Latin America – European Union. Forum 1996. Europe and Latin America: Two Ways of Integration for the 21st Century*, pp 189–191. European Commission, Brussels. p 189.
4. Hurrell, Andrew. 2001. The Politics of Regional Integration in MERCOSUR. In *Regional Integration in Latin America and the Caribbean: The Political Economy of Open Regionalism*, edited by Víctor Bulmer-Thomas, pp 194–211. Institute of Latin American Studies, University of London, London. p 203.
5. Dabène indicates that this problem was particularly characteristic of the 'first wave' of Latin American integration in the 1960s (Dabène, Olivier. 2009. The Politics of Regional Integration in Latin America. Palgrave Macmillan, New York. p 86).
6. Mattli, Walter. 1999. The logic of regional integration: Europe and beyond. Cambridge University Press, Cambridge.
7. Bouzas, Roberto, da Motta Veiga, Pedro and Torrent, Ramón. 2002. *Analysis of MERCOSUR integration, its prospects and effects on the market access of EU goods, services and investment*. Report presented to the European Commission. University of Barcelona, Barcelona. p 22.
8. Idem, p 126.

INDEX

A
Act of Colonia, 96, 116
Act of Economic Cooperation Uruguay-Brazil, 96, 116
Arbitration, 41, 109, 118

B
Benelux, 51, 78, 96

C
CAN, 111, 152–153
Cardoso, Henrique, 93, 102, 120, 190, 191, 205
CAUCE, 55, 96, 115–116
Constructivism, social, 14–16, 22–25, 26–27, 34–35, 211, 212, 221–224
Cooperation, definition, 2
Coordination, definition, 2
Customs code, 37

D
Díaz de Guzmán, Ruy, 141–142

E
Eclecticism, analytic, 8, 18
English, language, 154, 155, 157, 158
Europeanness/European identity/European culture, 10, 15, 22, 25, 90, 128–138, 162
EUROSUR, 189, 194, 195, 201, 209

F
French, language, 154, 155, 157, 158
FTAA, 72, 101, 180–181, 182, 189, 191, 193, 194–195, 205, 213

G
Gauchos/gaúchos, 143
German, language, 154, 155
Guaraní, language, 125, 140, 153, 156
Guaraníes, 139–140, 143, 161–162

H
Hegemony, definition, 16

I
Infrastructure, 45–47
Integration, definition, 2
Intergovernmentalism
  explanatory approach,
    11, 13–14, 20–24, 26, 34–35,
    88, 92, 211, 212, 221, 223, 224
  organisation of regional
    governance, 95, 114

J
Jesuits, 140, 161–162

M
Menem, Carlos, 102, 183–185
MERCOSUR Político, 105

N
NAFTA, 17, 98, 101, 102, 175, 191, 192, 195
NATO, 101, 102, 135, 175, 178, 179, 190, 192, 200, 213
Neofunctionalism, 11, 12–13, 20, 21–22, 23, 33–34, 41–42, 47–48, 53, 87, 216–217, 219
Neorealism, 16–17, 20, 23, 173, 174, 193, 197

P
PARLASUR, 107–108
PEC, 96
PICE, 96, 97, 151
Politics, definition, 87
Portuguese, language, 155–158
  Portuguese dialects of Uruguay, 156
PTAs, effects, 56–58

R
Race, 124, 125, 153
Religion, 124, 127, 153

S
Southern Cone, 91, 138–139
Spanish, language, 155–158
Supranationalism, 95–96, 114

T
Treaty of Asunción, 40, 49–52, 59, 96, 109, 152
Treaty of Buenos Aires, 151, 152

U
Unification, definition, 2

V
Venezuela, 1, 90, 91, 193, 195